BYGONE BRITAIN

ON THE MOVE

1900–1970

LONDON: HMSO

Researched and prepared by Publishing Services, Central Office of Information.

© Selection and introduction Crown copyright 1995

Applications for reproduction should be made to HMSO

First published 1995

ISBN 0 11 701884 8

Published by HMSO and available from:

HMSO Publications Centre
(Mail, fax and telephone orders only)
PO Box 276, London SW8 5DT
Telephone orders 0171 873 9090
General enquiries 0171 873 0011
(queuing system in operation for both numbers)
Fax orders 0171 873 8200

HMSO Bookshops
49 High Holborn, London WC1V 6HB
(counter service only)
0171 873 0011 Fax 0171 831 1326
68-69 Bull Street, Birmingham B4 6AD
0121 236 9696 Fax 0121 236 9699
33 Wine Street, Bristol BS1 2BQ
0117 9264306 Fax 0117 9294515
9-21 Princess Street, Manchester M60 8AS
0161 834 7201 Fax 0161 833 0634
16 Arthur Street, Belfast BT1 4GD
01232 238451 Fax 01232 235401
71 Lothian Road, Edinburgh EH3 9AZ
0131 228 4181 Fax 0131 229 2734
The HMSO Oriel Bookshop
The Friary, Cardiff CF1 4AA
01222 395548 Fax 01222 384347

HMSO's Accredited Agents
(see Yellow Pages)
and through good booksellers

Acknowledgments

We would like to thank the staff of the British Library Newspaper Library at Colindale
for their ready and cheerful assistance and co-operation, and for their expertise in problem
solving. The staff at the British Library at Bloomsbury have also helped in turning up rare
and distant journals. We are also indebted to the National Magazine Company, to the
National Federation of Women's Institutes, and to the Thomas Cook archive, who so kindly
allowed us to access to their archives. Copyright in the extracts quoted generally belongs to
the newspapers and the magazines concerned, and to their successors in business. Present
owners have been most kind in granting permission to quote, as have Reuters Ltd. In spite
of all our efforts, it has not been possible to trace all present copyright owners in the extracts
featured.

We would like to thank our colleagues in COI Pictures Section for helping us to choose the
photographs for this book.

PREFACE

By Sir Harry Secombe

There's nothing quite like coming across a 50-year-old newspaper or magazine – when you're moving house, perhaps, or having a particularly vigorous spring-clean. The shape and size of their yellowing pages may look familiar, but their contents seem to come from another world.

The Bygone Britain series explores our past through the pages of these old newspapers and magazines, which were only ever meant to be bought, read for a day or so and thrown away, but often end up lining people's drawers or wrapped round their crockery.

I find them endlessly fascinating. On the one hand here are events familiar through the reasoned analysis of history – battles, political upheavals – reported with vivid immediacy. Yet news items such as Chamberlain's successful appeasement mission to Berlin can only be viewed through the lens of hindsight. There are also the news stories that took a long time to happen: the earliest of many items about the Channel Tunnel in Bygone Britain is dated 1907!

Quite unselfconsciously, the articles, letters and advertisements reveal completely different priorities from our own. It is quite shocking that a small and ostensibly sentimental item about the discovery of an abandoned baby finishes with the casual disclosure that the infant was then consigned to the workhouse. Conversely, the behaviour of these aliens from another age has the power to amuse us in a way that would make them quite indignant: the excruciating niceties of visiting cards are surely no laughing matter, and what on earth is wrong with attempting to banish grey hair with radium? Likewise, in these knowledgeable days of niche marketing and core business, we find it absurd to see an advertisement urging hairdressers to sell the odd bicycle on the side.

But there are many hints that the people who populate these pages are not such strangers to us after all. Get-rich-quick schemes and dubious books already feature prominently in the small ads, and the slimming advertisements seem as widespread as in our own press. Some of the ideas voiced in the articles are ones that we thought our own generation had come up with: domestic science as a subject for boys, the dangers of too much exposure to the sun. And, needless to say, affairs of the heart loom large across the pages, whatever the decade.

The things that we can recall ourselves exert their own particular attraction. Coverage of events we remember, pictures of celebrities, advertisements for objects we coveted excite a warm glow of recognition and affection. Other pictures may arouse quite opposite emotions: horror and self-loathing to think that we ever went around with lapels like that! Our reactions to our memories are as much a gauge of how we as individuals have changed as of how society has changed.

So what conclusions can we draw from leafing through the pages of the Bygone Britain books? The increasing pace of technological change is evident, as is the growing informality – in manners, in language, and in address to the readers. The problem page letters confirm this. Early in the century, the letters themselves do not appear; all we see are the replies, addressed to a mysterious correspondent with a fanciful name: Heart's Ease or Sapphire. Fifty years later many writers think nothing of revealing their true identities along with their troubles. (In passing, let us be thankful for the demise of the enterprising service offered by the *Hairdressers and Toilet Requisites Gazette*, whereby people sent in samples of falling hair – and worse – for trichological analysis.)

Does the very different look of the articles in the 1900s and those of the 1960s – tiny, dense text with small headlines giving way to more spacious type with *Sun*-style screamers – mean that our powers of concentration are declining? That papers and magazines have to try harder to wrest our attention from television is obvious, but modern technology, availability of newsprint, and more widespread literacy have all played their part in shaping our contemporary press.

Whether you have a serious interest in British history and society, or you're an avid consumer of trivia; whether you can remember most of the first seventy years of this century, or you weren't even born, you will find plenty to wonder at, to mourn and to laugh about in the Bygone Britain series.

INTRODUCTION

By 1900 the communications revolution was well and truly launched. People had been speeding up for some time, but there were still advantages in, and adherents of, a more leisurely style.

'I hope', said Queen Victoria (on the subject of the motor car) to her Master of the Horse, 'you will never allow any of those horrible machines to be used in my stables. I am told that they smell exceedingly nasty, and are very shaky and disagreeable conveyances altogether'.[1]

In 1899 the Russian balletomane Alexandre Benois visited London. He and his wife had much to put up with: dirty boarding house; awful plumbing; appalling food. Yet they were forbearing, even complimentary, in their reminiscences. On his last Sunday in London, Benois took a ride from the Strand to Hampton Court on the top of a horse-drawn bus. He was tempted to get on by 'the inviting smile of the conductor' who 'firmly helped me in'. He loved the ride: 'one picture followed another' – being held up by a Salvation Army procession; Richmond Bridge; Bushey Park with 'masses of people dressed in their Sunday best . . . promenading . . . peace and propriety reigned'.[2]

Ten years later a driver in Somerset wrote:

> We dropped down from a breezy eminence to a
> low-lying, level drowsy land of deep green meadows
> watered by sluggish streams, wherein for miles we
> met only a farmer's waggon crawling slowly along.
> . . . Densely populated as England is, gridironed
> all over with railways, yet there are districts in
> it the very abode of loneliness, where the
> centuries come and go with little outward change,
> and the country looks much the same as it did in
> the days of the Stuarts, or even before . . .[3]

This railway system, which had played so vital a role in industrialising Victorian Britain and had made the fortunes of prospectors and shareholders, was tight and efficient. The Forth Bridge and Severn Tunnel, built in the 1880s, had greatly improved it. It discouraged other forms of transport and roads were left to decay.

Motoring was the pastime of the rich few, but the internal combustion engine had definitely arrived, and was not going to go away. Roads could nevertheless be treacherous, for they were often sprinkled with nails from horses' hooves. Punctures and breakdowns were frequent. In 1901 (when there were about 100 cars in the whole of Scotland) a journey from Paisley to Langwell in Caithness, some 300 miles in a 10 horse-power Arrol-Johnston, took three days.

Only since 1896 had a motor car been allowed to move without a man walking in front with a red flag. Cars at that time were made in specialist workshops. In the 1890s France and Germany had a lead on Britain as far as car and cycle building were concerned. Exports were healthy, but

> British businessmen hovered uneasily on the edge
> of the modern mass-production era, perhaps more
> doubtful than they should have been about their
> future markets both at home and abroad.[4]

In 1894, at the age of sixteen, William Morris had started his own bicycle firm in Oxford with £4 capital. It was to become one of the motoring giants of the century, which raised its founder to the peerage (Viscount Nuffield) and to immense wealth, liberally donated to charitable causes.

Pressure was put on King Edward VII to use a motor coach at his coronation in 1902, and he would have been willing to help the young motor industry by doing so. But when it

[1] 6th Duke of Portland, *Men, Women and Things* (London, 1937), p 136.
[2] Alexandre Benois, *Memoirs* (London, 1964), II, pp 174–80.
[3] J.J. Hissey, *An English Holiday with Car and Camera* (London, 1908), pp 79–80.
[4] Keith Robbins, *The Eclipse of a Great Power, 1870–1975* (London, 1983), p 54.

was pointed out to him that 'such a vehicle would have to be without noticeable vibration, noise, vapour or smell', he had to abandon the idea because no such vehicle yet existed.[5]

Cycling was popular. In 1895 Arthur Balfour, Leader of the House of Commons, wrote to Lady Elcho that he had dared to go cycling in London, but only on a Sunday afternoon. By 1900, however, the Cyclists' Touring Club had 60,000 members.

In 1900, Miss Vera Butler of Pall Mall was fined 40 shillings for driving her motor car at between 12 and 14 miles an hour, and the Metropolitan electric railway had been inaugurated, with dizzying effects (see p. 5). In 1901 the London electric tramway made its first journey from Shepherds Bush to Southall. By 1902 the Liverpool tramway system had been electrified and the Pedestrians' Protection League was being formed to 'suppress reckless motor-car driving'. Traffic jams were no new thing, but they were to become much more dangerous, and traffic controls and restrictions, and less and less carefree driving, were inevitable.

A small country (yet many people at the turn of the century had never been beyond their nearest market town) was becoming even smaller. The world was becoming smaller too. British seapower was formidable. The Manchester Ship Canal, opened on 1 January 1894, had transformed that city into the world's first inland port. The White Star liner *Celtic,* the biggest in the world, was launched in 1901, HMS *Dreadnought* in 1906, and in 1909 Edward VII reviewed 18 miles of warships in the Solent.

During 1900–1910 the Post Office was reassuring the public about the new telephone system, although no subscriber was allowed to use the instrument for more than six minutes continuously. Marconi was establishing transatlantic wireless telegraphy. Radio and Baird and television were little more than a decade away.

The stir caused by Blériot's flight in a monoplane across the Channel in 1909 was matched by the excitement of the first scheduled London–Paris air service and the airships in 1919. Pioneers of ever more rapid and far-flung movement included Alan Cobham in 1919 and Amy Johnson in 1930. Triumph and tragedy attended expeditions to the Antarctic, to the Alps and to Everest – Scott and Shackleton, Dorothy Lloyd, Mallory – and speed and distance records in the air and on water were repeatedly broken – by the Campbells, Malcolm and Donald, during the 1930s–1960s, Neville Duke and John Cobb, to name a few.

Verve and sophistication were the keynotes of the 1930s motor shows at Olympia, where some of Britain's latest models achieved instant classic status. The Mini's launch in 1959 showed that Britain had lost none of its design flair. Hurricane, Spitfire, Wellington, and the jet, helped to maintain Britain's reputation in the air, as air travel, like motor travel, gradually became more and more accessible. As early as 1954, BOAC enjoyed record profits, with over 300,000 passengers.

In 1966 the Harrier jump jet was unveiled and in 1969, Concorde made its maiden flight – two of the latest British achievements in the air. In 1963 Dr Beeching was wielding an axe on that dense railway network. Yet inventiveness was still with us. London Transport were testing an automatic train driver and experimenting with electronic ticket scanning machines. The QE2 was also launched in 1969. The Rolls Royce drophead coupé and Jaguar XJ6 were among the cars of the decade, and there remained a staunch following for the Ford Anglia and Morris Minor.

Today's conductor/drivers may often be too harassed to smile invitingly, but the best way to see London is still from the top of a bus. And, even today, it is still possible, in a much more densely populated country suffering the overwhelming effects of mass motoring, to find areas of stillness and solitude.

John Collis
COI
August 1995

[5] Sir Charles Petrie, *Scenes of Edwardian Life* (London, 1965), p 91.

1900 ▬ 1909

HER TRAVELS ENDED.

DEATH OF MISS MARY KINGSLEY IN SOUTH AFRICA.

A telegram from Capetown announces the death of Miss Mary H. Kingsley, the well-known traveller and writer.

Miss Kingsley left England in March last with the intention of renewing her travels in Africa. She went first to South Africa and assisted in the good work of looking after the sick and wounded at the front. She was taken ill and removed to Simonstown Hospital, where she died.

"My life can be written in a very few lines," Miss Kingsley once wrote in an autobiographical sketch. "It has been wholly without romance or variety. It has just been one long grind of work—work worth doing, but never well done—a perpetual Waterloo in a microscopic way."

Her life-work thus modestly described was filled with perils and adventures. Two expeditions to West Africa, penetrating regions where no white man had ever set foot, furnished experiences which she subsequently related in two fascinating volumes, "Travels in West Africa" and "West African Studies."

Miss Kingsley's object in her travels was the study of early religion and law, a purpose in which she declared she was rarely understood. Her love for the forests and rivers and people of West Africa forbade her remaining for any length of time in England, where everything to her was commonplace by comparison.

She was the daughter of Dr. G. H. Kingsley and a niece of the late Canon Kingsley.

Daily Mail **1900**

Dr Turner's advice on diet is also valuable. He is no foe to vegetarianism for those who have been accustomed to such a diet; in short, "I should advise each to go on in that way which he finds best suited to himself, being careful only not to exceed in any way." He emphasises the folly of trying "to ride hard or fast soon after a full meal. The stomach, when overloaded, presses on and interferes with the action of the heart, and many cases of fatal syncope have been caused by riding too soon after a meal." He deprecates, too, the use of any sort of alcoholic stimulant between meals, it being only so taken in order to screw the rider up to further exertions, and being bound to lead to a worse collapse in the end. As Dr Turner points out, "There is a reaction after every dose of alcohol, and that reaction leaves the rider more fatigued than he was before." The question of what to drink is, of course, a very difficult one. Tea should not be taken more than twice a day. It should not be strong, or allowed to stand more than five minutes on the leaves. I always ask for a jug and pour it off into that, diluting it with hot water if too strong. The practice of leaving it in the pot and adding hot water is strongly to be condemned. Ices and iced drinks should be avoided entirely when cycling.

Queen **1900**

The current number of the *C.T.C. Gazette* is particularly good, and leads one to congratulate oneself on membership in a club which secures the receipt of twelve such budgets yearly, full, as a rule, of valuable and interesting information. In the present number Part IV. of Dr Turner's "Physiology and Hygiene of Cycling" deals with "Clothing, Diet, and Accidents," and, like all sensible men, medical and otherwise, he makes woollen underclothing a *sine quâ non* for the cyclist. Indeed, he goes so far as to say that "no cotton or linen should, if possible, be allowed to enter into the composition of his garments, especially in the shape of a linen collar or a linen waistband. Anything of this sort is a most fruitful source of chills, colds, and rheumatism, besides being extremely uncomfortable. *All underclothing should be loose.*" Italics are mine, for there can be no doubt that the ordinary corset, with its unyielding whalebone, would stand absolutely condemned for cycling purposes if a really satisfactory substitute could be designed. Every sensible rider would then unhesitatingly dispense with what is practically an absolute bar to the free expansion of the lungs (especially the lower part), and consequent proper oxygenation of the blood. What woman would dream of going through a gymnastic course in corsets! Yet the exertion of a prolonged cycle ride, "up hill and down dale," demands an equal freedom of play for lungs and heart.

Queen **1900**

AUTOMOBILISMS.

Mr Joseph Pennell, the well-known artist and tourist, tried a Werner motor bicycle early in the season, and was not favourably impressed. Lately, however, he has been riding one again, and a great change has come over the spirit of his dream. His best time on a bicycle from Paris to Lausanne was five days; on the Werner he has done it in three, nearly one of which was consumed in fiddling with details. An ordinary bicycle takes long enough to get ready for a tour, so one can readily imagine what a motor bicycle must be in this respect.

Mr Pennell is no friend of the free wheel, never having properly mastered it; consequently he appears to have had quite an exciting time on the Furka Pass. His beloved back-pedalling was absent, and he had to rely entirely on his brakes. It will be interesting to observe whether the Werner will convert him to free wheels generally. He is very enthusiastic as to the special charms of a motor bicycle, which he considers are peculiar to it, and not possessed by either bicycle or motor car.

Certainly it looks as if the motor bicycle will prove a most important link between cycling and motoring. There are hundreds of cyclists who use their mounts as much for getting about as for mere pleasure and exercise. Most of them cannot afford a motorcar or motor tricycle, but they feel the need of an auxiliary power to enable them to make long journeys without excessive fatigue. At the same time they would like a reasonable amount of exercise. To this class the motor bicycle will appeal strongly; it is a free wheel that can be pedalled at any time, even if the engine breaks down or the petrol supply gives out; it is comparatively light, easily handled and stored, and only about double the price of a good bicycle.

Such a machine, however, needs some amount of skill and activity to manage, so that ladies will probably be slow to take it up. The mechanism does not at present admit of the frame being dropped, but a divided skirt would meet the case. Of course, in France the national ladies' cycling costume presents no impediment whatever.

Mr R. J. Mecredy, editor of the *Irish Cyclist* and the *Irish Motor News*, challenges Col. Magrath's remarks on Irish roads, which I quoted recently. In a letter to the *Autocar*, he says that while in co. Wexford, where the Colonel resides, the roads are notoriously bad, it is far from correct to say that all Irish roads are covered with loose stones and unfit for use in winter. Mr Mecredy ought to know if anyone does, for on cycle and motorcar he has covered nearly 90,000 miles of Irish roads. As regards pneumatics having a short life in Ireland, he informs me that the Dunlops on one of his cars have run over 1300 miles during the last two months, and are still in perfect order. He attributes the mishap to many of the tyres in the 1000 miles trial to the great weight of the cars.

The Cycling Editor.

Queen **1900**

THE HOUSE FOR
SMART MOTOR WEAR.
Gamage's
OF HOLBORN.

Our Latest

The "MERCIA" Automobile Coat (*as illustration*), **45/-**
Real Scotch Tweed, Dust and Waterproof ... ...

Ditto, in Donegal Tweed (Ready Made or to Measure **50/-**
same price) ... ...

The "DUCHESS" Hood, in Soft Silk or Chiffon, with
DETACHABLE VEIL for face, which can be detached
or thrown back without disarranging the other part of
wrap. Completely protects hair, hat, and neck from
dust, and presents a pretty and chic effect. In any **8/11**
fashionable colour, price .. ..

"L'AUTO." Ladies' Automobile Cap. Absolutely
exclusive design. The smartest ladies' cap yet made. **8/6**
Petal Straw, Leather Peak, Piped Crown, ..
Postage 4d.

MOTOR GLOVES
AND
ALL ACCESSORIES.

"THE QUEEN," of May 28th, 1904, says:
"The entire English Motoring world has come
to accept the fact that for all the accessories and
intricate spare parts that go to make up these
coveted possessions, there is no place like
Gamage's."

MOTOR LISTS POST FREE.

A. W. GAMAGE, Ltd., HOLBORN, E.C.

A LADY AND HER MOTOR CAR.

Miss Vera Butler, of 56a, Pall-mall, appeared at the
West London Police-court yesterday in answer to a
summons charging her with driving a motor car from
Fulham-road into Redcliffe-gardens, Kensington, at a
greater speed than was reasonable and proper.—The
Defendant's Father, who was riding in the car,
declared that the speed was not more than seven
miles an hour, but the evidence called by the police
was to the effect that the car was going at the rate of
12 or 14 miles an hour.—Mr. Rose imposed a fine of
40s. and costs.

Evening Standard 1900

A trial run for the Central London Railway, Shepherds Bush, prior to its opening in 1900.

HORSE SAUSAGES.

TO THE EDITOR.

Sir,—From time to time men are brought before the London Magistrates for cruelty to horses in driving old worn out and lame creatures to the docks to be shipped to Holland for the dead meat trade, as Mr. Mead termed it. I had often remarked that, if the Dutch liked old horse for food, why not let them have it and enjoy it? But imagine what was my astonishment last Summer, when I discovered that the old horses were never intended by the Dutch for their own food, but to be made, at Rotterdam, into sausages for the English.

These sausages are, I believe, imported into this country, and are sold by grocers and at small general shops. This is rather slim of the Hollander, but I think the trade ought to be stopped by the Customs or by the Food Inspectors, by prosecuting the sellers for selling as pork sausages that which is not pork, but horse.

I am, Sir, your obedient servant,
"CELT."

November 28.

Evening Standard **1900**

PIGEON POST AT THE CRYSTAL PALACE.

In connection with the inauguration of a pigeon post at the Crystal Palace, the first of a number of breeding lofts has been completed, and the remainder are in hand, and nearing completion. As a fitting "send-off" an exhibition of homing birds is being organised by Mr. E. S. Shrubsole, the curator. The exhibits, which will include many famous war pigeons, and the best of the racing birds in the United Kingdom, will number quite 2000. They will be staged in the south nave, and will remain on view during December 18 to 20.

Evening Standard **1900**

THE ELECTRIC RAILWAY.

At the Mansion House Police-court, a woman was summoned before the Lord Mayor for being drunk.—The Defendant, who was stated to be a general servant, did not appear.—Police-sergeant Criddle said the Defendant told him that if she appeared she would lose her situation. Her explanation was that she had been travelling on the Electric Railway, and that she took two glasses of port to recover from the effects.—The Lord Mayor said he hoped that that was not going to be the experience of everyone who travelled on the Electric Railway. He fined the Defendant 2s., and 3s. costs.

Evening Standard **1900**

SUBMARINES TARDILY COMING.

A submarine boat, one of five now being built at Barrow by Vickers, Sons, and Maxim, was launched yesterday without ceremony. The other four boats will be launched in about two months.

The new boats are of the Holland type. Their measurements are 63ft. 4ins. in length all over, with an 11ft. 9ins. beam; and a displacement (submerged) of 120 tons. The boat can expel torpedoes while stationary or while travelling at full speed above or below the surface.

The torpedo expulsion tube is situated at the extreme forward end of the craft, opening outwards 2ft. below the light water line. The exterior of the hull is free from projections likely to become entangled by ropes or other obstacles when under water, while the vessels are specially designed to minimise resistance when cruising on the surface. Propulsion is effected by a gasoline type of main engine, and the boats are expected to be capable of maintaining a maximum speed of about nine knots on a run of about 400 knots. Submerged, an electric main motor will give a speed of seven knots for a four hours' run.

Daily Express **1901**

COUNT VON ZEPPELIN'S AIR-SHIP FLYING OVER THE LAKE OF CONSTANCE.

The first voyage of Count von Zeppelin's air-ship was made last July, before some twenty thousand spectators. The weather was fine, with hardly any wind. The trip was very satisfactory, and the huge ship covered a distance of about six miles, turning about and ascending and descending with great ease. An interesting and full account of the air-ship appeared in *Pearson's Magazine* for September.

Queen 1900

[Photograph by Fradelle and Young, 283, Regent-street, W.

LONDON'S LATEST METHOD OF LOCOMOTION.
THE NEW ELECTRIC TRAMWAY FROM SHEPHERD'S BUSH TO SOUTHALL.—THE START FROM SHEPHERD'S BUSH.

Queen 1901

MORE ELECTRIC TRAMS.

MR. BALFOUR GIVES THEM A HEARTY SEND-OFF.

Mr. Arthur Balfour was one of the large company at the opening of the seven and a half miles extension of the West London electric tramways yesterday. He made an interesting speech on the problem of relieving congested London.

" I am not concerned," he said, "to discuss the prospects of this enterprise as a commercial affair. I am interested in it because it seems to me one of the greatest engines of social reform and amelioration which it has been the privilege of any great corporation to start.

"The question of congestion in all our great populous areas may always be stated in terms of time and cost. There will be no congestion if we can all move at no expense and with speed from the outskirts to the centre of London."

Mr. Balfour pointed out, however, that every fresh facility for bringing people from the outskirts increased the difficulty of the traffic in inner London. This must also be met.

He warmly welcomed the present scheme, which, when complete, would probably carry 150,000,000 people a year.

Mr. George White, the chairman of the company, said that by means of these trams the working man could get from Hanwell to Shepherd's Bush for a penny, and thence by the workmen's trains on the "Tube" to the Bank for another penny—twelve miles for twopence.

Prior to the opening ceremony, which took place at the headquarters of the company at Chiswick, the bulk of the guests enjoyed a trip over the new line.

Eight cream-coloured trams, decked out with roses and greenery till they looked like triumphal cars, made the procession. Enthusiastic crowds witnessed the departure from Shepherd's Bush, and nearly all along the route, through Acton and Ealing and Hanwell to Southall, people stood three deep and cheered and waved flags.

Daily Express 1901

Two Worlds 1902

Character in Walking.

STEPS that are quick are indicative of energy and agitation.

Tiptoe walking symbolises surprise, curiosity, discretion, or mystery.

Turned-in toes are often found with pre-occupied, absent-minded persons.

The miser's walk is represented as stooping, noiseless, with short, nervous, anxious steps.

Slow steps, whether long or short, suggest a gentle or reflective state of mind, as the case may be.

The proud step is slow and measured ; the toes are conspicuously turned out ; the legs straightened.

Where a revengeful purpose is hidden under a feigned smile the step will be slinking and noiseless.

The direction of the steps, wavering and following every changing impulse of the mind, inevitably betrays uncertainty, hesitation, and indecision.

Obstinate people who in argument rely more on muscularity than on intellectual power rest the feet flatly and firmly on the ground, walk heavily and slowly, and stand with the legs firmly planted and far apart.—*Liverpool Daily Post*

THE NEW TELEPHONE

SOME QUESTIONS ANSWERED BY THE POST OFFICE.

FREE AT FIRST.

Much doubt was expressed in the City yesterday as to the exact meaning of the Postmaster-General's statement regarding the new telephone system.

Though dubious of the benefits it would confer, business men were ready to suspend criticism until its details were understood.

Thanks to the courtesy of the Post Office, the " Express " is able to clear up several doubtful points.

In the first place, the canvassers are out, the installation staff is at work, and any day someone near the Central Exchange in Queen Victoria-street—the largest and most perfect exchange in the world—may have the honour of being the first to use the Post Office system.

As each exchange is opened it will be connected by junction lines with other Post Office exchanges and with the National Telephone Company's exchanges.

Many people are doubtful whether the connections between the Post Office and the N.T.C. will be complete and satisfactory. It would appear easy for the N.T.C. to hamper the operations of the Post Office system by dilatoriness in effecting connections between the two, but the Post Office is quite satisfied that the N.T.C. employees will act honourably in this matter, and that a call coming from a Post Office exchange will be transmitted to a subscriber on the N.T.C. system with promptness.

Will, however, the N.T.C. clear its own messages before dealing with Post Office messages? That is a question business men would like answered.

FREE SERVICE AT FIRST.

In reference to this question of interchange between its own and the N.T.C. lines, all the Post Office can say at present is that subscribers will be charged no fees until the service is largely extended and satisfactory inter-communication is assured. Subscriptions and payments, the " Express " understands, will not begin until the Post Office is able to give value for money.

Another point business men would like settled is the question whether the N.T.C. will allow those subscribers who have entered into five-year contracts to revise these agreements and adopt the new scale? There are many moderate users of the telephone who would prefer the " message rate" system, at one penny a call, to the £17 a year "unlimited service" system.

Here the Post Office can only say that where subscribers wish to continue contracts made with the N.T.C. they can do so, a concession of possible advantage to those who now pay the N.T.C. £10 a year for service within the county area. But in regard to the opposite proposition—viz., the revision of contracts, the Post Office can say nothing. It rests with the N.T.C., and at present the company is absolutely dumb to all inquiries.

City men who have a telephone at their office and another at home want to know what the Post Office will charge for the two. The charge will be £17 for the first and £14 for the second if unlimited service is required, or the home telephone can be on the message rate system.

CALLS ON PARTY LINES.

Will messages on the party line be heard by everyone who chooses to listen? And will a call to one subscriber ring up the other nine?

An answer to the latter question, the Post Office replies that if two persons use a party line a call signal will ring up only one of them. If ten are connected by one party line a call will ring up five of them at a time. It will not be necessary, however, for Mrs. Brown to run to the 'phone every time Mrs. Smith next door is called, unless she is very anxious to beat the butcher explain why Mrs. Smith's joint was not sent. Each of the five will have a separate signal, distinguished by one or more rings.

Six minutes will be the limit of time for which any one subscriber will be allowed to use the telephone continuously.

Daily Express 1901

BIGGEST SHIP IN THE WORLD.

TO-DAY'S LAUNCH OF THE CELTIC.

From Our Special Correspondent.

BELFAST, Wednesday Night.

When I visited Messrs. Harland and Wolff's shipbuilding works to-day 2,000 workmen were almost lost in the immensity of the White Star liner Celtic, the largest vessel in the world. Amid the din of hundreds of hammers all other sounds were drowned. From the adjoining slips, where two other big hulls are growing, came the same reverberating metallic chorus of many hundreds of busy workers. Standing on the highest of the nine decks of the ocean leviathan which is to be launched on the morrow, one looked out over the noble sweep of Belfast Lough in the distance, and then the eye travelled back from the blue waters to the towering height of the Celtic, and a feeling of awe took the place of mere curiosity as one glanced over the side to the slipway, over a hundred feet below, and grasped the immense proportions of this marvel of naval construction that in four or five months will be ferrying to and fro between the Mersey and New York. Seven hundred feet in length, she is about one-third longer than St. Paul's Cathedral. With an aggregate of 37,700 tons, she displaces almost the same amount of water as the three British battleships Centurion, Barfleur, and Victorious, our entire battle fleet in the Far East until a few months ago. She has a gross tonnage of 20,880, and, therefore, exceeds the Great Eastern by nearly 2,000 tons. When carrying her full complement of passengers, she will be a home on the Atlantic for 3,294 persons—the population of many a town of no mean importance. In comparison with this newest addition to be made to the White Star fleet, the largest battleship or cruiser afloat is a pigmy. She is the big sister of the Great Eastern, which, costing three-quarters of a million in 1858, was sold to a shipbreaker, about twelve years since, for £58,000. The proportions of the Celtic are so huge, and yet her lines are so graceful, that it would not be easy to describe her by any adjectives or phrases. She is a very giant, built for comfort and safety, slow in comparison with the speeds attained by the Oceanic, and yet more retrograde, it would appear, when contrasted with the Hamburg-American Deutschland of 23½ knots, and the Kaiser Wilhelm der Grosse. She is expected to develop only seventeen knots, which will enable her to cross the Atlantic in about eight days.

Daily Telegraph 1901

THE LOCOMOBILE.

From the hour when I first saw a Locomobile performing gyrations such as no other motor had ever done—cutting figures 8 and shaving imitation policemen, nursemaids, and German bandsmen in the arena of the Agricultural Hall—a longing seized me to experience the sensation of sitting on top of a boiler working at from 160 to 180lbs. pressure and doing " even time " without having my spinal column dislocated with vibration. " Everything comes to him who waits." I recently had the pleasure of a ride on a natty No. 3 Locomobile, an illustration of which accompanies this.

A run of twenty miles convinced me that my fears concerning the aforesaid boiler's juxtaposition were chimerical. Any lingering doubts which I might have had were finally laid to rest by an inspection of the internal economy of the 'Bile—as they call it in America.

It is astonishing how simple the various parts of the mechanism become, even to an unpractical mind,

THE LOCOMOBILE.

after a short rudimentary explanation, and what before seemed a complication of tubes, valves, levers, and tanks resolve themselves into an ordinary array, and are soon easily distinguished for their separate and conjoint functions. Even now I flatter myself that with a little supervision I could make that car do my every wish.

Motor-Car World 1901

TO PROTECT PEDESTRIANS.

A society, to be known as the Pedestrians' Protection League, it is stated, is now in process of formation. The chief object of the society will be the suppression of reckless motor-car driving, though the action of the league is to be also directed against horse-driven vehicles and cyclists.

The league will employ inspectors to watch for delinquents on the main roads, and report facts to the society.

Free advice will also be given to members of the league in cases of accident or negligence, and non-members of the poorer class will be assisted in obtaining compensation if justified.

Evening News 1902

MR. HARRY METCALFE, OF STRETFORD, CHESHIRE, WHO RECENTLY RODE FROM MANCHESTER TO CHESTER BACK-WARDS, WITHOUT A DISMOUNT. SOME FURTHER PARTICULARS WILL BE FOUND IN ONE OF OUR NEWS PAGES.

Cycling 1903

Illustrated London News 1903

THE NEW KEW BRIDGE.

For the third time, the river at Kew has been spanned by a bridge. The last and finest of the structures, the King Edward VII. Bridge, which was opened by his Majesty on May 20, has been building for three years. It consists of three elliptical arches, of which the centre one has a span of 133 ft. It has been constructed of granite from Cornwall and Aberdeen. The earliest

THE OPENING OF THE NEW BRIDGE AT KEW: THE CASKET PRESENTED TO HIS MAJESTY, MAY 20.

bridge, which replaced the old horse-ferry, was erected by one Robert Tunstall in the reign of George II. It was completed in 1759, and remained in use for nearly thirty years, when it was removed to make way for the second bridge. Pictures of the three bridges in oxidised silver appear on the golden casket presented to King Edward on the occasion of the opening of Kew Bridge. The Goldsmiths and Silversmiths Company, of 112, Regent Street, were entrusted with the work of preparing this souvenir of the event.

MARINE MOTOR NEWS.

THE HARMSWORTH CUP RACE.

FOR MOTOR LAUNCHES NOT EXCEEDING 40 FEET O.A.

OWING to the short interval between the publication of the conditions of this race and the date fixed for the event, none of the foreign competitors turned up, with the exception of the Mercedes launch, which was ineligible, owing to the boat being built in France, while the motor was made in Germany.

Consequently the only competitors were the three British boats entered by Messrs. S. F. Edge, F. Beadle, and J. E. Thornycroft. Of these three, only one was built up to the full length of 40 ft., viz., Napier, owned by Mr. S. F. Edge, both the other boats being 30 ft.

Mr. Edge's boat was the most powerful of the three, her horse-power being stated on the programme as 75, while Mr. Beadle's boat had 50 b.h.p. and Mr. Thornycroft's only 20 b.h.p. It is very doubtful if the actual b.h.p. of Mr. Edge's boat was known, for it did not appear to give more than 50 b.h.p., though several statements have been made in the papers that it was as much as 80 b.h.p., and we know this was the power for which the boat was designed. Judging by the size and weight of the machinery (13½ cwt.), it might well have been 100 b.h.p.

The best performance was undoubtedly that of the Thornycroft boat, with no more than 20 b.h.p., as she was only beaten by 5 min. 8 3-5 sec. on a course of 8.97 nautical miles. The winner did the course in 24 min. 44 sec., which would give a speed of 21.7 knots for Mr. Edge's boat. The speed of Mr. Beadle's boat was 19.5 knots, and Mr. J. E. Thornycroft's 17.7 knots.

The Yachtsman 1903

THE THORNYCROFT LAUNCH.

Righteousness and Temperance amongst Cabmen. By George McRobert.

British Workman 1905

ON one occasion Lord Beaconsfield spoke of the hackney carriage driver as "the Ishmael of civilisation, whose hand is against every man's and every man's against his." There may have been some measure of truth in the description, but happily those Ishmael days may now be numbered with "the good old times." Whilst cabmen are still a peculiar class, with habits, manners, trials and temptations all their own, a very marked improvement has come over them even during recent years. They now compare favourably with other classes of workers.

The contrast between the men who manipulate

Missionary distributing "The British Workman" among Edinburgh Cabmen.

the "ribbons" to-day and those of forty years ago is very marked. In some of the towns, both of England and Scotland, they look almost like another set of men. Morally, physically, and in outward appearance the driver of to-day is a vast improvement on the Jehu of a decade ago.

An abstainer, and especially a Christian, on the box in those days was a *rara avis* indeed, and those making any such profession came in for "a hot time of it" from their fellow whips. Now, however, that has been wholly changed. Christian men and abstainers are to be found on every cab rank, so much so that in London and Edinburgh there are stands known as the preachers' and the apostles' ranks; and some men would rather lose a hire than turn on to these, so completely have the tables turned.

Bath Daily
Chronicle and Argus
1903

MARCONI'S SUCCESS

England and America Linked in Mid-Ocean

The Press Association is informed by Mr. Henniker Heaton, M.P., that the Mayor of Canterbury last Thursday sent an invitation to Mr. Marconi addressed to him: "Marconi, Lucania, somewhere in the Atlantic," asking Mr. Marconi to luncheon on his visit to the ancient city. Mr. Marconi replied accepting the invitation, and stating that excellent results had attended the experiments made on the Lucania.

Mr. Marconi arrived at Liverpool this morning on the Lucania from New York. The inventor succeeded in establishing simultaneous communication when in mid-Atlantic with England and America. This is the first time that the two Continents have been linked from mid-ocean in this way, and Mr. Marconi regards the success of his experiments with great satisfaction. He told a Press Association representative that wireless telegraphy between passing vessels and the land was now an entire and practical success, and he confidently believed with increased power brought into play he would within six or eight months, perhaps within three months, establish Trans-Atlantic wireless telegraphy from shore to shore as a commercial undertaking. On Thursday a summary of Mr. Chamberlain's speech at Glasgow was published by means of Marconi's system on board the Oceanic. The passengers, mostly Britishers and Canadians, received the speech with enthusiasm.

OF GENERAL INTEREST.

The chief Friendly Societies of the United Kingdom, embracing in all 4,000,000 members, have a capital of £30,000,000.

The Lifeboat Institution's fleet now comprises 285 sailing and pulling lifeboats, 4 steam lifeboats, and 1 steam tug. There were 1,427 launches during the year for exercise or service, and rewards were granted for the saving of 709 lives. The income was £80,662, including £19,777 from the Lifeboat Saturday Fund.

Crusader 1904

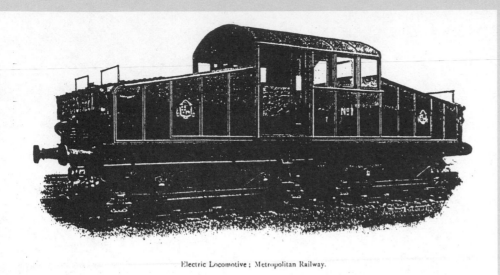

Electric Locomotive ; Metropolitan Railway.

Railway Engineer
1905

Electric Locomotives ; Metropolitan Railway.

THE first of ten 50-ton electrical locomotives has just been supplied to the Metropolitan R. by the British Westinghouse Company, the contractors for the electrification, and will shortly be put in service both in the Harrow and Inner Circle section of the line

They will be used for hauling the main line trains between Harrow and Baker Street, the steam locomotive that brings them up from Aylesbury, &c., being taken off at the former point and put on at the return journey. The trains used on this portion of the line are 120 tons in weight, and the new locomotives will propel them at a speed of 36 miles an hour on the level.

The same locomotives will be used on the Metropolitan half of the Inner Circle for goods traffic and for hauling the steam trains of other companies, possessed of running powers over it. The electrical locomotive will pick up the train at Edgware Road, being replaced by a steam locomotive at the point where the train leaves the Circle.

The new locomotives will be equipped with four motors of 300h.p. each ; and a feature of interest is that, owing to the terminus facilities being somewhat restricted, it has been necessary to use motors of a smaller size than usual equipped with forced ventilation, so as to keep down the length of the locomotives to convenient limits for handling at the termini.

This course of substituting electrical locomotives for steam is the only one possible for running trains that have been designed for steam propulsion over electrified lines, and within a reasonable time the electrical locomotive will doubtless become a familiar object. In a subsequent issue we shall give further illustrations of these locomotives.

The bogies, framing, &c., were constructed under a sub-contract by the Metropolitan Amalgamated Railway Carriage and Wagon Co., Ltd., of Birmingham.

Railway Engineer 1905

THE AUTOMOBILE ASSOCIATION.

A meeting was held at the Trocadero on Thursday afternoon, the 29th June, for the purpose of forming an association of motor road users.

Mr. Charles Temperley, who presided, explained that the meeting had been called in consequence of another meeting previously held, when the question of forming the association was decided. He explained that the new association would have as its objects the protection and advancement of the legitimate interests of motorists, and in particular to assist in the enforcement of the laws affecting all users of the highway. He explained that the association would combat in every form restrictions for the fair use of the public road by motorists.

Mr. Charles Jarrott spoke in support of the formation of the association, and said that already a considerable number of gentlemen had joined. He believed that the only way to secure fair treatment was to fight for it, and fight hard, and give nothing away. It was intended that the new association should have a strong legal department for the assistance of its members, and that an active policy should be undertaken to see that not only were the laws affecting motor cars fairly enforced, but that other laws relative to the use of the highway by other vehicles should be enforced in a similar manner. He saw no reason why the membership of the association should not run into thousands, and as the subscription has been fixed at a very small amount, a very large number would be able to join, who are debarred from joining any of the existing clubs.

The Chairman explained that the subscription was two guineas, and that application forms and particulars could be obtained from Mr. E. A. Bowden, hon. sec., 45, Great Marlborough Street, W. A general meeting of members to elect a committee and appoint officers is called for Monday next, 10th July, at 5.30 p.m., at the Trocadero Restaurant.

Autocar 1905

London
Bridge,
1905.

THE BOARD OF TRADE RETURNS.

The declared value of the Imports last month was 49,894,624l, showing an increase of 2,031,633l as compared with August, 1905, and an increase of 6,454,681l as compared with the corresponding period in 1904; the value of the Exports last month was 33,492,614l, being an increase of 3,974,778l as compared with the same period in 1905, and an increase of 7,132,734l in 1904.

SUMMARIES

EXPORTS of BRITISH and IRISH PRODUCE, &c. (Value F.O.B.a).

	Month of August.			Increase (*) or Decrease (†) in 1906 as compared with 1905.	Increase (*) or Decrease (†) in 1906 as compared with 1904.
	1904.	1905.	1906.		
	£	£	£	£	£
I.—FOOD, DRINK AND TOBACCO: Total, Class I	1,716,866	1,928,059	1,961,809	*33,250	*244,443
II.—RAW MATERIALS AND ARTICLES MAINLY MANUFACTURED: Total, Class II	3,872,903	3,112,947	3,773,935	*660,988	*901,032
III.—ARTICLES WHOLLY OR MAINLY MANUFACTURED:					
A. Iron and Steel and Manufactures thereof	2,216,563	2,627,859	3,568,611	*940,752	*1,352,049
B. Other Metals and Manufactures thereof	610,077	843,461	911,776	*68,315	*301,699
C. Cutlery, Hardware, Implements and Instruments	394,294	415,688	488,604	*72,916	*94,310
D. Electrical Goods and Apparatus b	106,897	505,843	586,580	*31,237	*480,683
E. Machinery	1,625,636	1,897,792	2,200,955	*303,163	*574,319
F. Ships (new)	325,805	642,251	494,692	†187,559	*161,887
G. Manufactures of Wood and Timber (including Furniture)	116,977	103,826	98,194	†5,632	†18,783
H. Yarns and Textile Fabrics:					
(1.) Cotton	7,943,530	8,807,535	9,160,827	*353,292	*1,217,297
(2.) Wool	2,701,238	2,776,600	3,091,984	*315,384	*390,746
(3.) Other Materials	1,005,849	1,135,082	1,301,967	*166,885	*296,118
I. Apparel	599,344	649,599	701,094	*51,495	*101,850
J. Chemicals, Drugs, Dyes and Colours	1,015,925	1,060,291	1,147,120	*86,829	*131,195
K. Leather and Manufactures thereof (including Boots and Shoes and Gloves)	426,142	506,611	569,025	*62,414	*142,883
L. Earthenware and Glass	297,727	272,926	333,080	*60,154	*35,353
M. Paper	147,204	154,749	166,710	*7,961	*19,506
N. Miscellaneous	1,815,805	2,103,692	2,472,425	*368,733	*656,620
Total, Class III	21,375,912	24,047,805	27,293,644	*3,246,339	*5,917,732
IV.—MISCELLANEOUS AND UNCLASSIFIED (including Parcel Post)	394,199	429,525	463,726	*34,201	*69,527
Total	26,859,880	29,517,836	33,492,614	*3,974,778	*7,132,734

a The values of the Exports represent the cost and the charges of delivering the goods on board the ship, and are known as the "free on board" values. *b* Other than Machinery, and Telegraph and Telephone Wire.

The declared value of the imports for the 8 months of this year shows an increase of 39,317,067l as compared with the corresponding period of 1905, and an increase of 42,693,222l compared with 1904. The value of our exports for the 8 months of this year shows an increase of 34,483,984l as compared with the corresponding period of 1905, and an increase of 52,268,963l compared with 1904.

Public Ledger 1906

LAUNCH OF A GREAT BATTLESHIP.

THE KING AT PORTSMOUTH.

[FROM OUR OWN REPORTER.]

PORTSMOUTH, Saturday.—As a spectacle the launch of H.M.S. Dreadnought by the King to-day was robbed of its brilliance. The King of Denmark's death not only prevented Queen Alexandra accompanying the Sovereign, as she had intended, but made inappropriate the elaborate decorations and other rejoicing which Portsmouth had contemplated to celebrate a striking event in the history of the British Navy. That the launching of the Dreadnought is such an event is one of the few points of agreement in the controversy which has been waged regarding the vessel. That controversy has been based mainly on conjecture, for the Admiralty officials have maintained a strict reticence regarding the design of their latest product. It has been agreed, too, both by those who approved and by those who denounced it, that the vessel marks an important departure in naval construction. Bearing a name honoured in the British Navy ever since "good Queen Bess's glorious day," the present Dreadnought will, when completed, be the largest, the swiftest, the most powerfully-armed, and the best-protected battleship in the world. In design she embodies the result of experience in the Far East naval struggle and of consultation with the most trusted British Admirals. In some respects an experiment, the cost of which is variously estimated at from a million and a half to two millions sterling, the new battleship is believed to combine all the features of an efficient fighting machine. For her speed of 21 knots an hour she will be indebted to turbines, which have been introduced for the first time in a line-of-battle ship, with modifications to give power of rapid manœuvring. Her armament will consist of ten 12-inch guns throwing 850 lb. projectiles, and so placed as to make six of the weapons effective for an end-on action ahead and eight for firing a broadside. Hitherto the most heavily armed battleship has not had more than four such guns. Unlike her predecessors, she will have no intermediate weapons. Her only other guns will be eight of 3 inches calibre for repelling torpedo attack. She will carry five submerged torpedo tubes, firing 18-inch torpedoes up to a range of 2000 yards. Her displacement will be 18,000 tons, and it is believed that the special design of the hull will make her unsinkable. Another feature of the Dreadnought's construction has been its rapidity. The keel was laid just eight days more than four months ago. It is hardly fair, however, to date the beginning of the ship from the 2d of October, as a great quantity of material had been collected and prepared before then. Even with that deduction, and allowing for the concentration of effort on one ship, the production of the hull in so short a time is a feat which has never been approached. It is at once the envy and the despair of other nations. In little more than a year from now it is expected that the Dreadnought will be commissioned.

The Scotsman 1906

THE Channel Tunnel is bound to come. The march of civilization makes it imperative, and no theories, or man's puny obstinacy, can withstand in the long run the obvious requirements of the race. When it does come it will in all likelihood be needed only for goods traffic and nervous persons, as light traffic and the great majority of passengers will prefer the more salubrious form of air transit.

AËRIAL navigation, or flight in the air, will render the Channel Tunnel devoid of all danger to this country, even in the minds of the most direful of Cassandras. When armies can manœuvre in the air they wont need to sneak through tunnels in the dead of night, or when the enemy has been kind enough to leave the far end open. The probability of being able to drop down large charges of awful explosives on any desired spot on the earth will cause wars to cease, or at least not be lightly entered into.

Health Resort 1907

THE OPIUM QUESTION.

THE discussion in Parliament last week on the trade in opium brings to the front again a problem which has admittedly hitherto been shelved rather than solved. Perhaps the present time is a more favourable opportunity to attempt its solution than we have had before. The old passions which gathered round the question have, to a large extent, died down. And the subject has recently been dealt with in one of those exhaustive surveys which are connected with the name of Rowntree. In his book "The Imperial Drug Trade," Mr. Joshua Rowntree quotes a mass of evidence bearing upon the history of the traffic, and our past and future policy in regard to it. Discussing the effects of opium on the Chinese, he maintains that the spectacle of their weakness in the conflict with England in the opium wars was one of the principal causes which led Japan to arm herself on European models. And what is more to the point, he holds that it was largely because they were demoralized by opium that the Chinese have presented such a remarkable contrast to Japan both in activity and military efficiency.

Church Times 1906

REPORT ON THE TRADE AND FINANCES OF THE REPUBLIC OF URUGUAY FOR THE YEAR 1905.

By Mr. Consul Kestell-Cornish.

The statistics of imports into Uruguay for the year 1905 show an increase under every classified heading over those for 1904, and, with the single exception of beverages, over the average of all classes for the five years ending 1904. This is no doubt due to the renewal of commercial activity and the restocking of commercial houses, which had been depleted during the Civil War. Exports show a decrease, owing principally to a diminution in the export of slaughter-house products and live-stock. No statistics are yet available which can show the participation of foreign countries in the trade of Uruguay for the year 1905 (even those for 1904 are not yet published), but it is hoped that with the existing material some useful information may be afforded.

It has, of course, to be borne in mind that 1905 was a good year, free from revolution, which was not the case with respect to 1904, but there is no doubt that Uruguay's trade with the United States has been, and still continues to be, steadily advancing.

The considerable growth in the general bulk of shipping at Montevideo is clearly demonstrated by the fact that at the date of writing these remarks (Sept. 19), 391 British ships are recorded at the Consulate as having entered the harbor in the year 1906, as against 322 ships at the same date in 1905 and only 293 ships during the corresponding period of 1904.

Public Ledger **1906**

The question of making choice of an economical and up-to-date method of sewage disposal for the town of Bedford has been pending several years. Circumstances of late have compelled more attention to be given to the subject, and it is understood that a proposal will be forthcoming ere long to adopt what is known as the "percolation system." One knows nothing whatever of the "percolation system," but one is assured, on very reputable authority that it answers its purpose so successfully that workmen on the sewage works where the system is in operation have been known to drink, with impunity, of the effluent produced from the purified sewage.

After this intimation we may venture to anticipate the recommendations of the Sewage Farm Committee somewhat on these lines: We can with great confidence recommend the adoption of the Percolation System, because not only is it perfectly efficient as a means of purification, but, by an adaptation of the Perpetual Motor Percolator, it will at once effect a marvellous economy and solve the water question for ever. By an ingenious application of the Archimedean rotating helix it will be possible to transfer the purified effluent to the mater-mains, and the same water can be used over and over again. It is obvious that this plan, so beautiful in its simplicity, will render the town independent of the Oolite rock, the Greensand, and the river Ouse, and at once get rid of all the expense incidental to pumping, filtering, driving headings, purchasing land, and all the rest of it.

Ampthill and District News **1908**

Mr. Albert Fletcher came specially from Manchester in his magnificent 48 horse-power motor-caravan, which was much admired. In this van he informed us he could travel 90 miles a day. He can sleep six comfortably, and the top, approached by a staircase from inside, affords a pleasant place for taking the air and seeing the scenery.

The World of Travel **1908**

In a leader on the Caravan Meet, the *Evening Standard* wrote: "To be free from hotels and waiters and tips, to be able to go to sleep in the country, and not in a noisy hostelry where people keep on arriving at unconscionable hours, and make the more noise the later they arrive, to sleep in a wood or on a moor, or by the side of a loch—these are some of the joys of caravanning. Our Teuton forefathers wandered over the vast steppes of Hungary, and through the still vaster forests of Germany, in rough caravans, and the instinct still lives strongly in every Englishman. 'Man is man and master of his fate' when he is in a caravan, and the Englishman, being the most independent person going, loves to caravan, provided he can afford one. We confidently predict that in the reaction from rushing about the country in motors we shall all take to the snail on wheels."

The World of Travel **1906**

Among the crew of the new Orient liner Orsova, which dropped anchor at Tilbury, recently, after her maiden cruise in the Channel, is a man with a strange record. He is a ship's barber, the match-making barber as he is called. "I have made 67 round trips to Australia," he said "and I can hardly recall a voyage upon which some young man has not met his 'fate' in the ship, and come to me to buy the ring to plight his troth. I do not keep wedding rings in stock, but I often get them made for passengers. A boiler fitter will make a plain gold ring out of an ordinary sovereign as fine as any ring can be bought at a jeweller's shop, and at a cost of only two shillings. Many couples who get engaged on the voyage like to have these as a memento and a novelty. I often tell the couples who come to me that I provide them with everything except a parson. I should say I have helped in at least 100 engagements.

Hairdresser and Toilet Requisites Gazette **1909**

THE FIRST FLIGHT ACROSS THE CHANNEL.

BRILLIANT ACHIEVEMENT BY A FRENCHMAN.

M. BLERIOT'S WONDERFUL SUCCESS.

ENTHUSIASTIC RECEPTION IN DOVER.

REMARKABLE SCENES.

M. Bleriot, the French aviator, successfully crossed the Channel on Sunday morning. His arrival was totally unexpected, and when a Marconigram had been dispatched from Les Baraques, near Calais, to say M. Bleriot had started, the exciting journey had already been commenced. The message had been sent shortly after 4.30, and the journey in crossing took about 43 minutes.

When the monoplane started, it quickly shot ahead of the French torpedo boat destroyer Escopette, whose commander had been hastily ordered to put to sea with all speed. Although the course of the flight was lengthened by the indirect line taken, the journey was then some twenty minutes quicker than the Channel boats from Calais to Dover.

It was twenty minutes to five when M. Bleriot started from the French coast, heading direct for Dover. The sea was then perfectly calm. The commander of the Escopette had been informed the attempt would be certainly made at sunrise, if the slightest opportunity afforded itself. The spot he had selected was between Shakespeare Cliff and Dover Harbour Jetty, where he hoped to land on the sand. The whole of the night was spent in vigil, there being no doubting the purpose of the determined aviator.

When M. Bleriot left M. Latham at midnight, the wind was gradually sinking, and he then determined to start at the break of dawn, and steal a march upon M. Latham. After a short sleep, he rose at three o'clock and went to Les Baraques. His aeroplane was quickly brought out from its shed, and taken to the middle of the field. M. Bleriot, who, owing to an injured foot, has been limping, threw away his walking-sticks, declaring, while taking his seat in the apparatus, "I shall not use them until I have been to England." He then carefully examined the machine and set the motor running.

A ten minutes' trial showed that everything was in working order. M. Bleriot gave instructions for the aeroplane to be taken to the point fixed for the start. The machinery whirred again. "Let go, all!" shouted M. Bleriot, and the aeroplane glided rapidly down the hill, amid the cheers of the spectators. It then rose triumphantly over the telegraph wires, flew for a few minutes across the dunes, and headed straight out to sea. She was soon lost to sight. Far in the distance all that could be seen was the smoke of the torpedo destroyer, attempting to keep up with the aeroplane.

Madame Bleriot, remembering the accident which had happened to Mr. Latham, had obtained permission to follow the flight on the Escopette. Her anxiety was very great as the destroyer continued its career out to sea with no sight of the aeroplane. Her fears were great that should any accident happen they would not be near her husband. It was not till the officer reported a boat was steering towards them with the news that her husband had reached England in safety that the lady's doubts were set at rest.

In the meantime, M. Bleriot, whose splendid start was made at about ten knots, by the aid of the wind was soon, with the assistance of his motor power, going at the rate of 40 miles an hour, which had quickly outdistanced the Escopette, she only speeding about 26 knots. In mid-Channel he lost some of the wind, but met a south-west wind nearer the English coast, which caused a very considerable drift, so that he had actually got within a reach of St. Margarets. He then turned his machine Dover-wards along the shore, and took a parallel direction for the Northfall Meadow, which further demonstrates his machine can be capably manipulated in the hands of a skilful operator.

The deflections in the currents were very trying at this time, and he found great difficulty in maintaining his stability, and the tendency of his craft to turn turtle caused him to take a seaward direction again. The south-west breeze was increasing, and he seemed to show less anxiety to land, as his objective was still the foot of Shakespeare Cliff. Suddenly, however, he caught sight of the valley where is situated Northfall Meadow, although at that time he was out beyond the harbour works. After three circles, his machine darted forward, and landed in the middle of the meadow, about 400 yards from the edge of the cliff.

Dover Telegraph and Continental Traveller **1909**

MONOPLANE FLIGHT ACROSS THE CHANNEL.

The flight from France to England was accomplished on Saturday by a Frenchman, M. Bleriot, in his monoplane "The Mascot." The distance is about twenty-one miles in a direct line.

In the early hours of the morning the aviator, after a ten minutes trial trip, flew from a spot near Calais, and in a brief period—about 35 minutes—landed safely in a meadow behind Dover Castle.

There was no hitch throughout the flight. A French torpedo-boat, the "Escopette," followed the flight, but it was left hopelessly behind by M. Bleriot, who travelled very rapidly. Mme. Bleriot was on board the torpedo-boat.

The news of the success of the flight was sent by wireless telegraphy to Calais, and led to a great outburst of enthusiasm.

Dover was asleep when, at about 5 o'clock, M. Bleriot landed. The town was quickly roused, and the aviator was given a most enthusiastic welcome from everybody.

North Devon Journal **1909**

THE KING AND THE NAVY.

REVIEW IN THE SOLENT.

EIGHTEEN MILES OF WARSHIPS.

The great Naval Review by the King in the Solent yesterday was favoured with magnificent weather. The vessels of the Fleet were ranged in six lines, each of which was six miles long. His Majesty therefore inspected eighteen miles of warships.

The yachts on which the members of the Royal Family had spent the night in Portsmouth Harbour cast anchor shortly before noon. The warships were gay with rainbow bunting, guards paraded on deck, while the naval bands played the National Anthem.

His Majesty, in the uniform of an Admiral, stood on the signalling bridge of the Victoria and Albert. On the same vessel were the Queen, the Prince and Princess of Wales, and the Lords of the Admiralty. The Duke and Duchess of Connaught were on the yacht Alexandra. In the procession were two other vessels—the Admiralty yacht Enchantress and the Commander-in-Chief's yacht Firequeen.

The flotilla went for a short cruise before anchoring off Ryde for luncheon, after which the yachts were joined by the White Star liner Adriatic, on which were members of both Houses of Parliament.

When the Review started, the wind became fresh, but the weather continued brilliantly fine, and the spectacle was one of great animation. As the Royal yacht entered the lines of the Fleet every ship was manned, and the bluejackets and marines, ranged in lines on the decks and superstructures, gave three hearty cheers for His Majesty. The whole of the Royal party stood on the bridge to acknowledge the reception.

Every ship carrying saluting guns fired a Royal salute of twenty-one guns, and as the cheering was taken up by ship after ship and line after line the effect was most impressive.

The Royal progress occupied about an hour, and the flotilla then anchored close to the Dreadnought, to witness a torpedo-boat destroyer and submarine attack on the flagship, which was carried out in realistic fashion.

His Majesty and the Royal party showed the keenest interest in the display, and afterwards received the principal officers of the Fleet aboard the Victoria and Albert.

While the firing of the Royal salute for the King was proceeding on the Téméraire, the 4in. gun had a back-fire, and four men in the turret were so seriously hurt as to necessitate their early removal to Haslar Hospital. The names of the men are Able Seaman Foran (the most serious case), Petty Officer Kennet, and Seamen Truscott and Jenkins. All are suffering from powder burns and shock.

Referee 1909

ORTON.

PRESENTATION TO RAILWAY GUARDS.—The Misses Wharton Duff of Orton House have, with their usual generosity, again this year presented each Highland Railway guard on the Inverness and Keith section with a pair of hand-knitted socks as a New Year's present. The Misses Wharton Duff's great kindness has been much appreciated by the recipients.

Northern Scot 1908

It's Never Too Late to Mend.

The following appeared in the daily papers last week :

PRINCESS'S KINDLY ACT.

The mother of the boy who was recently killed by the Duchess of Connaught's motor car has received from her Royal Highness a Christmas hamper and a cheque, in addition to the gifts made at the time of the accident.

This is a worthier answer to our appeal and questioning than Major Murray's first retort.

'Our relief fund will now be closed and its proceeds disposed of as Mrs. Coker may determine.

Clarion 1907

1910–1919

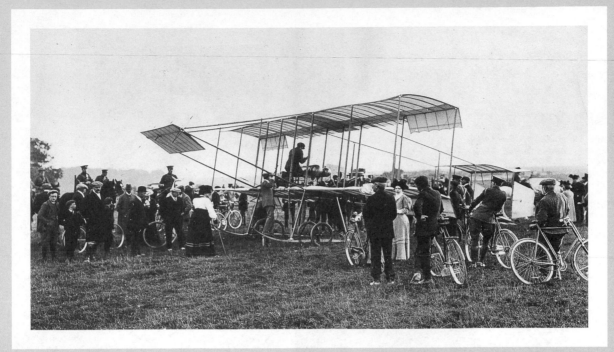

Salisbury Plain, 1910: a Bristol Boxkite biplane being prepared for flight during British Army manoeuvres.

ROLLS' RECORD.

MAGNIFICENT FLIGHT.

CHANNEL CROSSED & RE-CROSSED.

DOVER TO CALAIS AND BACK IN 1½ HOURS.

INTERVIEW BY THE "DOVER AND COUNTY CHRONICLE" REPRESENTATIVE.

Dover has had many disappointments over the Channel flight, but Thursday night was fully repaid for its long time of waiting, the Hon. C. S. Rolls not only leaving the English coast for the French cliffs (which were beautifully in sight the whole evening), but returning in full view of the thousands of spectators who lined the shore, the hills, and every point of vantage. It was throughout an ideal evening, and the Channel was clear from coast to coast, with only a dash of clouds here and there, but well above the aviator.

Mr Rolls left the high ground to the east of Dover Castle at 6.30, and in a few minutes was well on his way in direct course to Calais. At about 7.30 a telegram was received from Calais to the effect that he had safely arrived, a later message announcing his return to sea, and, in consequence, great excitement prevailed at Dover, especially as he was not accompanied by any faster vessels than the two tugs, the Lady Curzon and the Gnat, the torpedo vessels having had orders in the morning to leave the port and return to their regular stations. Everyone was on the tiptoe of expectation, with their eyes directed towards the French cliffs, where a haze was hanging.

At about ten minutes to eight Rolls' machine was observed immediately over the lightship outside the Dover breakwater, and in a line from the centre of the town. He was travelling at a tremendous pace, and rapidly approaching, taking a line the town side of Dover Castle. As he passed between the town and the Castle the airship presented a graceful spectacle, and a mighty roar of welcome and cheers went up that must have reached the first aviator to cross and re-cross the English Straits, and the first Britisher to cross the Channel. Having got above the town, Rolls, showing a remarkable control of his machine, gradually bent his course around the Castle to his garage, from which he had started an hour and a-half previously.

Dover and County Chronicle **1910**

THE FUTURE OF AVIATION.

The tragic death of the Hon. C. S. Rolls at Bournemouth has brought home the dangers of aviation to the people of this country as no previous occurrence of the kind has succeeded in doing. His brilliant exploits in the air, following upon equally notable achievements in motoring, had won him remarkable popularity, and to thousands who had never seen him, the news of his untimely death brought a sense of almost personal loss. Universal sympathy is felt for Lord and Lady Llangattock in their bereavement, while the nation realises that it has lost a man whom it could ill spare. The present month has added three more victims to the steadily lengthening death-roll of the new science, and the public are beginning to ask whether it is worth while. Indeed, many correspondents, in the columns of a London temporary, have answered the question emphatically in the negative. But we may be certain that, even though a considerable section of the public may be opposed to any further experiments in aviation, and would gladly see them prohibited, the science has come to stay, and will continue to attract many devotees. "Flying" appears to exercise the same fascination upon the human mind as mountaineering, so that even on the day following the tragedy at Bournemouth a number of persons were willing to be taken into the air as passengers, and were the envy of hundreds of others who would gladly have embraced a similar opportunity. But the death of Mr Rolls seems likely to have one good result. There is a growing feeling that the whole question of the future of aviation must be seriously considered. Is it to be pursued on scientific lines, and regarded as a thing of importance to the country? or is it to be looked upon as a pastime for sightseers, and reduced to the level of a "penny show"?

Dunstable Borough Journal **1910**

The first British pilot's licence, awarded to J.T.C. Moore-Brabazon on 8 March 1910.

CYCLE AND MOTOR AMALGAMATION.

It is reported that an official announcement will shortly be made of the amalgamation of the Birmingham Small Arms Company and the Daimler Motor Company, Coventry.

The B.S.A, which has an authorised capital of £1,000,000, for the past three years has paid an Ordinary dividend of 10 per cent.

The Daimler capital is £500,000. An interim dividend of 5 per cent. has been paid for the current year, but for the two preceding years no Ordinary dividend was declared.

Dunstable Borough Journal 1910

WORLD'S FLYING RECORDS.

It was officially announced at Lanark on Friday that in the course of his flight on Thursday, when for some time he was lost to sight in the clouds, Mr. Drexel attained the world's record altitude of 6,750 feet. His barograph will be submitted to Kew Observatory to check the accuracy of the instrument.

In an interview Mr. Drexel said he felt the cold badly in his flight. He climbed to 6,700 feet in one hour, and then the next 50 feet took him four minutes. Discovering that he was short of lubricating oil, he resolved to descend.

He was enveloped in cloud, and after an hour in descending he came in view of an expanse of water, which proved to be Cobbinshaw Loch, distant about fifteen miles from Lanark.

A farmer came to his assistance and provided some hot food. Getting a cycle, Mr. Drexel despatched telegrams to different places, and by midnight motors were with him. He was back in Lanark at one a.m., and so keen was he that an adjournment was made to the course to compare his barograph with the official theodolite.

Flying began on Friday, with the wind blowing twenty-four to twenty-eight miles an hour. The starting competition was first entered upon. This test is for the quickest rise from the line, and Mr. McArdle was the third to ascend. He was caught in a gust and blown towards the hangars. The chassis and the propeller of his machine were smashed, but the aviator was unhurt.

By starting in a distance of 57 feet, Mr. Radley has made a world's record. The previous world's record was by Paulhan at Budapesth a month ago, when he rose in 77 feet.

Dunstable Borough Journal 1910

BALL MOTOR PARTY'S TERRIBLE SMASH UP.

SERIOUS INJURY TO MISS DOROTHY COURT, MIDDLEWICH.

OFFICER'S LEG BROKEN.

A motor-car returning from a ball at Ashbourne early yesterday ran into a telegraph pole on the Derby-road about a mile and a half from Ashbourne, and three persons were severely injured.

The ball was that of the Dove Valley Harriers. The party in the motor-car consisted of Miss Dorothy Court, of Middlewich, Cheshire, Lieut. F. Arkwright, Capt. Talbot, and the chauffeur, Tuck. They were driving to Ormaston Manor, when the car got on to the grass, skidded for thirty or forty yards, and ran with great force against a telegraph pole. Lieut. Arkwright, who was driving, was thrown into a ditch. The car was smashed to pieces, and portions of it clung to the pole which it had struck. Miss Court was found among the fragments at the back of the car. The chauffeur was pitched through the glass screen. Capt. Talbot was the most fortunate, escaping with some bruises and a shaking.

The early mail car driver, Hodgkins, was coming from Derby. Hearing the smash and cries for help, he got down and with his lamp promptly gave assistance. He lifted Lieut. Arkwright from the ditch and removed Miss Court from the wreckage. The chauffeur was wandering pitifully about the road with his hands over his face, and Capt. Talbot was also distracted. Another motor-car returning from the ball was stopped, and the injured received attention.

It was found that Miss Court's collar bone was broken, and that she had deep cuts on the face. After attention she was sent back to Ormaston Manor. Later in the day it was reported that she was in a critical condition, that a specialist had been called in. Both Lieut. Arkwright's legs were broken, and his thigh was fractured, and Tuck's face was terribly lacerated.

Miss Court is daughter of Mr. W. Roylance Court, of Middlewich Manor, joint master of the Cheshire Hounds, and Lieut. Arkwright, who only came of age a short time ago, is the son of Mr. F. C. Arkwright, of Wollersley Castle, Cromford.

Chester Chronicle 1912

The People 1911

MUSCULAR PARSON

ROWS THE CHANNEL IN RECORD TIME.

A remarkably fine record for sculling across the Channel was set up by the Rev. Sidney Swann, Vicar of Crosby Ravensworth, Westmoreland, who rowed from Dover to Sangatte, near Calais, in a racing skiff in the extraordinarily short time of three hours fifty minutes.—Mr. Swann was accompanied by the motor launch Win, in charge of Mr. P. Walker. A start was made from Dover outer harbour at 4.50 in the morning, the weather being favourable to the event, but not ideal, for there was a fresh breeze against the sculler right across the Channel. The sea was inclined to be choppy and the strong spring tides are still running. Mr. Swann, who is an old 'Varsity Blue, having been included in the Cambridge eight for three years, is an accomplished sculler, and pulling a long steady stroke his skiff shot out of the harbour and into the Channel. At the end of the first hour no less than seven miles directly across Channel had been covered by Mr. Swann, whose long sweeping strokes gave no idea of the great pace at which the skiff was being driven across the Channel currents, so easily and comfortably did the clerical athlete appear to be taking his work.

In Difficult Water.

After taking a glass of cold milk Mr. Swann again got under way, and in less than half an hour was in mid-Channel over 10 miles from Dover. About this time the oarsman had a rather uncomfortable experience, getting a good deal of wash from a large East India steamer. The manoeuvre to pass had taken Mr. Swann somewhat out of his course, but he soon set the skiff's head right again for the French shore. He was still making an average of 27 to the minute,

The Rev. Sidney Swann.
[Photo by Barrett.

and this he maintained almost without variation for the rest of the voyage. The distance was rapidly reduced by five miles, then the breeze got stiffer and lumpy seas were met with, which made the sculler's task a very difficult one. It needed very careful handling of the light craft if she were not to be swamped on the last stage of a record row. Another mile was covered with the conditions becoming steadily worse. In the last mile, which was being closely watched by the interested onlookers ashore, white-capped waves broke over the frail craft and she became almost waterlogged. Mr. Swann had to manoeuvre his boat in the last pinch to avoid the sandbanks, but at 8.40 he safely grounded his boat on the shore and landed. At Sangatte the spectators heartily congratulated Mr. Swann on his notable achievement.

HANDSOME LIMOUSINE BY HOLMES AND CO. ON A 17 H.P. FOUR-CYLINDER MAUDSLAY CHASSIS.

Queen 1912

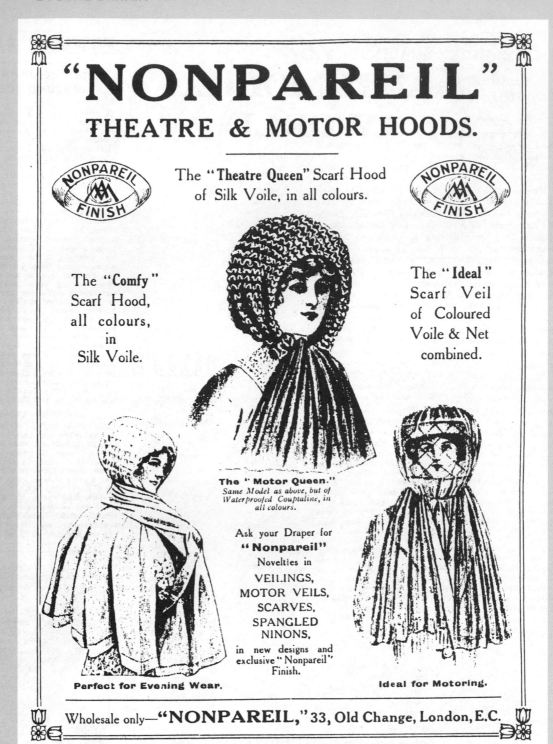

"NONPAREIL"
THEATRE & MOTOR HOODS.

The "Theatre Queen" Scarf Hood of Silk Voile, in all colours.

NONPAREIL FINISH

The "Comfy" Scarf Hood, all colours, in Silk Voile.

The "Ideal" Scarf Veil of Coloured Voile & Net combined.

The "Motor Queen."
Same Model as above, but of Waterproofed Couptaline, in all colours.

Ask your Draper for "Nonpareil" Novelties in VEILINGS, MOTOR VEILS, SCARVES, SPANGLED NINONS, in new designs and exclusive "Nonpareil" Finish.

Perfect for Evening Wear.

Ideal for Motoring.

Wholesale only—"NONPAREIL," 33, Old Change, London, E.C.

TO CORRESPONDENTS.

CLAUDE ORPEN.—There is no motor-car on the market in this country which has a ground clearance of 20 inches. To secure that would necessitate the use of road wheels over 4 feet in diameter. Of course, such could be supplied, no doubt, but solid tyres would be an inevitable consequence. The largest clearance you will secure in a standard car built for colonial use is about 11 inches—involving the use of 36 inch wheels, with propellor shaft drive. The firms we would advise you to get into communication with are Argylls Ltd., Alexandria, Scotland; Clement-Talbot Ltd., Burlby-road, North Kensington, London, W.; S. F. Edge Ltd., 14, New Burlington-street; Star Engineering Company, Wolverhampton; and Wolseley Tool and Motor Car Co. Ltd., Adderley-park, Birmingham, who make special colonial models with low gears and maximum road clearance, and would meet your other requirements.

A Fine Limousine.

The bodywork of the limousine illustrated is by Messrs Holmes and Co., it is mounted on a 17 h.p. Maudslay chassis. The weight of the body has been curtailed to a marked degree, so that it is only about 1¼ cwt. heavier than a Torpedo touring car with screen and hood. Frameless windows are fitted throughout, which helps to take away from the heavy look often associated with this type of body, and the Clement patent fittings enable the windows to move over the plate fitted on the doors and prevents rain entering the window runs. The lines of the side panes and the sweep of the roof from back to front are good, the curve of the latter not being exaggerated. There is good accommodation for three persons on the back seat and two on the extra seats, fitted at the back of the driving seat. The cushions are comfortable and the fitting and finishing of the car generally is in good taste. A similar car is now being built for Her Royal Highness the Princess Christian.

Queen 1912

DAZED MAN'S AWAKENING

—

STRANGE STORY OF RECOVERY UNDER A HOSE IN MID-OCEAN.

How a man regained his senses after an illness and found himself on a ship crossing the Atlantic was described at Brighton Bankruptcy Court by Mr. Charles Stride, formerly well known as an auctioneer, of Chichester. He denied that there was any truth in the recently-published reports that he lost his memory while travelling from New York last May, or that he had been robbed in that city. Learning by cable that a bankruptcy petition had been presented against him he went straight to the docks and got on the first boat he could find, to come to England to reply to it. He said:

I had been ill, and suffered from the heat. I became dazed, and the next thing I knew was that I was on a ship at sea. I was on deck, and members of the crew were flourishing a hose which, through not seeing me, they turned on my head. (Laughter.) They helped me down to the saloon, where the stewards found me in the morning when they got breakfast. I had been without anything to eat for 48 hours. They asked me my name, but at the moment I said I did not know. I could not reply to 20 questions at once. They made up a tale about a man who had lost his memory. They told me I could not have got on board without a ticket, but I said I did. I never told them I had been robbed. That was an invention, and I think the reporters are as bad in England as they are in New York. (Laughter.) On arriving my sons paid my passage.

Mr. Stride valued his Chichester estate at £83,000, and denied that his estimated surplus of £50,000 was fanciful. His difficulties had arisen through a bank objecting to his paying a Stock Exchange loss of £6,000 out of business account. He thereupon transferred the business to his two sons. He declared that he was perfectly solvent. In America he was doing well in a real estate office, but through being followed about by detectives he had to give it up. He stopped one of the detectives and asked him what he wanted. The detective prevaricated, saying he knew friends of his in England. At one period his overdraft at the bank was as much as £20,000.

News of the World 1912

MEN WERE SPLENDID!

GAVE UP CHANCE OF LIFE FOR WOMEN.

Continuing, Mr. Lightoller said that Boat No. 6 was filled under his supervision. He handed the women in himself, taking them by the wrist as they dropped in. He reassured the passengers by telling them that apparently there was a passenger vessel in the distance which would probably pick them up. He did not think at that time that the ship was going down.—President: Some of the boats carried considerably more than 40 passengers?—Yes; 65 in some cases.—Speaking of the lowering of the last collapsible boat on the port side, witness said there was some difficulty in getting the boat filled with women. "On one occasion, at least," he said, "someone standing close to the boat said, 'There are no more women,' and with that several men began to climb in. Just then someone cried out at the back, 'Here are a couple of women,' and so the men got out again and put the women in. I think this happened on two occasions."—The Solicitor-General: When you say men got out, do

MR CHARLES LIGHTOLLER

you mean men passengers?—I cannot say now.—They gave up their places?—Yes.—When that boat was filled and ready to go were there, so far as you could ascertain, any more women about?—None whatever. I am under the impression that I could have put more women into the boat, and also some more men; but I did not feel justified in giving the order for more men to get in, as it was the last boat leaving the ship, so far as I knew, and I thought it better to get into the water safely with the number she already had—in other words, I did not want the boat to be "rushed."—Were there men passengers about?—There were a good many people about.—Was good order being maintained then?—Splendid.—Was there any attempt to "rush" that boat?—None whatever, except that men began to climb in when they knew there were no more women.—Was there no man in any of the boats you saw lowered?—None, with the exception of a Major Peuchin, whom I ordered in. Mr. Lightoller then described in calm tones his thrilling experiences during his last minutes on the Titanic. After the last boat was lowered, he went across to the starboard side of the officers' quarters to see if he could do anything, but could not. There were other officers there, including the first officer, who was working at the falls of the starboard emergency boat.—The Solicitor-General: Then what happened?—She seemed to take a bit of a dive, and I

JUST WALKED INTO THE WATER.

Chester Chronicle 1912

APPALLING DISASTER
TO
THE TITANIC.

1,453 LIVES LOST

ONLY 705 SURVIVORS.

RECORD CATASTROPHE.

Message of Sympathy from the King and Queen.

ARRIVAL OF THE RESCUED PASSENGERS.

THE BAND PLAYED A HYMN AS THE SHIP WENT DOWN.

Chester Chronicle 1912

BOATS FOR ALL.

LESSONS OF THE TITANIC CATASTROPHE.

FAR-REACHING REGULATIONS NOW RECOMMENDED.

North Eastern Daily Gazette 1913

"Boats for all" would seem the one outstanding lesson enforced by the Titanic disaster on the members of the Merchant Shipping Advisory Committee of the Board of Trade. After many weeks' deliberation this committee has now issued its report "respecting the statutory regulations as to boats and life-saving appliances and other means of ensuring safety at sea," and its recommendations are of a far-reaching character. The chief of these are:—

Boat and raft accommodation for all on board.
Two efficient boat hands for each boat carried under davits.
With a lascar crew, two lascars and an officer or petty officer able to communicate orders to them, should be allotted to each boat.
Ships should go at moderate speed in the known vicinity of ice.
Searchlights would be inadvisable.
Binoculars for look-out men are inadvisable.
There should be a periodical inspection of ships' boats.
Measures for safety should be enforced on the basis of an international agreement.
There should be means of access to the bulkhead deck from each compartment below.
All foreign-going vessels with more than 50 passengers should be compelled to maintain a constant watch by wireless.
One expert operator, with an assistant able to recognise a danger signal, would be sufficient.
Wireless stations should be established at all points on shore where they would be most useful, "as a national duty."

The committee are of opinion that boat accommodation is of less importance than making a ship as nearly unsinkable as possible. "The circumstances attendant on the loss of the Titanic," it is stated, "have demonstrated the extraordinary difficulty, even in calm weather, of using to the full in a passenger vessel carrying large numbers the boat accommodation already provided, and thereby emphasised the view we expressed in our report of July 4, 1911, as to the necessity for taking all possible precautions to provide for

THE BUOYANCY OF THE VESSEL

Chester Chronicle 1912

RAILLESS TROLLEY CAR PROPOSALS.

BOURNEMOUTH.—A company propose to install a railless trolley car service from the County Gates to Canford Cliffs and the Sandbanks, in the vicinity of Bournemouth, with a view to develop one of the most charming districts on the South Coast. Replying to objections urged against the scheme, the promoters' engineers state that the poles they propose to erect would not be of the tramway type, but light poles erected wherever possible in a line with the trees, in positions where they would be practically out of sight; that the type of current collector to be used is practically noiseless; and that the wear on the roads would be considerably less than that caused by the operation of the existing petrol vehicles.

YORK.—At their September meeting the City Council referred back to the Tramways Committee for further consideration their recommendation to apply for powers to run railless trolley cars along two routes to Heworth and Haxby Road. Councillor Sharp, who moved the adoption of the report, in reply to a question stated that the terms offered with the demonstration motor omnibus which was brought to the city were altogether prohibitive. Councillor Clarke observed that the only objection that was made at the time of the trial was that the omnibus did not hold sufficient people.

ABERDEEN.—The shareholders of Aberdeen Suburban Tramways Company have given the directors authority to work railless trolley cars or other mechanically-propelled vehicles in connection with the undertaking. Replying to a shareholder, the chairman said the directors were alive to what had been accomplished in connection with 'buses in London. It would not be wise to say definitely what vehicles would be best, but there was a strong feeling in favour of motor 'buses among the directors.

MARCONI.

GIVING OF CONTRACT JUSTIFIED.

TECHNICAL INQUIRY'S

VINDICATION OF MR HERBERT SAMUEL'S

BUSINESS JUDGMENT AND ACUMEN.

The report of the Technical Committee on the Marconi contract, which has been received by the Postmaster-General, was handed to the Select Committee, and has been laid on the table of the House of Commons. It is a document of great importance and must influence the future course of the inquiry.

Broadly speaking, so far as it deals with rival systems of wireless telegraphy, it is an emphatic justification of the Postmaster-General and his expert advisers.

The Technical Committee reports that the Marconi system is at present the only practicable long-distance system. If that be so after a year of rapidly advancing experiment, how much more must it have been so in March last year when the Postmaster-General entered provisionally into the agreement?

On the other hand, the Technical Committee, going perhaps a little outside its terms of reference, has given its sanction to the main points put forward in the evidence before the Select Committee given last autumn by Sir Henry Norman and Sir Croydon Marks.

TRUTH ABOUT MARCONI SYSTEM.

We report, therefore, that, according to our investigation, the Marconi system is at present the only system of which it can be said with any certainty that it is capable of fulfilling the requirements of the Imperial chain.

Votes for Women 1913

"A Tram emulates the Suffragists" is the *Daily Graphic's* title for a picture of an accident at Birmingham on January 30, when a car ran into a shop window.

Tramway and Railway World 1913

Protection from Vibration.

One of the greatest bugbears connected with swift travel is vibration. Even the least sensitive person understands the wearing effect of perpetual vibration of the wrong sort. The best car can hardly be said to be entirely free from it. It is therefore that the air foot-rest made by Messrs Pontifex, of Buckingham Palace-road, is so welcome to lady or invalid motorists. The difference it makes to one's comfort is very considerable, for vibration reaches the spine through the legs and produces a sense of weariness, and even headache after a long run. The inflating motor foot-rest is the greatest help in eliminating this nerve-destroying factor of motoring.

Queen 1914

"VALE"—A DIRGE.

No more along our ancient streets shall roll
  What was of yore the glory of the town;
"Thy doom is sealed," and ne'er again will run
  The one-horse tram.

"When first our eyes beheld the verdict harsh,
  The only outcome of the modern world,
What thoughts of sorrow filled our hearts for thee
  Thou one-horse tram."

"Thy death will truly be a loss to some,
  Ears will be strained to hear thy trundling wheels."
Eyes seek in vain their well-beloved friend,
  Their gentle, safe and slow old one-horse tram.

"The country-woman who didn't trust before
  Her ancient limbs confidingly to thee
Must plod henceforth on weary feet along,
  Fearing thy rough supplanter, one-horse tram."

And of the aged beasts themselves, who long
  Have made the toilsome journey to and fro,
What is their fate? Will no one weep for them?
  The patient workers of the one-horse tram.

The Granta 1914

TRAFFIC LAWS FOR BRITAIN'S AIR.

All Craft from Abroad Must Land at Fixed Places.

PROHIBITED AREAS.

Permits from British Consuls and Fees for Continuing Voyage.

NO CAMERAS OR PIGEONS.

Britain has tabulated her first code of laws controlling her aerial highways.

Very drastic indeed are the rules concerning the traffic on Britannia's airway, which have been drawn up by the Committee of Imperial Defence, and are now issued by the Home Office.

It is provided that every person in charge of an airship leaving a foreign country for the United Kingdom—

MUST obtain authorisation from a British Consul, giving full particulars of himself and every person on board.

MUST state the intended time and place of his landing at one of only eight specific strips of coastline.

MUST inform the Home Office by letter and telegram of his intentions.

MUST report himself on landing and pay £3, and must not proceed further without special permit.

MUST carry no camera, carrier pigeons, explosives, firearms, mails or dutiable goods.

MUST land immediately in response to certain specific signals giving warning of the prohibited area.

But this aerial board of control—the A.B.C. foreshadowed in a then incredible airship romance written a dozen years ago by Rudyard Kipling—exercises a rigid control also over flying men who start within the United Kingdom.

No fewer than sixty-eight prohibited places are named within three miles of which no man may fly, whether he comes from Hendon or Heligoland, and any airship which attempts to fly over a prohibited area is liable to be fired upon.

Six months' imprisonment and a £200 fine are the extreme penalties for contravention of the orders, but espionage makes a man liable to seven years' penal servitude.

Daily Mirror 1913

Ypres, 1914: a naval armoured car on the Menin road.

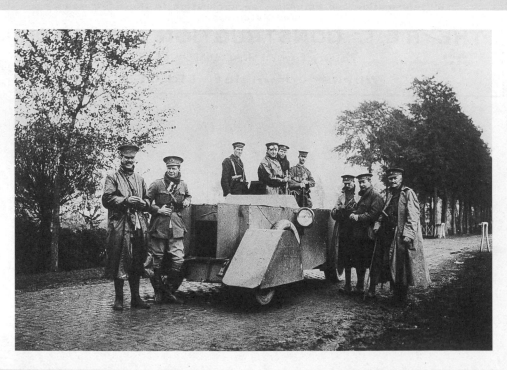

POLE THROUGH BUS

Passenger's Remarkable Escape in Whitehall.

An extraordinary accident occured in Whitehall last night in which a gentleman in a motor-bus had a miraculous escape.

A pair-horsed van collided with the bus, and the pole of the van crashed through the side of the bus, pinning the passenger, who was seated on the opposite side. The man was extricated and conveyed to Westminster Hospital, where it was found he had escaped injury and was merely suffering from shock.

It was a marvellous escape, for had the pole been an inch nearer the man would have been transfixed. As it was, the pole passed between his top coat and waistcoat.

The Star 1914

WHY THE OKLAHOMA WAS LOST.

Rescue Work Handed On From Ship To Ship.

Five more survivors of the Oklahoma, the oil tank steamer which sank in the Western Atlantic, have been brought into New York, making the total number saved 13.

There is some mystery about the loss of the vessel. Captain Graalf, of the Bavaria, in a wireless message to the Hamburg-Amerika Line, states that there was no explosion, and he cannot account for the vessel breaking in two.

Captain Bonet, of the Spanish steamer Manuel Calvo, says they left the Oklahoma when darkness fell, as the vessel had no searchlight and the tanker was unlighted. The weather rendered it dangerous to cruise near. A searchlight, the captain declared, would have saved the situation.

Apparently the tendency of the home vessels was to assume that some other attempt at rescue was being made, and a tramp handed the job to the Spaniard, who in turn entrusted the tanker to the Georgic.

The Bavaria and the Glasgow steamer Tenadores raced at full speed to the rescue, the Bavaria being the first to arrive.

Daily Sketch 1914

On the Road in War Time: Cautions.

One does not expect to see much optical evidence of the war in Fleet-street, yet in crossing to the south side of it the other day I was held up by a smart Rolls-Royce with polished aluminium tapered bonnet, bearing the official letters, O.H.M.S., instead of the ordinary number plate. Two khaki-clad officers alighted, and arrested the attention of a group of passers-by. Elsewhere one can see plenty of cars without number plates bearing instead the letters W.D., or the broad arrow signifying Government property. For such cars there is apparently no speed limit in the neighbourhood of mobilising centres or in one of the towns at present garrisoned, policemen giving precedence to them and holding up other traffic for their benefit. On the other hand private cars have their liberty justly restricted at the moment. Those touring outside the district indicated by their number plate are liable to be held up and searched. Many drivers have been stopped and asked to show their licences. The police of High Wycombe are authorised to search all motor-cars that pass through the borough. It is hardly necessary to point out that all such interruptions must be taken in good humour. As to driving at night, in their own interests, motorists are advised to drive with care, and to obey instantly any command by the military. Troops have precedence at all times,

Queen 1914

Practical Flying.

A quite delightful, readable, yet practical book has been produced by the collaboration of one of our finest fliers and a well-known journalist who also has his pilot's certificate, and the names of Mr Hamel and Mr C. C. Turner are sufficient guarantee of the accuracy of any statements made. The book is called *Flying: Some Practical Experiences*. Mr Hamel has a faculty for expressing himself on paper, and some of his picturesque descriptions are vivid word pictures. I was especially interested in his observations during cross-country flying of the effect produced on the air, and consequently upon the behaviour of his machine, by the colour of the fields over which he was passing. The brown of a ploughed field approached from green fields produces quite a bump, while in a lesser degree the passage from the latter to a field of yellow flowers—and one thinks of the colza fields of Normandy—gives quite a noticeable disturbance. This argues the sensitiveness of the air to colour. The sad accident which cost the young sergeant of the R.F.C. his life last week is a confirmation of the authors' statement in the chapter on accidents and their prevention. Over-confidence and youthful foolhardiness have perhaps been responsible for half at least of all the flying fatalities on record. Of no science can it more truly be said that a little knowledge is a dangerous thing.

Queen 1914

Two Years' Travel in a Napier.

Mr Oscar Asche and his wife have made an extensive tour during their absence from England, having visited Australia, Mr Asche's native land, New Zealand, and South Africa. During this two years' theatrical campaign they have made their journeys chiefly by motor-car, and have driven upwards of 34,000 miles. Their car was a Napier landaulette, and it is an interesting fact that, in spite of all kinds of roads and all sorts of weather, there was not throughout the entire journey the slightest hitch with the car itself, though naturally tyres had to be renewed. This is splendid testimony to the good work turned out by this famous firm. Since the Olympia Show, where, as a rule, one finds all the 1914 models, Messrs Napier have introduced a new model, which takes its place between the popular 15 and the 16-22 h.p. types, with R.A.C. rating 19·4 h.p. The engine is similar to that of the 16-22, while the remainder of the chassis follows the practice of the 15. There are four speeds, and gear change is easy to make. The springing is on a good principle, which renders shock absorbers almost unnecessary. This is attained by the thin leaves of the springs, which give a sensitive support without any considerable rebound. The front springs are of the semi-elliptical type, while the rear has rather unusually long three-quarter ellipticals.

Queen 1914

The War Work of the Aeroplane.

How often at Hendon and elsewhere have I heard the pessimist or the unimaginative man deride the aeroplane as an aggressive armament, and declare that its only practical use would be as a scout. Their prophecies have been falsified by recent occurrences, and now the Army aviators are getting experience of real warfare we shall probably hear of still more remarkable doings. It is happily not true that Garros lost his life in an attempt to ram a Zeppelin. But M. Pegoud, of looping fame, has stated that a military aviator has succeeded in destroying the airship hangar near Metz and its contents, a Zeppelin and three Taube aeroplanes. There could hardly be a less appropriate name for a war aeroplane than *taube!* M. Pegoud himself has been under fire, and in the course of an aerial raid of close on 200 miles over the frontier his aeroplane was pierced ninety-seven times by bullets and twice by shells. But his bombs took deadly effect in blowing up two German convoys. The piercing of the aeroplane disproves, on the other hand, the assertions of the optimist that it would not be possible to hit a fast-travelling machine. Yet to hit the aircraft and to bring it down are evidently not two things in necessary sequence. It seems possible for the wings and fuselage to suffer considerable damage before a descent becomes compulsory.

Queen 1914

The Pianomaker 1915

Instead of the cry being "A kingdom for a horse," for the moment many piano manufacturers are crying, "A ransom for a packing-case." The railway companies do not realise the importance of "returned empties," and are holding empty cases back in large numbers. A managing director of a large firm informed me the other day that he had quite a large number of pianos hung up, not being able to obtain his empties from the dealers through the dilatoriness of the railway companies.

Not only is there difficulty in this direction, but more trouble is being caused by pianos and players not being delivered at their destinations by the railways. Doubtless the companies are still at the call of the Government, but it is a serious matter when business is arrested in this manner.

Ten Months' Wine Clearances.   No Real Improvement.

The official statistics concerning our trade now possess more practical interest and significance as they deal with periods covering completely the beginning and continuance of the great War, which has brought, and is destined to inflict, such a vast amount of irreparable injury upon the world. In dealing with the September figures we pointed out that the marked increase in imports and clearances of Wines shown by them should not be taken as an indication of improved demand, for, as we further remarked, most shippers and merchants had unnecessarily added to their obligations in fear of further taxation. This panic-stricken state of affairs is past, and the Trade is now getting upon a firmer and more normal footing than at any period since the European conflict started. The imports for last month amounted to 987,117 gallons, a gain of 88,674 ; and the total loss on the year is consequently reduced to 691,416 gallons. The clearances during October were upon 910,383 gallons, an increase of 13,321 gallons, and the total deficit on the twelve months is now reduced to 404,291 gallons.

Wine and Spirit Gazette 1915

Queen 1914

The British Music Trades' Ambulance.

SOON after the outbreak of the War, Mr. Wilfrid Holmes, son of Mr. Henry Holmes (Mortimer Street, W.), started an idea of supplying a motor ambulance for the use of the British Red Cross Society. He communicated with Mr. Dent, of the B.R.C.S., and was informed that a lady had kindly given a chassis on the understanding that it was to be used as an ambulance by the B.R.C.S.,

The Pianomaker **1915**

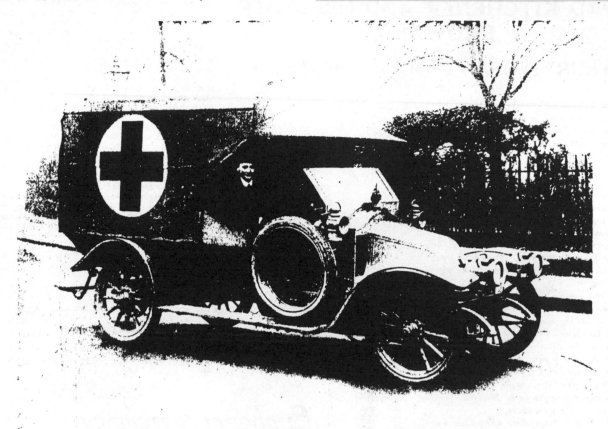

providing a body was supplied. Mr. Holmes immediately approached some members of the piano trade for subscriptions to purchase a body suitable for conveying wounded soldiers, and the result up to the present has been that he has succeeded in collecting £57 out of the £75 required. He, acting as chauffeur, has already made several journeys from various London termini to hospitals and convalescent homes.

Abergele Visitor **1916**

WOUNDED'S WEARY WALK.

The sight of some eighteen or twenty wounded soldiers—some of them severely broken in the war—being marched from Pensarn station to Kinmel Camp, a four mile tramp, occasioned considerable comment in the town the other day. At intervals the poor fellows had perforce to halt for rest, and passers-by noted tears welling into the eyes of not a few of them as they slowly passed along. Possibly it never occurred to the authorities to ask Mr. J. Williams, Harp Hotel, or any other local car-proprietor, to provide conveyances to take the gallant party to their destination. We know nothing would afford them more real pleasure than to have provided the facility—absolutely free of cost.

NAVAL DISASTER OFF THE ORKNEYS.

H.M.S. HAMPSHIRE SUNK BY MINE OR TORPEDO.

LORD KITCHENER AND HIS STAFF DROWNED.

NO SURVIVORS FROM LOST WARSHIP.

The Secretary of the Admiralty on Tuesday issued the following telegram received from the Commander-in-Chief of the Grand Fleet at 10.30 (British summer time) on Tuesday morning:—

I have to report with deep regret that his Majesty's ship Hampshire (Captain Herbert J. Savill, R.N.) with Lord Kitchener and his Staff on board was sunk last night about 8 p.m. to the west of the Orkneys either by a mine or torpedo.

Four boats were seen by observers on shore to leave the ship. The wind was north-north-west, and heavy seas were running.

Patrol vessels and destroyers at once proceeded to the spot, and a party was sent along the coast to search, but only some bodies and a capsized boat have been found up to the present.

As the whole shore has been searched from the seaward, I greatly fear that there is little hope of there being any survivors.

No report has yet been received from the search party on shore.

The H.M.S. Hampshire was on her way to Russia.

The War Office makes the following announcement:—

The special party consisted of Lord Kitchener, with

Lieut.-Colonel O. A. Fitzgerald, C.M.G. (Personal Military Secretary).

Brigadier-General W. Ellershaw.

Second-Lieutenant R. D. Macpherson, 8th Cameron Highlanders.

Mr H. G. O'Beirne, C.V.O., C.B., of the Foreign Office; and

Mr L. S. Robertson, of the Ministry of Munitions.

Mr L. C. Rix, shorthand clerk; Detective Maclaughlin, of Scotland Yard; and the following personal servants—Henry Surguy-Shields, Walter Gurney, and Driver D. C. Brown, R.H.A.—were also attached to the party.

Aberdeen Weekly Journal 1916

CHANNEL TUNNEL IN 35 DAYS.

REMARKABLE PLAN OF NEW YORK ENGINEER.

A machine for tunnelling the English Channel in 35 days has been brought to the attention of the British Government by Mr. John K. Hencken, a civil engineer, of Fifth-avenue, New York, who states that he has official approval of his scheme.

The scheme contemplates boring four tunnels by means of eight machines that will cut through earth and rock at the rate of 100 feet per hour; and provides not only for a trackway in each tunnel, but a driveway along which motor-lorries could be driven from England to the supply bases in France.

Mr. Hencken asserts that he can have the tunnels complete and ready for operation within a few months' time, and declares that should the scheme be carried through it would release most of the shipping now used between England and France, thus making available for other uses more ships than could be built in the shipyards of the world in several years.

He offers to finance the scheme by floating a bond issue, which could be paid off within a few years, and then to make the tunnels a present to Britain and France by the United States, and states that he has the sanction of the American Government in making this offer.

Mr. Hencken's plan (says the London *Express*) is to have eight of his machines in use, under engineers of the three nations concerned—one machine at each end of the four tunnels, and another set boring the approaches at the same time.

Nottingham Evening Post 1917

Sunbeam Supremacy on every hand

supreme on land—supreme in the air —Sunbeam productions are nobly upholding the reputation of British engineering skill as is represented in the

SUNBEAM

cars and ambulances, as well as

SUNBEAM-COATALEN AIRCRAFT ENGINES.

The fact that the entire output of Sunbeam works is still being retained for Military and Naval purposes, signifies the soundness of Sunbeam productions.

THE SUNBEAM MOTOR CAR CO., Limited.
Head Office and Works: Wolverhampton. Manchester Showrooms: 112, Deansgate. *Agents for Cars for London and District:* I. KEELE, LTD., 72, New Bond St., W.

The Royal Air Force in the First World War: SE 5a aircraft of No. 85 Squadron with their pilots at the controls, at St. Omer aerodrome, France, in June 1918. The RAF was at this time less than three months old.

The FIRST and LATEST MORGANS to be RUN ON GAS.

SPECIAL interest attaches to the two photographs on this page. The first depicts a 1914 sporting Morgan converted to run on coal-gas by Mr. Charles Potter, a Leeds motor agent. He had it running on the 13th November, and claims it to be the first Morgan to be equipped with a gas bag. The second illustration shows a 1915 Grand Prix Morgan fitted with an overhead gas container by Messrs. Edwards and Parry, 89, Wigmore Street, London, W.

A comparison of the two outfits will interest all owners of Morgans who are thinking of converting

The first Morgan to be fitted with a gas bag, by Mr. C. Potter, of Leeds.

their machines, and good points in design and construction can be gleaned from each.

Mr. Potter has designed an overhead tray for the bag supported by four iron uprights. The tray has lattice sides, 12 ins. high, hinged so as to fall down to allow the car to enter the garage. The length of the bag is 8 ft. 6 ins.; width and height 4 ft., and when filled registers 170 cubic feet. The carburetter fitted for petrol was an Amac. To the air intake of this was fitted the spraying chamber (only) of a B. and B. carburetter with controls to the steering wheel, the gas being fed into the jet opening by a ¾ in. pipe. When using coal-gas, the Amac control levers are left full open and the engine is driven on the B. and B.; when using petrol the opposite arrangement comes into operation. No difficulty is experienced in starting up on gas, one charge (costing ninepence) being sufficient fuel for 22 miles.

The equipment fitted to the 1915 Grand Prix Morgan by Messrs. Edwards and Parry differs in a great many respects.
A8

MR. AND MRS. CHURCHILL.

NARROW ESCAPE IN MOTOR ACCIDENT.

Mr. and Mrs. Winston Churchill had a narrow escape in a motor accident yesterday. They left their residence at Lullenden, near Lingfield, Surrey, on their way to London. When they had reached four cross roads at a very dangerous spot, another motor car coming down a blind road, ran into their car and knocked it over on its side.

Fortunately, neither Mr. nor Mrs. Churchill was injured, though somewhat shaken. The car was much damaged and the chauffeur was slightly injured. The occupants of the colliding car were not injured.

Mr. Churchill proceeded to London in another car.

Nottingham Evening Post 1917

The latest Morgan fitted with a gas bag, by Messrs. Edwards and Parry.

LONDON-PARIS
BY
AEROPLANE.

DOUBLE TRIP IN 4¼ HOURS.

ALL MACHINES ARRIVE.

Yesterday the regular air service between Paris and London was inaugurated, three machines in all performing the trip, with several passengers and a considerable amount of goods. Airco 4 did a remarkable round journey. Her times were as follow:

Left Hounslow ... ... 9.10 a.m.
Arrived Paris (Le Bourget) 11.25 a.m.
Left Paris ... ... 12.15 (noon).
Arrived Hounslow ... ... 2.45 p.m.

The double journey was thus done in 5 hours 35min, but the actual flying time, deducting the stop at Le Bourget, was only 4 hours 45mins.

Airco 16 left Hounslow at 12.40 p.m., and, according to a Central News telegram received at midnight, arrived after a trip of 2½ hours.

A big Handley-Page machine started from Cricklewood at 8.30 yesterday morning, the intention being that she should fly to Paris and back in the day. She had eleven or twelve passengers on board.

A Reuter's telegram from Paris, received late last night, states:

"The Handley-Page which left London this morning with London editors on board, has arrived after a successful flight, but is detained here, and will not return to London until to-morrow."

Daily Telegraph **1919**

BOOT ALLOWANCE.

That this Conference views with disgust the action of the Department in failing to increase the amount of 5d. granted in lieu of boot allowance, which sum has been paid to member serving in H.M. Forces, and demands that the full equivalent based on the increased allowance be paid forthwith.—LIVERPOOL (Parcels).

Owing to the great advance in the price of boots the present allowance of one guinea is totally inadequate, and demands that this sum be increased to 42s. half-yearly issue.—LIVERPOOL (Parcels).

That this Conference demands that the boot money be increased to 1s. 6d. per week, and part-time officers to be paid according to number of hours worked.—STOCKWELL.

That this Branch of the Postmen's Federation instructs our Executive to urge the Department to supply all Postmen with boots every six months in lieu of boot allowance.—STOKE-ON-TRENT.

That the boot allowance be increased by £1.—NEWPORT, MON.

That this Conference demands that boot allowance be increased to £3 3s. per annum.—MANCHESTER, SALFORD AND DISTRICT.

To increase the boot allowance from £2 2s. per annum to £4 4s. per annum, as owing to increased and increasing cost of boots and repairs, combined with inferior quality of materials used in making boots, this increase is justified.—LEICESTER.

That the boot allowance be raised by 1s. 6d. per week.—GREENOCK, GLOUCESTER.

That we press for a 50 per cent. increase on boot allowance.—BOW.

That this Conference instructs the E.C. to ask that a boot allowance equivalent to what Postmen receive should be made to Hall Porters.—BELFAST.

That the boot allowance be further increased by 100 per cent.—LIVERPOOL (Indoor), MULLINGAR.

That our Executive push forward the claim for half boot allowance for our Auxiliary comrades.—EALING.

That all Auxiliary Postmen should receive one guinea (21s.) per annum for boots in consequence of the high price of same.—FETHARD (TIPP.), BUCKFASTLEIGH.

Boot allowance to be 1s. 6d. weekly.—W.D.O., LONDON.

That steps be taken to obtain an allowance for boot repairs for Telegraph Messengers.—W.D.O., LONDON.

That the incoming Executive be instructed to press for the boot allowance to be paid to Auxiliary Postmen in proportion to the time worked.—FINSBURY PARK.

Postman's Gazette **1919**

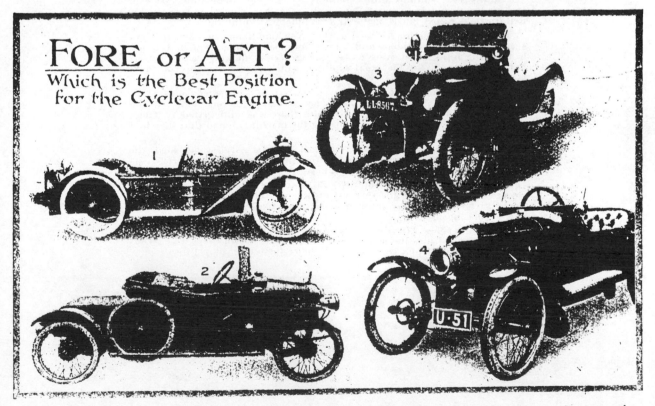

FORE or AFT?
Which is the Best Position for the Cyclecar Engine.

Considerable difference of opinion exists as to whether a water-cooled engine can be placed most advantageously in the front or rear of the car:—(1) The Carden monocar and (2) The G.W.K., which have the engine in the rear. (3) The Morgan and (4) The G.N., with the engine in the front.

Light Car and Cycle Car **1918**

ATLANTIC FLIGHT

Vimy-Vickers Success

LANDING IN IRELAND.

A Fight with Fog and Drizzle.

"FLYING UPSIDE DOWN"

After a voyage of sixteen hours, hampered at the start by fog difficulties, the Vickers-Vimy aeroplane, with Capt. Alcock and Lieut. Brown on board, has crossed the Atlantic in one flight.

The announcement was received at the "Sunday News" office this morning in the shape of a message from the "Daily Mail," which said:—

THE VIMY-VICKERS' MACHINE LANDED AT CLIFDEN, IRELAND, AT 8.40 THIS MORNING.

"Stop Press" editions of the "Sunday News" were immediately issued, and we are now able to give fuller details of a feat which has secured for Britain the coveted laurel of the first complete Atlantic flight.

The preparations for the start at the Newfoundland aerodrome had necessarily been enormous, and a large number of labourers had toiled in levelling hillocks, blasting rocks, and generally making ready for a jumping-off track for the great biplane which required plenty of room to get a rising headway.

The tuning-up for the flight was a concern of the closest detail. Days ago it was Capt. Alcock's intention to be content with one test, but the wireless difficulty proved more obstinate than was anticipated. Then, quite recently, the airmen, overhauling the machine, found that they had sprung the axle in landing.

When the damaged part was replaced and the wireless adjusted, the postponement of the great Transatlantic flight for a £10,000 prize was due solely to the prevalence of a high south-west wind.

A start, however, was made at 4.13 yesterday afternoon, and after a voyage which imposed the severest strain on the endurance of the intrepid airmen, the latter reached Clifden on the West Coast of Ireland at 8.40 this morning.

In an interview Mr. Harry Hawker, whose plucky attempt to essay the flight gained him the admiration of the whole world, pays a generous tribute to the skill and courage of his more fortunate competitors.

Sheffield Sunday News 1919

Captain John Alcock (left) and Lieutenant Arthur Whitten-Brown about to set off on their pioneering flight across the Atlantic in June 1919.

After its successful crossing, their twin-engined Vickers Vimy aircraft landed in a bog at Clifden, Ireland.

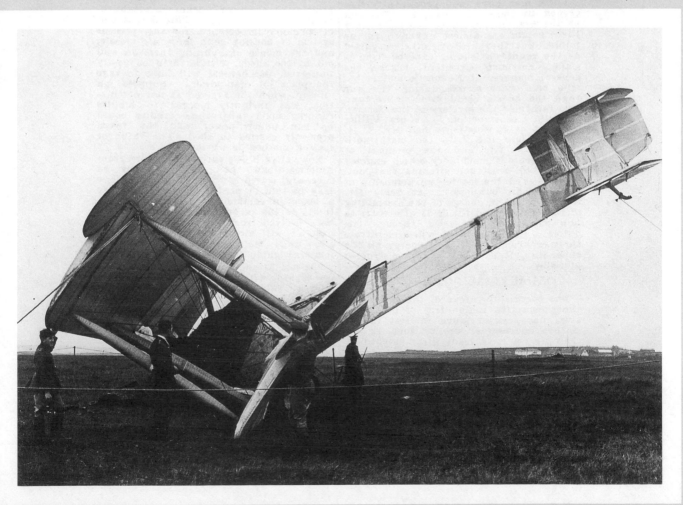

SUPER AIRSHIPS.

LEVIATHANS OF THE IMMEDIATE FUTURE: R39 GETTING READY.

SUNDAY NEWS SPECIAL.

The old-time rivalry between the Tyne and the Clyde in the matter of ship-building is to be revived in the construction of great airship liners. The Clyde built R 34, having now twice crossed the Atlantic, the Tyne-siders are anxious to see their vessel the R 33, upset the record as did the Mauretania (built on the Tyne) the ill-fated Lusitania (constructed on the Clyde), and they hope to see that accomplished before the end of the present flying season. "If," they say, "the R 34 can go to the U.S. and back, our R. 33 can easily make the double voyage to India." They are now awaiting and betting upon the success of such a trip.

Although, as was pointed out in last week's issue of the "Sunday News", the R 33 was assembled at Selby, she was actually conceived and created at the great aerodrome of Messrs. Armstrong-Whitworth on the historic Town Moor at Newcastle, where the world's super-dirigible, the R 39, is being prepared. She will be despatched in organised sections to be put together at Selby. This is one of the £500,000 airships the Admiralty are having constructed, and she will be much larger than either the sister ships R 33 and R 34.

Three men have been prominently concerned in these dirigibles, and because of the erstwhile need of official secrecy their names are almost unknown to the public, but they are officially recognised as the country's leading experts. One is Capt. Fairburn Crawford, R.A.F., the general manager at Newcastle and Selby, who held more secrets during the war than the public could ever realise, and who fathomed the mystery of the German Zeppelin construction. As his willing assistant at Newcastle he had Mr. S. H. Phillips, late R.N.V.R., the mathematician of the trio, and the producer of some ingenious machinery which enabled Britain to construct airships that outrivalled even the master workmanship of the German builders. At Selby Mr. Golightly was in charge of the assembling of the vessels, and the R 33 demonstrates how effectively he carried through his duties. Now the three will concentrate their experience, skill and energy on the super ship, R 39, about to be constructed at Selby.

COMMERCIAL POSSIBILITIES.

The successful voyage of the R 34, and the prospective Indian trip of her sister ship, has aroused much interest in the future commercial use of such lighter than air craft. Already great shipowners are making inquiries as to the possibility of shipping lines to augment their overseas mail traffic by means of airships. The day may not be far distant when the greyhounds of the air and sea may act in conjunction to give a more rapid transport of mails and parcels. This idea was discussed with Mr. Phillips, who kindly furnished the "Sunday News" special representative with some interesting information.

"A significant fact about the successful dual voyage of the R 34," said Mr. Phillips, "should not be overlooked by the large transport companies of the world, both shipping and railway concerns. These will probably soon realise, if they have not already done so, that the possession of half a dozen or so of airships will be a decided progressive step, and one which will become imperative in the very near future. A sense of proportion must, however, be observed by the public in discussing the relative advantages of air and marine ships. It will not be possible for an airship like R 33 to convey a cargo of 5,000 tons from Liverpool to New York in 48 or 60 hours. On the other side, it would not be practical for a steamship to dash across the Atlantic with a ton of urgent mail matter in the same time. The importance of a combination of the two modes of transportation thus becomes obvious.

THE LESSONS LEARNT.

"The lesson learnt from the Atlantic experiment is the need of harbourage. There was nearly a disaster through the absence of a proper anchorage establishment on the other side. This is a matter of primary importance, for the present system of housing such large air vessels, and the modes of running them in and out of the sheds, will have to be vastly improved. Mechanical will have to take the place of man-power. Suppose an airship, when she arrived at her destination, was instantly moored to cradles running upon rails, these cradles could be run under power and the vessel promptly carried to shed. The value of such a method is obvious.

Now, after R 34's successful return from America, and the possibly equally as successful a trip of the R 33 to India, one may be safe in predicting something like a boom in commercial airship construction. As the ocean liners of to-day have been evolved from the steamships of the past, so will airships grow and grow in size until we may have vessels of 10,000,000 cubic feet of gas-bag.

"The R 33 and R 34 are about 750 feet in length, with a gas-bag capacity of 3,500,000 cubic feet, a total lift of 105 tons, a mail or cargo carrying capacity of about 12 tons, and a range of voyage of about 4,000 miles. Such ships, however, will be dwarfs alongside the super-aerial liner, possibly of the near future, possessing a length of 1,000 feet, a gas capacity of 9,250,000 cubic feet, a cargo of 55 tons, and able to do a voyage of 9,000 miles without a stop. Such ships, or even larger, are sure to come."

Sheffield Sunday News 1919

1920–1929

A mason in a motor-car giving the sign to a brother mason indicating his probable destination should he not rapidly betake himself elsewhere.

Pearson's Magazine 1921

HIGHER LONDON FARES.

THE TROUBLESOME HALFPENNY.

TUBE STATION SCENES.

Revised fares on the Underground, the tramcars, and the motor omnibuses were responsible for a wave of excitement in London yesterday, and at lunch time the all-round advance in the cost of travelling had displaced the threatened coal strike as a topic of conversation.

Many people, in spite of the effective poster campaign which has been conducted by the Underground management, left home in the morning completely ignorant of the new demands to be made on their purses, and even the forewarned were uncertain what they would have to pay for their journeys.

The first result of the alterations in the scale was a hunt for halfpennies. Most people had come to the conclusion during recent months that the halfpenny was becoming an obsolete coin, but yesterday there was not a sufficient number to secure the smooth working of the London transport system. This was due to the substitution of three-halfpenny for penny fares. The new penny ride, where it survives at all, is a shrunken thing, which seems to stop short of any useful point. On the Underground it is limited to short stages on a section of the District Railway between Bow Road and Aldgate East. On the tramways it is confined to a distance one-third as long as obtained in 1914. On the omnibuses it is governed purely by tramcar competition. As a general rule it may now be taken that a journey of a mile costs three halfpence whatever the form of transport. That is why the coin known in the North as a "meg" was in such unprecedented demand yesterday.

The additions to the old fares are not popular, but when the first shocks caused by their extortion have passed, most of them will probably be accepted as being reasonable as well as inevitable. If an average is struck, the new scale shows an increase of about 100 per cent. over 1914 charges and the cost of most things has advanced to a much greater extent in the last six years. On the Underground the increase is rather less than 100 per cent., but many of the new three-halfpenny fares are resented, and will yield little revenue. Thousands of people cheerfully paid a penny to travel from Victoria to St. James's Park, Blackfriars to the Temple, or Charing Cross to Piccadilly Circus. Now they will walk the distance.

The Times
1920

The R38 airship disaster at Hull, 1921.

Lost Diamonds on the Lusitania.

MUCH more of tragedy than of mere romance attaches to the German sinking of the *Lusitania* with over a thousand lives nearly five years ago; but a decided touch of the latter quality is to be found in a story that long has been current in Ireland. It is said that not long after the great Atlantic liner was sunk a registered parcel was addressed to the Postmaster-General in London, containing four parcels of diamonds to the reputed value of £23,000, which was on board the *Lusitania* at the time of her destruction, salved from the sea some days later by a fisherman and his crew, and delivered by them to the Receiver of Wrecks at Baltimore through the coastguards at Castletownshend, County Cork, and forwarded to the General Post Office, London: that this action on the part of the fishermen enabled the postal authorities to deliver the registered parcels to the respective addresses, thus saving the carriers and the postal authorities a heavy loss in compensation to the owners.

Jewellers' and Watchmakers'
Trade Advertiser 1920

TRANSPORT BY AIRCRAFT.

A Leeds Cargo via the Humber Aerodrome.

On Saturday, March 6th, a "Kangaroo" airplane, piloted by Mr. R. W. Kenworthy, flew from the Brough (near Hull) air-ship station, carrying a cargo of wearing apparel from Leeds manufacturers consigned to Holland.

The landing was made at the Soesterberg aerodrome, near Amsterdam, and the goods were delivered in good condition.

It had been arranged that Mr. Kenworthy should return via Roubaix and pick up a cargo of gabardine cloth, but a cable was received saying that the stuff would not be ready. In the meantime a Bradford manufacturer made arrangements for the pilot to make a return journey with a cargo of aniline dyes. The dyes, which have been held up at Rotterdam for some time, weigh about 1,400 lbs., and are valued at £5,000.

Hull Trade and Transit 1920

MOTORISTS' CHANGED CONDITIONS.

NEW YEAR DUTIES EXPLAINED.

PENALTIES FOR NEGLECT.

Motorists are reminded that from next Saturday onwards they will come under a markedly different *régime*. Every motor-vehicle will have to be registered afresh, and the new licence and registration book will belong to the car and be transferable with it. In place of the excise duties on cars a new system of duties payable to county or borough councils will come into force. Motor-bicycles will be taxed by weight, with an extra tax for a side-car. Private motor-cars will be taxed by horse-power, and commercial vehicles by weight.

The money thus collected, together with all fines and penalties, will be paid into a road fund, which will be applied solely to road maintenance and improvement. It is hoped that £8,000,000 will be raised for this purpose under the new regulations.

A month's grace is allowed to owners for the fresh registration of motor vehicles. In other words, applications for the new licences must be sent to the local authorities before January 31. The following details must be filled in on the application form for private cars :—Actual horse-power, existing registered number, type of body, colour of body, name of car, manufacturer, chassis type, letter and number, number and date of manufacture of engine, and number of cylinders and internal diameter. Where a registered number is already in existence, the old number will be retained.

The new licence will be of stout paper, with different colours for different periods. It must be carried in a conspicuous position on the near side of the vehicle, so that it is visible at all times by daylight to an observer standing at the near side. The registration book will be a folding card and need not be carried. It should be pointed out that the licence which has to be shown on the car has no relation to the driving licence, which will still be obtained in the present way.

The annual duties will in future be as follow :—

PRIVATE MOTOR-CARS.

	£ s. d.
Not exceeding 6 h.p., or electrically propelled	£6 0 0
Exceeding 6 h.p., for each h.p. or part	1 0 0

MOTOR-CYCLES OR "SCOOTERS."

	£ s. d.
Not exceeding 200lb., unladen	£1 10 0
Exceeding 200lb.	3 0 0
Sidecar or trailer, an extra	1 0 0
Tricycles	4 0 0

Customs duties on imported motor spirit are abolished under the new legislation, and the corresponding reduction in price has already been announced. The excise duty on licences taken up by dealers will also be dropped.

There are various pains and penalties for anyone who has not complied with these regulations by February 1. It is difficult for the average motorist to understand the official language in which the regulations are set out by the authorities, and those who do not want to offend unwittingly are recommended to obtain one of the various booklets which are now being issued, putting the regulations into plain English. One of the most useful and comprehensive of these is the handbook issued by Messrs. Mann and Egerton. It carefully explains all the parts of the Act that affect the motorist, and adds a handy table for calculating the taxation on different types of vehicles.

The Times 1920

We regret to hear that Mr. E. J. Spare's "Wild Hero," £5 pool winner in the 1920 Marennes race of the Midland Combine, dropped dead on Monday last. Collision with the telegraph wires adjacent to the loft upset the kit of birds, who flew until exhausted, "Wild Hero" pitching on the loft and when picked up was dead.

Homing Pigeon 1921

SHACKLETON WEIGHS ANCHOR

The Tiny Quest Sets Out On Her Big Voyage.

EXPLORER'S LAST TRIP.

"The Call of Far Places Gets Into the Blood."

Leaning out from the glass-enclosed bridge of the good ship Quest as she yielded to the straining of her little tug, Sir Ernest Shackleton waved his soft felt hat in response to the cheers of the crowd assembled at St. Katharine's Dock to see the expedition off.

The 30,000 miles voyage of discovery to the Antarctic had officially commenced. There yet remained scenes of enthusiasm in Thames-side, and a call will be made at Plymouth for an 18ft. copper plate—an "earth" for her wireless—to be fixed, but metaphorically, at any rate, the anchor was weighed at one o'clock.

If we do all we hope to do this time I am singing my swan song, Sir Ernest told the *Illustrated Sunday Herald.* **This is my last trip.**

"This is My Life."

He laughed, and added:

That is what I say now. This is my life, and the call of far places gets into the blood.

Half an hour before the Quest sailed the King's flag was hoisted. Sir Ernest handed it to the two Scouts Marr and Mooney, who hoisted it to the fore-mast.

"The expedition is novel in many ways, especially so in the fact that there is no crew in the accepted term on board," Sir Ernest said. "Nearly everybody on board is interchangeable, and I am hoping that the small complement will represent, in the interests of the Empire, a crew of double their number.

"I am proud of the Quest; she is a wonderful ship."

Taking Ice to the Antarctic!

Sir Ernest had much ado to cast off at anything like the appointed time. Hundreds of personal friends and well-wishers of every member of the ship's company came to wish them the best of luck.

Packing away the final consignment of stores was a work of difficulty, interrupted by continual hand-shaking. At mid-day the deck was still littered with a strange assortment of frozen mutton, bags of lettuce, boxes of onions, poultry and huge blocks of ice.

Sir Ernest never answered so many questions in so short a time.

"Where shall I put these, sir?" said one of the crew, indicating a crate of onions.

"Get them below, anyhow. We'll get them squared up at Gravesend," was the reply.

Bills for the Penguins?

One of the most unexpected items of the cargo were two huge boxes, bearing the seal of the Stationery Office, and labelled "Forms—to be kept dry." Perhaps Sir Ernest is expected to act as distributor on behalf of the Income-tax Commissioner in the Antarctic!

Mr. Rowett, by whose financial assistance the expedition has been made possible, was on board early, taking photographs of the scenes of acitivity.

Coming out into the Thames below Tower Bridge, the Quest had to face the cheers of a ten deep crowd on both sides of the bridge. Thousands more lined the waterside at the Tower of London.

Steaming slowly up stream the Quest turned by London Bridge, black with a fringe of spectators.

Where She Will Call.

After touching Madeira, the Quest will sail for St. Paul's Rocks, a small island near the Equator, from which she will go to Trinidad and Tristan da Cunha, a lonely island whose inhabitants will receive mails and gifts from the Quest.

Gough Island, in mid-Atlantic, has only once before been visited by an expedition of this kind. Capetown will be the base from which the Quest will start on her voyage of discovery. It is hoped to explore unknown seas and little known islands.

Illustrated Sunday Herald 1921

Bristol Jupiter and Lucifer radial piston engines at various stages of assembly, c. 1922.

27,200 FEET UP ON MOUNT EVEREST.

HIGHEST YET: 1,940 FEET FROM SUMMIT.

THRILLING CLIMB.

Captain G. Finch and Captain G. Bruce, with one Gurkha, camped for two nights on Mount Everest at 25,000ft., and finally attained 27,200ft., using oxygen.

GENERAL C. G. BRUCE, leader of the Mount Everest expedition, announces this further wonderful feat in a telegram dated Phari Jong (Tibet), Wednesday.

The altitude now gained is 400 feet higher than the point reached by Mr. Mallory, Mr. Somervell, and Major Norton on May 21, and 1,802 feet only short of the summit of Everest—the highest mountain in the world.

Below we print extracts from Mr. Mallory's own thrilling narrative describing the climb to 26,800 feet on May 21, achieved without oxygen. All these despatches are copyright of the Mount Everest Committee through *The Times*.

CANDLE-LIGHT DESCENT.

Cutting Steps in the Ice: Race for Shelter.

Mr. Mallory, in his account, says:—

On May 20 at 5 a.m. the party were roused, when I learnt that all the porters were unwell. Four were seriously affected by mountain sickness, but five others were eventually willing to come on.

We started at 7 a.m. and quickly made our way to the North Col (the high ridge connecting Everest with the lower peak of Changtse, north of it), whence a broad snow ridge ascends at a gently increasing angle. Presently we became aware that the day was by no means perfect; the sun gave no real warmth and a cold breeze sprang up from the west.

The rocks which we had been following ended abruptly, and we had to race for shelter on the east side of the ridge. It is always hard work cutting steps (in the snow or ice with ice-axes) at high altitudes, and 300 feet of such work in a hurry is extremely exhausting.

We were glad at last to shelter under rocks at 25,000 feet. One site after another was tried for a camp till we found a steep slab, and here ultimately the tents were pitched, 50 yards apart.

Deep Breathing.

At 8 a.m. we were ready to start, though none of us felt at his best after a long night of headache. Morshead was so ill that he had to say, "I think I won't come with you; I should only keep you back."

We three (Mallory, Somervell, and Norton) went on without him. Fresh snow covered the ledges and concealed loose stones, but we were disappointed that the angle was not sufficiently steep to require strenuous use of the arms, as the arms seem to relieve the monotony of footwork.

Our power of pushing upward depended on lung capacity; our lungs governed our speed, making our pace miserable, but we found by drawing our breath deep that it was possible to proceed. For a long time we had good hope of reaching the north-east shoulder of Everest, but remembering the descent we decided to turn back at 2 p.m.

At 2.15 we reached the head of the rocks and were still 800ft. below the north-east shoulder, commanding a clear view thence to the summit. The barometer registered 26,800ft. We turned for the long task of the descent.

Westward the slope looked easier, but slabs covered with treacherous snow compelled us to get back and follow the line of our ascent. We picked up Morshead and traversed [proceeded along] a ledge, but immediately recognised that fresh snow had made it dangerous.

Race Against Darkness.

A nasty slip occurred, when three of us were held up by a rope belayed round an ice-axe. With extreme caution we then proceeded, racing against darkness, cutting steps down a great snow ridge. Our difficulties did not end. Morshead, though climbing most pluckily, had reached the tether of his efforts, and could proceed only a few steps at a time.

Sinister grey clouds, flickering with lightning, made one of the most amazing mountain views seem full of malice. We reached the crevasses in dim starlight and lighted a lantern. We found our way to the edge of a small cliff. Here it was necessary to leap down 15ft. into snow, but alarming as the leap was it was safely accomplished.

The rope which we had fixed previously was buried under the snow and our last candle burnt out. We began to go down at a steep angle, doubting if this was the way, when someone hitched the rope from under the snow; and ten minutes later we were in our camp.

But the most essential thing was missing. The porters had gone down taking the cooking pots, and we had to swallow frozen milk mixed with jam and snow.

If the most remarkable fact in our experience is that three of us at a height of nearly 27,000ft. felt little more physical discomfort than here, at the base camp, it remains a fact that at great heights any moment any person may feel as Morshead felt. The margin of safety is small.

WIRELESS FOR ALL AT LAST.

SCHEME THAT WILL COST £200,000 A YEAR.

EIGHT NEW STATIONS.

The Daily Mail is able to state that agreement has been reached between the Postmaster-General and the newly formed British Broadcasting Company on all points connected with the company's scheme for general wireless broadcasting operations.

The committee appointed by the company to negotiate with the Post Office authorities will meet to-day to present their report and to announce the details of the scheme that have been agreed upon.

"One of the first things to be done, an official of the company told a *Daily Mail* reporter, "is to build seven or eight new broadcasting stations at important places up and down the country. Two hundred thousand pounds a year will be spent on the running of the scheme—arranging concerts, etc."

THE NEW WATERLOO.

One war was won on the field of Waterloo, and Waterloo Station had a great deal to do with the winning of a bigger war. The Londoner has his separate sentiments for each of the chief stations, as was shown in the reply of one journalistic visitor to the chairman of the vast and magnificent Pennsylvania station in New York. "Anything in London to compare with that?" asked the America. "Ah, we've one station in London," was the reply, "the like of which you can see nowhere else." "What's that?" "Ludgate Hill."

Little Charing Cross station is the World's End, so to speak. Euston is a roaring busy-body; the Great Central such a tidy fellow that if a porter wears his tie crooked people shiver. Waterloo is a warrior station, leading you in khaki carriages to Aldershot and Salisbury Plain. Also it is the station, perhaps, for the prettiest women—or has Victoria that distinction? Certainly Waterloo wins in Ascot Week. Therefore it is right that the new Waterloo should have the honour of opening by the Queen—who takes the place of the King, his Majesty being indisposed. How many splendid sailors and soldiers it sent to the war! How many of them, alas, never saw London again after the last glimpse of its cheering and tearful crowds!

Letter received from the Argentine by a British manufacturer :—

"Always has been my illusion of young man to possess a good great and robust moto-cycle; but they are of very tall cost, and I have not money for purchase it, by what I them might stay infinitely thankful if you regale to me an; then in yours immense factory she is a gout of water. I change I were the more enthusiast propagator of your moto-cycle."

We understand that the writer has not received the motor-cycle, but has been allowed to retain his "illusion."

Punch 1922

Society in the Air.

LADY DIANA DUFF COOPER is living up to her reputation for originality by announcing that she intends to learn to fly. The Hon. Elsie MacKay, Lord Inchcape's charming daughter, has just secured her "Pilot's certificate," so that Lady Di will not be the first Society woman to create a new sport for the aristocracy. Aviation in these days has reached a stage of safety that makes it possible for the fair sex, and the flying schools recently have had an increasing number of lady pupils.

The Queen of Belgium is an enthusiastic airwoman, and she invariably flies to this country in company with her husband when she is visiting London. She has designed a leather hat for flying, which with a few minor adjustments at the conclusion of a flight can be converted into a smart head-dress for town wear. Now that so many aeroplanes contain comfortable wind-proof passenger cabins, however, it is possible to cross the Channel by air wearing the daintiest millinery without fear of it suffering from the effects of the flight.

Everywoman's Weekly 1922

From a description of the new air-service to Cologne :—

"So low can one fly with safety on one of these great machines that we saw a flock of ducks take to the water in terror as the great dark bat swooped by their playground—at one little level crossing they ran to open the gates in case we should be landing there."
                                        Evening Paper.

We fancy we know the breed of canards to which these intelligent birds belong.

Punch 1922

Box and Cox.

Consecutive announcements from the tape one morning last week :—

"11.13.—M. Venizelos has returned to London from Paris and is staying at the Ritz Hotel."
"11.14.—The Aga Khan left the Ritz Hotel this morning for Newmarket."

Punch 1922

While being driven to slaughter at Coalville, Leicestershire, an ox ran up the stairs leading to a solicitor's office. We can only conclude that it knew very little about solicitors.

Punch 1922

A convincing test of the robust character of the "Austin Seven" is found in the experience of Captain Arthur Waite, who won the Easter Small Car Handicap on Brooklands track. His racing "Austin Seven" had only been out of the works for a few short runs, but on Easter Monday he drove it from Banbury to Brooklands, and after winning a race of 5¾ miles journeyed back to Bromsgrove, a distance of about 116 miles. His driving time for the day's total of about 190 miles was just six hours and the car was running better at the end of the day than during the race. Except in regard to gear ratios and body it differed little from the standard model.

Business Man: Birmingham 1923

Another Headache for the Historian.

At the State opening of Parliament:

"The Prince of Wales walked briskly in a minute before the King and Queen. He has lost all traces of lameness."—*Daily Paper.*

"He was quite lame—the result of his recent injury—and all the ladies gave a sympathetic sigh as he passed on."
                                        Another Daily Paper.

Punch 1922

TRANS-ATLANTIC BROADACSTING.

It was announced last night by the British Broadcasting Company that all their stations in this country are heard in America at three o'clock in the morning. A continuation of the experiment is to take place to-day, when America will transmit to British stations from 3 until 3.30 A.M.

The Scotsman 1923

MME. CLARA BUTT'S "ARIA"-PLANE.

LAST MINUTE RUSH FOR FORGOTTEN MUSIC.

A note of surprise was expressed by Dame Clara Butt yesterday as she was leaving Waterloo to catch the White Star liner Pittsburgh for Halifax on a three months' tour to Canada and the United States with her husband, Mr. Kennerley Rumford.

In the rush of leaving Compton Lodge, South Hampstead, she discovered a few seconds before the special train left that her portmanteau containing all the music for her use during the tour had been left behind.

A message was sent to South Hampstead immediately, and thence a messenger was sent by motor to Croydon Aerodrome with the missing case. He then flew with it by aeroplane to Southampton and arrived just before the Pittsburgh sailed.

The People 1923

TELEPHONING TO AUSTRALIA.

WORDS HEARD 11,000 MILES AWAY.

MARCONI TRIUMPH.

"Hullo! Hullo! Is that Australia? England speaking!"

From being a romantic possibility, such a message has become historical fact.

On Sunday night the voice of a man speaking in England was, for the first time, distinctly heard in Australia, more than 11,000 miles away, on an ordinary wireless receiver. The words were heard, one-eighteenth of a second after they were uttered, by Mr. Fisk, the managing director of the Amalgamated Wireless Company, at his home in the suburbs of Sydney, New South Wales.

These successful tests have been carried out at the Marconi experimental station at Poldhu, Cornwall. Mr. Marconi said to a "Daily Express" representative last night that the tests were of a preliminary character and partially carried out on the new "beam" system. A current of slightly under 20 kilowatts was used; under the "beam" system proper one-tenth of a kilowatt should give equally good results.

"When the system is brought into operation," he said, "it will be available for high-speed wireless telegraphy to Australia, and, when necessary, for telephony also."

Daily Express 1924

3 "EARTHQUAKES" IN ENGLAND

MIDNIGHT TERROR OF COAL-MINING TOWNS.

CHIMNEY CRASH.

"Daily Express" Correspondent.
NOTTINGHAM, Friday.

Three earthquakes shook the entire Nottingham and Derby coalfields last night and this morning, brought people in towns and villages from their beds, smashed crockery; and threw tiles and chimney-pots into the streets.

A large chimney stack fell at Sutton-in-Ashfield.

Men employed in pits left their working places in alarm, fearing a calamity. The theory that the tremors are due to a subsidence caused by colliery workings is discounted by the fact that the earthquake was felt over an area thirty miles across.

"I had just gone to bed," said a Radford teacher to me to-day, "when the floor shook so much that it rattled everything on the washstand."

There were shocks in many parts of the district last Monday at midday, but they were small in comparison with last night's roaring and rattling visitations.

LIKE AN EXPLOSION.

The first occurred at eleven o'clock, and lasted four seconds. It was felt most in the Nottingham district. Thousands of people in houses thought that there was a procession of lorries in the next street. Others thought that there was a colliery explosion. Lights up peared in windows and moved from room to room as people searched their houses for signs of damage.

The second shock was at one o'clock. It was most severe at Sutton-in-Ashfield.

At four in the morning the whole district was roused by another shock; windows rattled and crockery fell from shelves. Terrified people ran to the streets. Dogs barked and cocks crowed. The third shock was felt most at Ilkeston and neighbouring villages.

Daily Express 1924

EDITORIAL COMMENT.

NICKNAMED at its inception the "Million Pound Monopoly Company," and referred to in the agreement made by the Air Ministry with the British, Foreign, and Colonial Corporation, Ltd., as the Imperial Air Transport Co., Ltd., the new combine which took over, on Tuesday of this week, the services hitherto operated by four separate companies, will be known, in future, as Imperial Airways, Ltd.

Imperial Airways, Limited
This is certainly a less cumbersome title than that suggested in the agreement, and, doubtless, the company will speedily adopt and be known by the initial letters "I.A.L." Incidentally, it may be noted that, by coincidence or otherwise, these letters are the same as the initial letters of the Instone Air Line. The new company, it may be recalled, has been formed with a capital of £1,000,000, while the Government is committed to another million spread over ten years, the amounts payable by the Government each year being so apportioned as to become smaller and smaller every year. A certain minimum mileage has been stipulated before these subsidies become payable.

Flight 1924

Gentlemen attempting to enter Trinity College by Great Gate are asked not to wear nailed shoes when climbing over the inmates' motor cars. When lifting Austin Sevens out of the way, it is usually considered more polite to put them down top side up.

The Granta 1924

FLIGHT
The AIRCRAFT ENGINEER & AIRSHIPS

First Aero Weekly in the World.

Founder and Editor: STANLEY SPOONER

A Journal devoted to the Interests, Practice, and Progress of Aerial Locomotion and Transport

OFFICIAL ORGAN OF THE ROYAL AERO CLUB OF THE UNITED KINGDOM

Flight 1924

DIARY OF FORTHCOMING EVENTS

Club Secretaries and others desirous of announcing the dates of important fixtures are invited to send particulars for inclusion in the following list :—

April 23 .... Visit to National Physical Laboratory. Teddington. Inst. Ae. E.

April 25 .... Aero Golfing Society Team Match, Oxhey Golf Club.

May 31–June 9 Third Czecho-Slovak International Aeronautical Exhibition, Prague

June 15 .... Gordon Bennett Balloon Race, Belgium.

June 21 .... F.A.I. Conference Opens, Paris.

July 24–Aug. 10 Tour de France for Light 'Planes.

Aug. 4 .... Aerial Derby at Lympne

Sept. 8–13 Light 'Plane Competitions at Lympne

Times Literary Supplement 1924

NEW NOVELS.

A PASSAGE TO INDIA.

Not the least distinctive of Mr. E. M. Forster's qualities is his fairness ; his judgments are marked by an unfailing sincerity. The accurate blending of observation and insight is his outstanding virtue. His new novel, A PASSAGE TO INDIA (Arnold, 7s. 6d. net), is the first he has published for fourteen years—since "Howards End." Its artistry is of the same finished kind, its vision as original, as that of the foregoing novel : it has the beauty and pathos which belong to Mr. Forster's best work. But because it is essentially a definite picture rather than a creative imagining, it is a different kind of achievement from "Howards End" or "A Room with a View" ; its form is stricter, its appeal more precise.

The Granta 1924

THE EUPHRATES LARGE ADVERTISEMENTS

Insertion of Advertisements in these columns is at the rate of nine shekels a word.

A CAMEL—two humper, ½ rhinoceros power, super sheik model, slightly desert soiled, kick-starter, straight through exhaust, very fast, did 5 m.p.h. on Mespot Grass Track, and guaranteed 300 miles to a peck of rice. Engine recently overhauled by the veterinary surgeon to His Excellency the Sultan's chief wife, no spare parts.—For sale, 3 piastres, or would accept. Llhama skin.—Box "A. 1.!!"

M. MAKFAILI eagerly desires to obtain a pre-Memphitic sackbut, or would be content with an overstrung zither of the same period.

M. MAKFAILI's rooms are situated in the sole petuni houseboat, Lower Euphrates, G, Bowside, and prospective salesmen should be prepared to demonstrate the finer points of the above-named instruments there between the hours of the worshipping of Allah in the watch towers to the going down of the camels to the sheep butts.

M. MAKFAILI will disburse many shekels for the right sackbut or zither.

MOHAMMELS KISMET contract to instal punkahs in all heated places of inconvenience, such as theatres, cinemas, and political meetings. Charges moderate, punkah wallahs supplied with punkahs, no backsheesh.—Box "W. L."

Wireless—A Peep into the Future.

By H. POWELL REES.

MORNING'S NEWS SUMMARISED.

With music already in the ether for anyone's enjoyment at no more pains than the turning of a handle, it is a short step to conceive oneself listening at breakfast time to a summary of the news of the day broadcasted by one's favourite newspaper. One imagines such a summary being prepared as a gramophone record in the small hours of the morning after the paper has gone to press. This record automatically broadcasts itself wirelessly every ten minutes between 7.30 and 11 o'clock. Subscribers to the newspaper are supplied with a small receiver containing a loud-speaking apparatus from which, at the pressure of a button, the news issues while the bacon and eggs are being put away.

On the way to his office the subscriber reads in detail the news which the summary has enabled him to select without loss of time as most interesting or important to him at the moment.

NEW OFFICE METHODS.

On arrival at his office his desk is singularly clear of correspondence, due not so much to a secretary's efficiency as to "wireless," which has become the invaluable handmaid of the man of affairs, large and small. As he sits a faint whirr issues from a small box on the desk, and simultaneously there flows from a moving stylus a printed message agreeing to the terms of a proposed contract followed by the necessary signature hand-written at a distance and wirelessly transmitted, of course. Most of the correspondence throughout the day is carried out in this manner.

During the afternoon our imaginary business man is inspecting the progress of a new factory building he is erecting in the depths of the country, and it unexpectedly becomes necessary for him to stay overnight in the neighbourhood. He therefore plants his stick firmly in the ground, takes a watchlike piece of apparatus from his pocket, and attaches its chain to the handle of his stick. From another pocket he takes a small earpiece, the cord of which he also attaches to his stick. He then informs his wife that " Business detains," etc. One or two remarks pass, the watchlike apparatus and the earpiece are returned to their respective pockets, the operation is finished, having lasted exactly 15 seconds.

Westminster Illustrated 1925

The Aero-Taxi

One of the most significant, possibly one of the most prophetic, events of the week is the wonderful flight of Mr. A. J. Cobham in a light aeroplane. He flew from Croydon to Zurich and back, leaving Croydon at 4.54 in the morning and arriving back in the evening at 7.30. The time occupied by the double flight, which amounted to 1,000 miles, was thus 14 hours 36 minutes, of which 13 hours 49 minutes were spent in the air. The cost of the flight was £4 12s.—slightly over a penny per mile—and the " Moth" aeroplane in which he travelled is so small that one man can wheel it with one hand. Since the immortal hour in which Bleriot crossed the Channel by air few things have occurred in the realm of aerial navigation so likely to impress the imagination of the man in the street. It hints at the coming time when suburban houses will have their private aeroplane shed as well as, or instead of, their garage, and when amateur aviation will be as common as, let us say, motor-bicycling is to-day. Owing to the strong wind, Mr. Cobham flew only a hundred feet off the ground all the way back. "That is the advantage of this kind of light aeroplane," he told a representative of the *Morning Post*. "You can afford to fly low, because you can land in any field." The ordinary wayfarer, considering these matters, may well tremble at the traffic problem of the future, and begin to practise circumspection perpendicularly as well as horizontally. Luther spoke about the sky raining Duke Georges, and that was a hyperbole; it is no hyperbole after this week to say that the sky may soon rain amateur aviators in difficulties.

British Weekly 1925

NOISY MOTOR-CYCLISTS.

MAGISTRATES' £10 WARNING.

In view of the statement by the Home Secretary, Sir William Joynson-Hicks, in the House of Commons on Monday that he had instructed the police to enforce strictly the law relating to the use of silencers on motor-cars and motor-cycles—4,000 prosecutions for breaches of it having been made in London last year—

Mr. H. C. Bingley, the Marylebone magistrate, yesterday announced his intention of increasing the fines for future offences of this nature.

"Many motor-cyclists have very little thought for other people, and I shall ask the Bench to assist me in suppressing this nuisance," said the Wolverhampton chief constable, Mr. David Webster, when two motor-cyclists were summoned yesterday for having inefficient silencers.

In imposing fines of 40s. each, the mayor said if the present cases did not act as a warning the maximum penalty of £10 would be imposed in future.

Daily Mail 1926

On Monday night people in parts of England as far apart as Cumberland and Kent were astonished by a blinding flash of blue light which illuminated the sky and lasted for several seconds. There is little doubt that it was caused by a meteorite, but it is seldom that the light is so intense. The *Manchester Guardian* says that one of the most remarkable meteorites on record was that of August 18th, 1783. It was seen along a line from Shetland to Rome, and gave more light than a full moon.

The Spectator 1926

WIRELESS ADVANCE

EUROPEAN TESTS A SUCCESS.

NEW WAVE-LENGTHS EXPERIMENT.

"Highly satisfactory" was the official verdict on the first of the international broadcasting wave-lengths tests in the early hours of yesterday morning.

So far as this country was concerned the results were gratifying. One English listener, however, reports that two foreign stations were "cutting each other up" on a wave length of about 440 metres.

The highest wave-length used was that of Budapest (572 metres); the lowest that of Hanover (290 metres).

A few minutes after the test began, Newcastle reported that it was being heterodyned by a Continental station, which turned out to be Gratz in Austria. The explanation was that the Continental station had forgotten to change its wavelength after its evening concert, but the trouble was soon rectified to the satisfaction of Tyneside.

Bournemouth in Trouble.

Bournemouth on 387 metres apparently was in trouble all night. It was interfered with by Oslo, which uses similar power and a wave-length of 392 metres, and also by several other stations with a wave-length below 387 metres.

On the other hand, Manchester (377) and Frankfort (382) were able to operate without clashing. Among the stations "jammed" were :

Edinburgh (327) by Helsingfors (325).
Glasgow (420) by Munich (414).
Hull (335) by Le Petit Parisien.
Liverpool (314) by Hamburg (317.5).

"Le Petit Parisien" station, after some experiment, was able to adjust its wave-length so as to leave the field clear for Hull.

The B.B.C. observers received valuable reports from listeners and from the new Hayes station, whose partially completed apparatus was in practical use for the first time.

The second test takes place from mid night to-night.

Northern Daily Telegraph 1925

VISION BY WIRELESS

I SPENT an amazing morning yesterday at Motograph House, Upper St. Martin's Lane, with Mr. J. L. Baird, who has invented a practical way of conveying pictures over the ether. I sat before a galaxy of lights, a great disc studded wheel began to whirr, and away in another room my face appeared to a friend. Then we exchanged places and, on a screen some six inches square, I saw the features of my friend flicker into life, apparently out of flowing crescents of light which seemed to stabilize and solidify themselves into his lineaments. It was a fair likeness, easily recognizable, and had been wirelessed to me through several walls.

Television has occupied scientists for a great many years. In 1880 it was confidently predicted that we should be able to see by telegraph. When, however, the transmitting machine came to be constructed, the light-sensitive cells failed to respond to the immense speed required and the experiment was a failure. Within the last year or two pictures have been transmitted both by telegraph and wireless, but by a system which is relatively slow, and would be inadequate to catch life and motion on the rebound, so to speak. Briefly put, the problem of television is to show on a screen in London a man speaking in Manchester and to represent his actions as accurately as we can already reproduce his words.

TRAFFIC CONTROL BY SIGNALS.

MAN IN PICCADILLY CABIN.

HOW IT WORKED YESTERDAY.

When the Piccadilly traffic control lights came into use yesterday seven main thoroughfares were filled with traffic or completely emptied by the action of one man.

A *Daily Mail* reporter found Piccadilly's traffic "general"—a keen-faced police constable in uniform—in the box at the junction of Piccadilly and St. James's-street that is his headquarters.

Before him was a map of the district on which were dotted tiny replicas of the lights he was flashing in the different thoroughfares wherein he controlled the traffic.

EIGHT LEVERS.

Beneath the map were eight levers about six inches high, like those in railway signal cabins.

By moving two that operated two sets of lights in Piccadilly, one opposite Bond-street and the other opposite Berkeley-street, he filled the road with traffic or emptied it to the quietude of a country lane.

The other six levers released the cross-traffic when the main thoroughfare had been emptied. The names on his levers described at what corners the sets of lights were to be found, and they were inscribed :

Piccadilly west-bound.	From Dover-st.
	From Albemarle-st.
Piccadilly east-bound.	From Bond-st.
	From St. James's-st.
From Berkeley-st.	From Arlington-st.

Onlookers who sought to peep into his cabin saw him pull two levers towards him and then watched the effect on Piccadilly. The traffic police at the two signalling devices in Piccadilly saw the green lights change to white. That told them that a red light was coming. Then the red light shone, and in obedience they stopped traffic from entering the controlled area.

THE THREE LIGHTS.

The traffic "general" moved six more switches. The drivers massed in the side streets saw the red lights that held them there change to white and then green, and they raced across the empty Piccadilly.

The signals were to the police and not to drivers. The point duty men did their usual duties, except that their "general" told them when to act instead of allowing them to choose their own course of action. The result was that confusion was entirely eliminated from one of London's most congested areas, although it will be a few days before it is known whether traffic is speeded up or slowed down by the new system.

DIFFICULT TO SEE.

The biggest flaw, however, which once or twice led to confusion for a minute, was due to the police finding it difficult to see which light was in use. The lights were visible at 400 yards but almost invisible to the police watchers beneath.

Daily Mail 1926

The Spectator 1926

MR. COBHAM'S GREAT HOME-COMING.

"End of Yet Another Historic Flight."

Mr. Alan Cobham, on his return to London yesterday on the completion of his 28,000-miles flight from England to Australia and back, had a wonderful reception that reflected the nation's admiration of his achievement.

From the moment he crossed the English coast at Hastings until he alighted on the Thames at Westminster his was a triumphal home-coming.

The climax was reached on the Terrace of the House of Commons, which Sir Samuel Hoare, the Air Minister, in his speech of welcome described as " one of the most historic centres of the British Empire, where for generations past men of service in the State have been received year after year."

Here, in the presence of a distinguished company, Sir Samuel read to Mr. Cobham the following message from the King :—

On your safe return from Australia I offer you a cordial welcome home and congratulate you heartily on the successful termination of yet another historic flight.   GEORGE R.I.

When Mr. Cobham stepped on to the Terrace, he said : " How do you do, everybody? Glad to be home again. It's a very wonderful reception, and I thank everybody very much indeed."

PERFECT LANDING.

At 2.12 p.m., flying slowly at about 200ft., Mr. Cobham appeared at Westminster greeted by ships' sirens, which he could hear above the roar of his engine. Then, waving a greeting from his cockpit to those gathered on the terrace of the Houses of Parliament, he disappeared in the haze towards Hammersmith Bridge.

A few minutes later more cheers indicated his return. Making two wide circles, he throttled down his motor, and, after a final half-turn near the County Hall, glided across, 30ft. above the heads of spectators on Westminster Bridge, and made a perfect descent on the river between Westminster and Lambeth Bridges at 2.26 p.m.

His machine was immediately taken in tow, and he himself, with his two mechanics, Sergt. Ward, R.A.F., and Mr. C. S. Capel, left in motor-launches for the Speaker's steps, being cheered enthusiastically by the crowds on both sides of the river.

The first launch put Mr. Cobham ashore at the foot of the steps, and he ran up them to embrace and kiss his wife, the first person to greet him.

He was bareheaded, and clad in his travel-worn flying suit. The 500,000 miles which, in his many flights, he has flown over mountains, rivers, deserts, and seas, have left their imprint on his face. It is the face of one ever on the alert, with eyes even more farseeing than those of the seaman; eyes accustomed to sweep vast vistas from a bird's-eye view thousands of feet aloft.

Daily Mail 1926

Alan Cobham lands his de Havilland seaplane on the Thames at Westminster.

The Sporting Event of the Year

The First International Motor Race ever held in Great Britain will take place at BROOKLANDS on Saturday.

This will be the greatest test of endurance for cars and drivers ever seen in this country. For the Grand Prix of the R.A.C.—one of the series for the Championship of the World—the track has been adapted to reproduce the gruelling conditions of a Continental road race.

The Course, 287 miles long, will be taken in 110 laps by 14 competitors; cornering at 80 miles per hour; "S" bends at 30 to 40 m.p.h.

Starts, finishes and repair pits will be in full view of spectators. This is an event no motorist should miss.

FIRST
GRAND PRIX
IN GT. BRITAIN

ADMISSION (including tax) -	5/-
TRANSFER TO RESERVED ENCLOSURE - -	15/-
CARS TO COURSE - -	10/-
CARS TO GARAGE - -	5/-

Frequent trains from Waterloo to Weybridge (S. R.)

BROOKLANDS
Saturday Aug. 7th. Start 2 p.m

ROYAL AUTOMOBILE CLUB, PALL MALL, LONDON.

Yorkshire Post 1927

AEROPLANE SPRAYER.

25 MINUTES INSTEAD OF 2 DAYS TO STOP POTATO DISEASE.

Mr. George Caudwell, of Weston, near Spalding, Lincolnshire, a large grower of potatoes, chartered an aeroplane to spray a field of potatoes with powder to protect them from disease.

The powder was contained in two pipes on either side of the fuselage, and an operation which would take two days in the ordinary way was completed in 25 minutes

Daily Mail 1926

BROADCASTING.

POSSIBILITY OF AN EMPIRE SERVICE.

(From Our Correspondent.)

During the week-end the London programme was relayed in India, Australia, New Zealand, and South Africa for the first time since broadcasting was begun. There is no broadcasting station in the British Isles capable of reaching the Dominions direct, especially on moderately long waves, and the transmission was carried out by the wireless station at Eindhoven, in Holland (call sign PCJJ), which picked up Daventry and transmitted the programme direct to Australia on a 30-metre wave. In the case of New Zealand the station at Sydney also relayed the programme.

Cables from the Dominions concerned show that reception was good—" as clear as a local programme." The items included an orchestral performance, news, cricket scores, and a description of the Davis Cup lawn tennis matches.

Empire broadcasting regularly is one of the ideals of the B.B.C., but it is recognised that short waves will have to be used by any service instituted, and it is stated that the development of this side of radio does not at present justify the opening of a regular service.

The Corporation are now experimenting with short waves, and plans are already in hand for the erection of a short-wave station at Daventry. In an interview an official of the B.B.C. said:—

" All experiments such as the one from Eindhoven are helpful, and we are watching them carefully. We are experimenting to find the means of making continuous programmes to the Dominions practicable. Distortion and fading are the two factors that now stand in the way of regular transmission."

Yorkshire Post 1927

FLIGHT TO AUSTRALIA.

BRITISH AIRMAN'S CASUAL ANNOUNCEMENT.

A man alighting from a D.H. Moth at Croydon Aerodrome last night said to an official, " Can I leave my machine here? " " Yes," said the surprised official; " When do you want it? " The airman replied, " To-morrow morning."

It was later discovered that the airman who left his machine in so casual a manner was Mr. Dennis Rook, who intends to take off this morning on a flight of 10,000 miles to Australia. He has not flown for about eight years, but he now owns his own machine, and his intention is to fly it to Australia in easy stages. It is purely a sporting flight.

DARING 13,000 FEET CLIMB BY PERILOUS RIDGE.

Woman Scientist With Mountaineering as a Holiday Pastime.

HISTORIC ONE-DAY CONQUEST.

The Jungfrau group with the Eiger on the left.

ONE of the most interesting women in industrial scientific research in Britain, Dr. Dorothy Jordan Lloyd has to-day added to her laurels in another sphere—that of Alpine conquest.

In one day—a feat, it is believed, never before achieved—she climbed the Eiger (13,040ft.) by a very difficult ridge, returning by the same route. The Eiger is one of the highest peaks of the Jungfrau group.

Dr. Lloyd directs research work for the British Leather Manufacturers' Association—a woman with a staff of experts under her control. They study the chemistry and structure of hides.

Evening Standard 1928

THE SCOUTS' OMELETTE.

Hundreds of Eggs Smashed in Collision.

A lorry load of London Boy Scouts and a private car carrying between 500 and 600 eggs collided at Aston Clinton, near Aylesbury, late last night. The car was thrown 30 yards and the driver was smothered with smashed eggs, and also slightly injured. The Scouts were unhurt.

Bath and Wilts Chronicle 1927

WATERPROOF SADDLE.

The Dunlop waterproof saddle is an interesting newcomer, and since the sale of these articles has been taken over from Flexible Saddles, Ltd., many details have been improved. After standing in a downpour of rain for several hours, the saddles can be wiped bone dry with a duster. All types and sizes are made, and all are non-sagging. Anyone who has experienced the dangers and disadvantages of a wet and sodden saddle will appreciate this Dunlop improvement.

NEW PARKING PLACES IN LONDON.

ADDITIONAL LIMITATIONS.

The Minister of Transport makes the following announcement :—

The Minister of Transport has, on the recommendation of the London and Home Counties Traffic Advisory Committee, made revised regulations under section 10 of the London Traffic Act, 1924, in respect of parking-places in London to come into force on January 3, 1928. Under these regulations, which will supersede the London Traffic (Parking Places) Regulations, 1925, made on September 11, 1925, the following additional limitations are imposed :—

(1) That vehicles shall not wait so as to obstruct the entrances of any buildings, gardens, or courtyards ;

(2) That no person shall use any vehicles in connexion with the sale of any article to persons in the street or the selling or offering for sale of his skill in handicraft or his services in any other capacity ;

(3) That no driver or other person in charge of any vehicle bearing General or Limited Trade plate shall cause or permit such vehicle to wait upon any parking place at any time ;

(4) That no driver or other person in charge of any vehicle which has left any parking place after waiting thereon shall, during the period of one hour after so leaving, again cause or permit such vehicle to wait upon that parking place ;

(5) That while any vehicle is standing on a parking place no person shall sound any horn or other instrument provided on the vehicle for the purpose of giving audible warning of its approach except immediately prior to changing the position of the vehicle or departing from the parking place.

Under the new regulations the following parking places authorized under existing regulations have been abolished :—

Baker-st., Marylebone	Ebenezer-st., Shoreditch
Baldwin-st., Finsbury	Wardour-st., Westminster
Brook-st., Westminster	Whitcomb-st., Westminster
Brixton-st., Westminster	

The limits of the following parking places have been curtailed :—

Ambrosden-avenue, Westminster	Hans-rd., Kensington
Basil-st., Kensington	Hodford-rd., Golders Green
Britannia-st., Shoreditch	Whitehall Court, Westminster

NEW PARKING ACCOMMODATION.

New parking accommodation has been prescribed in the following streets :—

Trinity-sq., E.C.3	The Butts, Brentford
Charterhouse-sq., E.C.1 (South side)	Alexandra-rd., Brentford
Pulross-rd., Brixton, S.W.9	Stile Hall-gardens, Chiswick, W.4
Ferndale-rd., Brixton, S.W.9	Geraldine-rd., Wandsworth, S.W.18
Broomhill-rd., Wandsworth, S.W.18	Burston-rd., Putney, S.W.15
Putney Embankment, S.W.15	Ravenna-rd., Putney, S.W.15
Bedford-sq., W.C.1	Balham-grove, Balham, S.W.12
Matthew Parker-st., S.W.1	
Caxton-st., S.W.1	Ormeley-rd., Balham, S.W.12
Orchard-st., S.W.1	Laitwood-rd., Balham, S.W.12
Lowndes-sq., S.W.1	
Radsworth-st., E.C.1	St. Luke's-rd., Clapham, S.W.4
Soho-sq., W.1	
Portland-place, W.1	Market-place, Hertford
Finsbury-circus, E.C.2	Queens-rd., Hertford
Finsbury-sq., E.C.2	Great Northern Station, Approach-rd., Hertford
West Smithfield, E.C.1	
Royal-crescent, Notting Hill, W.11	Mill-road, Hertford
Victoria Embankment, S.W.1	

A board indicating the limits, method of parking, parking hours, and maximum period of waiting will be exhibited at each authorized parking place. It is also intended to arrange for the " limits " of each park to be indicated by markings in the carriageway, and experiments are being conducted to determine the type of material best suited for use on the varying road surfaces. So soon as the most suitable material has been determined, the limits will be clearly marked in the carriageway with an arrow indicating the direction in which the park is situated. It is also proposed to exhibit a prominent notice bearing the words " Car Park."

The Times 1928

Proprietors
SIMPSON PUBLISHERS LTD.,
PUBLISHED
MONTHLY

Vol. 6 No. 60. JULY, 1929

TALBOT HOUSE,
ARUNDEL STREET,
LONDON, W.C.2
Telephones:
CENTRAL 2122
Telegrams:
KARTOPS ESTRAND

A Motorist's Diary
By P.D.Q.

HAVING recently been experimenting with two or three well known American cars of large horse power that are selling very well on the English market, I have come to the conclusion that their chief reason of appeal to the British public lies in the very simple fact that they have a large engine. There is a certain performance to be obtained with a large engine even if it is slightly inefficient that can never be given by the most highly efficient small engined car. The taxation in this country has killed the production of the big engined car, therefore, it is impossible to obtain big engine qualities in a British car unless one can afford a car running well into the four figure mark. There is an extreme comfort with a big engine, providing it is free from vibration, and one must admit that the Americans are able to give this with their engines, providing, that revolutions are kept within a reasonable limit. Probably because of this large horse power available, the power-weight ratio of the average American car is always in favour of the power. This again gives the comfort which is not obtained through a medium powered car which relies on high revolutions for a high average speed. I do not think that the average American car compares at all well with the average British production in most other respects, except of course that the Americans with their large output are constantly adding those various little improvements to the equipment of their cars, which undoubtedly make for greater comfort. The British manufacturer is slower in this respect, due undoubtedly to the fact that his output being smaller, he cannot alter his standard equipment so frequently whilst selling at such competitive prices as exist to-day.

* * *

A novelty in the shape of London garage procedure has been adopted by the Piccadilly Garage of Denman Street. This novelty consists of the issuing of a season ticket for one or more number of months to an individual car owner, he paying a set sum for the use of the pass. This procedure is to be highly commended as undoubtedly there are hundreds of visitors to London daily or weekly who would like to feel that they do not have to pay their 1s. 6d. for all odd half hours garage when in London. The Piccadilly Garage which was opened quite recently heralds a beginning of these large and commodious garages designed especially for that use which London requires so urgently, and I am glad to note that the prices for garage are so thoroughly reasonable.

It was not so long ago that for the privilege of confining one's car in an ill lighted and dirty back mews, one had to pay something in the neighbourhood of 3s. 6d. for a brief period of an hour. It is no wonder that people sought to abuse the privileges of official parking places.

* * *

R 101 PROVES SHIP OF LUXURY

Less Vibration in Saloon Than in Big Liner

COMMANDER'S STORY

FROM OUR SPECIAL CORRESPONDENT
CARDINGTON, Monday.

"It was a wonderfully successful flight," said Major Scott to me after the R 101 returned to Cardington, "and I am perfectly satisfied with the ship in every way.

"With only three engines running our cruising speed was fifty-eight miles an hour—equal to the R 33's fastest speed.

"We reached London at 12.30 p.m., by way of Cricklewood, and flew at 2,000 feet.

"Trafalgar-square seemed to us to be pretty full of people, and we could hear distinctly the hooting of sirens from steamboats, tugs and railway engines.

"Our engines were extraordinarily quiet. At luncheon we sat as if were in the restaurant of a big liner. There was even less vibration.

WHISPERING HUM

"All we could hear was a sort of whispering hum.

"The chairs on which we were seated were not secured, but they did not move from their positions.

"When passing over schools, we were delighted to see that the children had been given permission to leave their desks to give us a cheer.

"There will be four trial flights—probably beginning on Wednesday—before we can really pronounce the ship ready for a long-distance flight.

"Our final trial will probably last for twenty-four hours."

While R 101 was being attached to the mooring tower a cable came in contact with the envelope and tore the fabric several inches.

I was informed, however, that the damage was immaterial and could be repaired in a few minutes.

Daily Mirror 1929

(Right) Hand control for the automatic gearbox on the 30 h.p. Armstrong Siddeley.

The Motor 1928

ARMSTRONG SIDDELEY . . . 67

AN IMPROVED 30 H.P. CHASSIS.
Self-changing Gearbox Standardized.

THE chief point of interest on the 30 h.p. Armstrong Siddeley car is the new self-changing silent four-speed gearbox. This gear is claimed to be dead silent in action and very simple to operate. A selective control is mounted on a quadrant above the steering wheel and enables the driver to select his next gear before actually requiring it, the change being made later on, merely by depressing and releasing a pedal. Other points of interest on this car are the new scuttle, the upswept frame—which enables the body line to be lowered—and a 21-gallon rear petrol tank.

The engine remains unaltered in any material respects, the bore and stroke being 88.9 mm. and 133.4 mm. respectively, which gives a capacity of just under 5 litres and an R.A.C. rating of 29.5 h.p. Overhead valves are operated by push-rods and all the major bearings of the engine are fed from a forced lubrication system. The chassis is shown fitted with an enclosed landaulet body seating two persons on the main seat, two on folding seats and one beside the driver. The car has distinctly pleasing lines and is luxuriously equipped. The price, with four-speed silent gearbox, is £1,350. Armstrong Siddeley Motors, Ltd., Coventry.

Here's congratulations to the Hon. Mrs. V. A. Bruce who quite recently broke the 24-hour record at an average speed of 89.57 miles per hour. The most remarkable point of this achievement is the fact that she broke this record absolutely single handed, driving consistently for 24 hours. It is really a marvellous performance considering that the previous holders of the record were Kaye Don, E. A. D. Eldridge and G. E. T. Easton. The previous single holder of this record was Mr. T. Gillett who with a 1,985 c.c. A.C. averaged 82.59 miles per hour as far back as 1925. This record illustrates once again the outstanding reliability of the Bentley, which car the Hon. Mrs. V. A. Bruce drove for the whole 24 hours.

Daily Mirror 1929

Daily Mirror 1929

BRITAIN'S BID FOR STILL GREATER AIR SPEED

Schneider Team Captain to Challenge World Record in 'Plane That Won Trophy

VICTORY AT 328 MILES AN HOUR

Two Italian Pilots Escape Disaster in Forced Landings —Atcherley Disqualified After Great Feat

Following her wonderful victory in the Schneider Trophy race on Saturday, Britain will to-morrow attempt to set up a still higher world's speed record.

The attempt will be made by Squadron-Leader Orlebar, the captain of the Schneider Trophy team, and he will use the 'plane in which Flying-Officer Waghorn won the race at 328 miles an hour. A second 'plane will be tested by Flight-Lieutenant Stainforth and may also make an attempt on the record.

The record at present stands at 332 miles an hour, the speed reached by Flying-Officer Atcherley, who had the misfortune to go off the course and be disqualified. The best Italian average speed was 284 miles an hour, and two of their 'planes came down, one pilot being injured.

Squadron-Leader Orlebar, who is to make an attempt to beat the world's air speed record to-morrow.

CAN NOTHING MORE BE DONE ABOUT LONDON'S TRAFFIC PROBLEM?

Delays Adding Ten per Cent. to Cost of Traffic: The Doldrums in the West End: Piquant Ideas of The Ministry of Transport.

WHITEHALL WAITS, TOO.

A one-way traffic block at the Mansion House.

By a Special Correspondent.

IS the London traffic problem insoluble?

Ingenious brains have devised "roundabouts" and one-way streets; statisticians tell of millions of pounds added to traders' annual bills; sardonic Americans have spoken of the advantages of a bus-top in the Strand for a long sleep; and still the immense blocks of vehicles continue.

I have spent days in riding or walking the streets to study the blocks at first hand. I have timed blocks that have lasted for ten minutes. I have seen lorries, piled high with freight, crawl along choked thoroughfares. I have seen private drivers become exasperated.

HAVE TO TURN BACK.

Never has it been more strikingly proved that time is money. Some of the big firms estimate their loss at £350 a week. I spoke to-day with a departmental manager of one of the leading firms of traffic contractors. He said:

"Traffic delays add quite 10 per cent. to the cost of transport in London. Drivers' lost time and wasted petrol consumption are two of the biggest items.

"Quite often lorries sent to the docks are held up so long that it is too late to unload them when they arrive, though we try to make sufficient allowance for stoppages. That means an extra journey the next day and possible serious delay in export. Added to

---

Farcical Travel.

Travelling by car in the Metropolitan area is becoming something of a farce. The greater the speed of the machines, the slower you travel.
—SIR IAN HAMILTON.

that is the congestion at the docks themselves. If a lorry arrives after 4 p.m. it is too late to touch the goods."

ADVANCING BY JERKS.

So much for the interference with business and trade. To show the annoyance with which the ordinary citizen has to put up I give the followin gtime-table of a journey by bus along Oxford-street, New Oxford-street, and Holborn :—

11.45 a.m.—Boarded a bus at Marble Arch.
11.47.—Held up for two minutes.
11.51.—Held up again; this time four minutes.
11.56.—Advancing towards Oxford-circus in earnest little jerks.
12. 0.—In the Doldrums. Ahead and behind a line of buses and motorcars as far as the eye can see. Much irascible blowing of horns.
12. 5.—A sudden spurt.
12. 6.—Three restful minutes to allow vehicles to cross from Regent-street.
12.10.—Stubborn progress towards Tottenham Court-road.
12.15.—Held up for two minutes.
12.17-12.32.—Crawled to Holborn-circus.

Evening Standard
1928

Oxford Mail **1929**

TRAFFIC EXPERIMENTS.

Electric Signalling Tests at Danger Spots.

Experiments with automatic electric signalling apparatus are shortly to be made by the London Traffic Advisory Committee at the Albert Gate—Knightsbridge crossing and the junction of Baker-street and Marylebone-road.

Traffic at these notorious danger spots will be controlled as in the New York streets by red and green lights.

When red is shown all traffic must stop to allow pedestrians to cross.

"It is unlikely that it will be decided to recommend that the pedestrian who disobeys the signal lights shall be punished by law," said a Transport Ministry official to an Oxford Mail representative to-day.

Daily Mirror
1929

COMMONS REJECT LONDON TRAFFIC BILL

Majority of 123 Against Scheme for Big Combine

CONFERENCE HINT

Amid Socialist cheers the London County Council (Co-ordination of Passengers) Traffic Bill was rejected in the Commons last night.

Rejection was carried by 295 votes in favour to 172 against; majority, 123.

The overwhelming demand for further traffic facilities in London was stressed by Sir Kingsley Wood, who spoke in favour of the third reading. "We ought to have more tubes and buses," he said.

Mr. Percy Harris (L.) moved the rejection of the Bill on the ground that it was an attempt to exploit an essential service to the disadvantage of the public.

This was a bad Bill based on wrong principles.

The object of the Bill was to create a monopoly, and such a monopoly should be under public control and supervision. It was nothing short of blackmail to say there would be no extension of tube facilities unless their Bills were passed.

1930—1939

Working on the tubular welded steel fuselage of the Avro X Commercial ten-seater aircraft, c. 1930.

BRISBANE IN LOVE
WITH AMY

Strenuous Time at Receptions
Compels a Rest

PRAYERS CROSSING THE SEA

BRISBANE, Friday.

MISS AMY JOHNSON'S feminine charm has captured the hearts of the people of Brisbane, and when she attended a conference to-day of the Women's Christian Temperance Union the conference rose and sang the Doxology.

This prompted Miss Johnson to reveal to the audience her spiritual faith. She said that while crossing the Java Sea she was terrified by the rainstorms and black clouds, and she prayed for Divine guidance. Immediately afterwards her buffeted aeroplane was surrounded by a rainbow, and she saw an opening in the clouds. Every day, she said, she prayed that she might be brought safely through her great adventure, and she felt sure somebody was watching over her.

Miss Johnson has had such a strenuous time at receptions that a doctor ordered her to bed early. Her damaged plane is now being repaired, and it is hoped that it will be ready for a trial flight on Sunday.—Central News.

An Air-minded Family.

Miss Johnson's parents, Mr. and Mrs. J. W. Johnson, and Molly, her 18-years-old sister, arrived at Filton, Bristol, Aerodrome yesterday in a plane from Hull, where they left Betty, the 11-years-old sister, making toy paper aeroplanes. From Filton they proceeded by Moth to Whitchurch, to take part in the Bristol Air Pageant. "Amy will be delighted," said Mr Johnson, "to hear of our flying to the pageant We are becoming a very air-minded family indeed."

Freedom of Hull?

When Lord Wakefield received the freedom of the borough of Hythe yesterday, he made the suggestion that Hull should confer a similar honour on Miss Amy Johnson. "My opinion is," he said, "that Hull would honour itself by conferring its freedom upon her.

"I had the pleasure of meeting Miss Johnson before she set out upon her eventful journey, and I was struck as much by her practical energy as by her courage—great as that is. Her long flight will probably prove to have been one very important factor in hastening the practical development of civil aviation.

"She will be honoured not only as the heroine of a very splendid and adventurous project, but also as one of those few practical pioneers who helped to bring us nearer to the day of flying for all. From either point of view, her journey has been a remarkable success, and her city of Hull is rightly proud of her."

Morning Advertiser **1930**

CHANNEL TUNNEL
DECISION

Government's Detailed Reasons for Rejecting the Proposal

POTENTIAL MILITARY DANGER

THE WHITE PAPER, promised by Mr. Ramsay MacDonald in the House of Commons, detailing the Government's policy on the question of the Channel Tunnel and their reasons for rejecting the proposal, was issued yesterday. The statement concludes:—

"The Committee of Imperial Defence were unable to discover a single advantage from a military point of view which would follow from the construction of a Channel Tunnel. On the contrary, it would result only in an increased military commitment, involving in certain happily remote contingencies an element of danger,' to provide against which a heavy capital and annual expenditure would have to be incurred.

"Following on the meeting of the Committee of Imperial Defence, the whole matter was examined by the Government, which, in addition to economic and military considerations, reviewed possible diplomatic reactions.

"Having regard to the element of doubt as to the feasibility of construction, the weakness of the economic case, the great cost, the long period before which the capital expended could fructify, and the small amount of employment provided, the Government have come to the conclusion that there is no justification for a reversal of the policy pursued by successive Governments for nearly 50 years in regard to the Channel Tunnel."

Morning Advertiser **1930**

Bystander **1930**

MISS ELEANORE MITCHELL

The European Typewriting Championship holder, likes an Austin Seven Saloon for keeping her special demonstration appointments, and with a compact Corona Portable mounted on a tripod, proves conclusively that the front seat affords ample room for working. This device is a sound idea for travellers who need to send in interview reports, orders and so on, and who wish to keep in touch with headquarters while on the road. The companion, Minx, is an additional luxury, but, as a park-guard, one well worth while

In Scotland, 499 drivers of vehicles were prosecuted for being drunk in charge and 384 were convicted. In 1925 the figures were 404 and 293. The figures are regrettable, but the increase is not out of proportion.

The Automobile Association has established another record in the history of British motoring. The number of badges issued to members has now passed the one million mark. The first A.A. badge of the new series will be numbered 1A.

Motor World
1930

Not every motorist has grasped that the new regulations for the storage of petrol cover the petrol even in the tank of his car, and that unless he empties the tank every night he must keep a fire-extinguishing apparatus of some kind in his garage. This has given a tremendous fillip to the sale of fire extinguishers, for although a bucket of sand meets the requirements of the law it is practically useless in the event of a fire, and cannot be carried about; while a comparatively small fire extinguisher that can be carried on the car itself complies with the new regulations.

• •

Bystander **1930**

Four Cars for £800.

In introducing the Tramways Committee minutes, Coun. Gledhill, alluding to the four tramcars proposed to be purchased from Exeter Corporation for £200 each, observed that so much had been said about economy lately, and it had been reflected during the evening, that he could not allow his committee to miss the chance of a bouquet for economy. They had been asked by a correspondent in the Press what they were doing. Well, these tram cars were built in 1928, and went into service in 1929. They were of modern construction, fitted with two 50 horse power motors, patent brake arrangements and with transverse seats exactly like the latest cars the committee had put into commission. They would cost at least £8,000, but owing to the fact that Halifax had a gauge of 3ft. 6in. like Exeter, and that the market for such in this country was restricted they had been able to buy what were worth nearly £8,000 for £800. That should be worth noting by the economists who wrote to the Press.

Ald. Stirk seconded.

Halifax Courier and Guardian **1931**

ROLLS-ROYCE
The Best Car in the World

ROLLS-ROYCE LIMITED, 14-15 CONDUIT STREET, LONDON, W.1.

Coun. A. H. GLEDHILL, J.P.
A soliloquy by the Chairman of the Tramways Committee.

Halifax Courier and Guardian **1931**

The RAF Supermarine S6B is lowered down the slipway on the day of the 1931 Schneider Trophy race. It went on to win the race.

The ACCIDENTS *you* MIGHT HAVE CAUSED
By The Editor

IF, in reading the accounts of the various daily road accidents in his newspaper, the motorist were to remember that luck as much as skill had prevented him from having a similar accident, the safety factor would become more heavily weighed in his favour. That is the point that M. Launay had in mind, no doubt, in a recent article in a Paris newspaper, which showed that in France, as in this and other countries, the abnormal number of road accidents is causing the authorities very great concern.

Some satisfaction is to be gleaned from the statistics that prove that, while in the last ten years the number of road fatalities in each year has exceeded that of the previous twelve months, just recently a reduction has been shown. We live in an age of speed; indeed, speed has become a craze.

It is interesting and all to the good that motor racing should take place at Brooklands, but it is not right to encourage such feats as racing express trains between Edinburgh and London, or any other two cities in this country. The recently reported race between Edinburgh and London may have been a wonderful feat; indeed, it was, but it was the more wonderful because there were no accidents.

It can be truthfully asserted that a race with an express train from Scotland to London cannot be done unless the driver is prepared to " chance it " at crossroads, level crossing, and going through towns and villages, and this, no matter whether the performance is during the day or during the night. A northern evening paper commented on the recent record run, and took the view that we were getting so used to speed that in course of time the roads might become as the railroads are now, but the important thing to remember is, that road arrangements just now do not permit of record - breaking speeds over long distances. It is a fact that many standard models, even of light cars of to-day, could create road records when driven by a skilful and experienced driver prepared to take risks. But the risks he would take would not only be of his own life, but of the lives of other road users. There is neither sense nor reason in ordinary road racing, and the authorities would be justified in taking whatever steps might be necessary to stop it.

We hear a great deal of the " Safety First " movement to-day. It may be that this movement can justifiably claim to be responsible for the recent decrease in road fatalities. On the other hand, people are no doubt getting used to speed, and taking greater precautions. While the law of averages over periods of time obtains, yet there is also this to be remembered, that, owing to depressed trade conditions, there were probably fewer actual novices on the road during the last twelve months than for any of the previous few years.

In fairness to motoring, a matter that is generally overlooked is that the risks to life to-day are altogether much greater than, say, twenty years ago. It is true that, despite lessons on safety first in the schools, the children do not hear sufficient of the dangers of the street, and of many other dangers, too. Probably, too much of the emphasis is laid on the need for looking for traffic before crossing the road, at the expense of other matters. Modern life holds many dangers of which children should be warned in the schools, in addition to road dangers.

There is the old story of the earthenware pot meeting the pot of iron. The tree has replaced the pot in conversation, and when it is not a tree it is a wall, another car—or a pedestrian—that the careless motorist comes into contact with.

I saw, the other day, a car which had " won " a tree. It was not a pretty spectacle —the front of the car was flattened, and the shock had been so violent that one wheel was lying nearly fifty yards away. The windows were broken and blood stained the car seats. The driver and passengers had been taken to hospital. Naturally, it is always the fault of the road or the car when there is a skidding accident, of the other driver in a collision, or of anybody or anything—but the motorist involved in an accident, who is seeking causes! The mental attitude of the average driver after an accident, gives a reason for a hundred daily accidents; his conversation is about the excessive speed, the bad judgment, the carelessness—of the other party involved. It is always the other party, or the road or the car—never his own foolishness or clumsiness.

GUY LAUNAY, in *Le Matin*.

The Motorist 1931

LAND FOR AERODROME.

The Finance Committee have considered a letter from Messrs. Frank Lane and Lane, offering for sale certain land for the purposes of an aerodrome.

The letter was referred to the Aerodrome Sub-Committee for consideration and report.

Councillor Mrs. F. E. Laney said she hoped the Council would have the opportunity of saying something about the matter before the Council were committed to the scheme, because she had received a number of letters and inquiries as to what was proposed to be done. " Some people are very much alarmed," she added.

The Mayor said the resolution would not commit the Council to the scheme.

Councillor Benwell suggested that the Town Planning Committee should meet the Aerodrome Committee in regard to the matter.

Alderman C. H. Cartwright: There is not the slightest intention of buying land for an aerodrome at the present moment. (Hear, hear.)

Bournemouth Daily Echo 1931

THE DIESEL ELECTRIC CAR.

SUCCESS OF SECRET TRIALS.

POSSIBLE REVOLUTION IN RAILWAY WORKING.

The trial of the Diesel electric rail car, built at the Scotswood works of Messrs. Armstrong, Whitworth and Co., Ltd., is stated to have been of a highly satisfactory character.

It is hinted that the railway officials who accompanied the trials, which were made in secrecy on railway lines near the works, were greatly impressed in regard to the future possibilities, particularly in view of the electrification of the railways generally.

The importance of the new invention is that no live rail is needed, and that the railway companies would not need to relay the permanent way installation on the lines adopted on the Tyneside electric horseshoe system.

60 MILES AN HOUR.

The new car, it is stated, achieved the 60 miles an hour which it was claimed could be accomplished although this trial was only of a limited nature.

The cost of electrifying the whole of the railways has been estimated at £341,000,000, but it is declared that the cost of installing the Diesel electric system will be less than half that sum —or £150,000,000. This car generates its own electricity.

Northern Echo 1932

The taxi rank at Waterloo Station, c. 1933.

WIRELESS WHILE MOTORING

SET WHICH IS BUILT INTO THE CAR

By ROBERT W. BEARE

Wireless reception while motoring has been attempted by many car owners who are also possessors of portable radio sets, but in most cases it has been given up as a bad job, and the set used merely to enliven the picnic party and for similar purposes, and eventually the set is left at home on account of its considerable weight and bulk.

A new type of motor-car wireless set has been developed, however, which is built as an integral part of the car, and occupies no otherwise useful space.

A demonstration showed that wireless reception is possible while the car is in motion even in the midst of London traffic.

A powerful superheterodyne set and a moving coil loud speaker are carried out of sight under the scuttle of the car. Low tension current is derived from the car's own accumulator and H.T. from a dry battery hidden under the driver's seat. All that is visible is a small tuning plate fitted over the steering column below the wheel.

A notable feature of the design is the provision of automatic volume control, which entirely eliminates the tendency of wireless reception towards great variations of volume as the reception conditions change in the progress of the car between high buildings, through cuttings and so on.

This control automatically boosts the signals when they are weak and holds them in check when they are overstrong.

An adaptation of the set is in extensive use by American police authorities in their war on gangsters, and it is understood that Scotland Yard has the apparatus under consideration.

Gloucestershire Echo 1932

Car's Zig-zag Course.

DRIVER FOUND UNDER INFLUENCE OF DRINK.

CAR OF 1926 VINTAGE.

There was a long drawn out case at Abergele Petty Sessions last Saturday, when Richard Donald Lewis, commercial traveller, Wallasey, appeared before Lord Clwyd (chairman) and other Magistrates to answer charges of driving a motor car whilst under the influence of drink and driving in a dangerous manner on the Abergele—Llanddulas road on March 16. Defendant pleaded not guilty to both charges, being defended by Mr. T. Arthur Hughes.

Supt. Philip Tomkins, in outlining the case, said that at about 10 p.m. on March 16 Mr. J. R. Saronie, cinema proprietor, Prestatyn, was returning home by car from Bangor and when in the vicinity of Gwrych Castle Lodge he observed a car in front of him travelling in a very erratic manner and sometimes getting on to the footpath. He followed the car very carefully for some distance, and when he at length saw a hand apparently signalling him on he managed to get past it. On reaching Abergele Mr. Saronie made a complaint to the police, and after seeing P.C. A. T. Hughes stop the car which he had passed he went on to Prestatyn. P.C. Hughes, having seen the car coming along Market Street in a zig-zag manner, informed the driver, defendant, of the complaint he had received about his driving, and he made no reply. His passenger, a Capt. Smith, however, asked who the hell had made the complaint and became very abusive. P.C. Hughes at length came to the conclusion that both defendant and his passenger were under the influence of drink, and as he would not allow defendant to proceed the passenger wanted to take charge of the car, but he would not allow that either. Defendant was eventually taken to the Police Station, where he was examined by Dr. M. Ffoulkes, of Abergele, and declared to be under the influence of drink to such an extent that he was not in a condition to be in charge of a car.

Rhyl Journal 1932

Millions of Listeners to Christmas Message of Good Will

'FROM MY HOME AND MY HEART'

Remarkable B.B.C. Feat—Memorable Scene in St. Paul's Cathedral

The magnificent achievement of the B.B.C. in transmitting seasonable greetings between widely sundered outposts of Empire, culminating in the King's message to his subjects, was the central feature of this year's Christmastide.

For the first time millions of people at home and abroad, including the great Dominions of Canada, Australia, New Zealand and South Africa, were enabled to listen to a royal message of good will and good cheer.

A phrase in the King's broadcast which awakened a responsive echo in all hearts was: "I speak now from my home and from my heart to you all . . . To all—and to each—I wish a Happy Christmas. God bless you."

While the message was heard clearly many thousands of miles away, residents in parts of Kent found their receivers silenced by an electric light breakdown.

Daily Mirror 1932

BATTLE OF WATERLOO BRIDGE ENDS IN TRUCE

L.C.C. will Accept Govt.'s Rebuilding Plan

AFTER NINE YEARS

Complete Reversal of L.C.C.'s Previous Opinion

The "South London Press" understands that the fate of Waterloo Bridge will be settled by the L.C.C. on Tuesday.

The Improvements Committee will recommend acceptance of the Government's £685,000 reconstruction scheme, and it is certain that the Council will agree, though with many dissentients.

The Improvements Committee met privately on Wednesday to consider the Government proposal and there was a sharp division of opinion before the committee framed its advice to the Council.

FOUR TRAFFIC LINES

The reconstruction scheme is a complete reversal of previous L.C.C. opinion, which has always been for a new bridge capable of carrying six lines of traffic.

The reconstructed bridge will carry four lines.

There will be a " free " vote at the L.C.C. debate and the withdrawal of party whips will result in a vote for the Government plans.

The 60 per cent. grant which the Government scheme carries will influence members, because the L.C.C. is unwilling to proceed without assistance from the Treasury.

In any event, the Council will require a guarantee that any scheme which is agreed will not be thrown out by Parliament—the fate which met the L.C.C. plans last year.

DANGER OF COLLAPSE

The battle of Waterloo Bridge has been waged for nine years in spite of the fact that for long engineers have told the L.C.C. that the bridge is in as dangerous a condition as it can be without collapsing.

Propping-up work and maintenance of the old structure has cost to date £206,000—more than a third of the amount now required to make Waterloo Bridge safe for another generation.

South London Press 1933

BRIGHTON ELECTRIC

6 TRAINS PER HOUR ALL DAY

You don't need a time-table!

**FREQUENCY AND COMFORT
CHEAP FARES DAILY**

Ask for special Fares and Time-Table Folder at any Southern Electric Station or Office

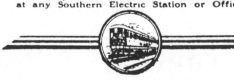

1933: The first flight over the world's highest mountain, in a Westland biplane powered with supercharged Bristol Pegasus engines.

Croydon Airport, 1933.

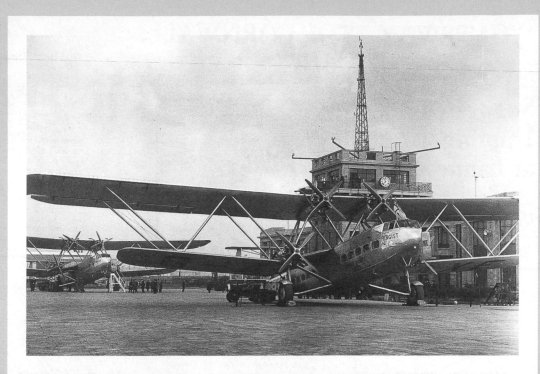

SIR H. ROYCE DEAD.

Genius Discovered by Rolls.

FIRST CAR BUILT AS HOBBY.

Didn't Know at That Time How to Grind a Valve.

[BY A LOCAL MOTORIST.]

Praise of an outstanding person often calls forth the retort that nobody is indispensable, but history has many times belied the assertion, so I have no hesitation in saying that at the moment there is nobody to step into the place vacated by the death of Sir Henry Royce on Saturday.

Royce was a genius, whose name must be written prominently in the annals of progress. Yet he might scarcely have been heard of had progress been a little slower, for it is with the motor-car and aeroplane that his name will ever be associated, and he was already almost middle-aged before he turned his attention seriously to the former. And even then, but for Rolls, with whom his name is so inseparably linked, his genius might never have found an adequate outlet, for his first car he built with no thought of manufacturing such vehicles. Disgusted with the motors that were then being turned out, he made one for himself largely as a hobby, because he felt sure he could build something much better. Fortunately Rolls heard of it, and was led to believe it was just the car he was in search of. The Hon. C. S. Rolls was a man of ideals. "I want a car," he said, "which will become a household word, just as we associate to Broadwood with pianos." Many would say now that Royce had even surpassed that ideal; certainly Rolls had already seen it realised before his death in a flying accident in 1910, not long after he had made the first flight across the Channel and back.

Yet in these days it is hard to realise what a contrast those early Rolls-Royces were to the other cars of those times. More amazing still is it to know that when Royce built his first car neither he nor any of the men helping him knew quite how to grind in a valve.

Sheffield Daily Telegraph 1933

SOUTHERN ROADS TANDEM "50"

Vegetarians Win Fastest Time, Second Handicap and Team Awards

THE Vegetarians began their annual collection of racing prizes in earnest during the week-end.

Three pairs of meat-haters rode in the Southern Roads Tandem "50"; one crew was not so fast, but the other two won the fastest-time award, the second handicap prize and the team medals. "Not bad for a start," said Mr. Davey.

W. G. Phillips and A. G. Oxbrow put up the fastest time of 1.56.22, and, incidentally, won second handicap prize as well. This is the Vegetarians' first important win this season, but it was by no means a runaway victory, for a pair of short-markers, E. Gravely and A. Parsons, of the Southern Wheelers, were second, only 13 secs. slower.

Wessex of recent years has produced several good tandem riders, and they have usually done creditably well in this event, so that by clocking third fastest time and winning third handicap prize A. J. Milton and W. A. Hills, of the Hants Road Club, upheld a tradition begun in such fine style by Hathaway and Jukes. Their time was 1.57.21.

Cycling 1933

The winners, Phillips and Oxbrow.

"GATEWAY TO CORNWALL BY AIR"

Suggested Landing Ground at Launceston

"TOWN MUST BE ON THE MAP"

Council to Go into Question at Once

THE MAYOR (Mr. G. E. Trood).

Launceston, the gateway to Cornwall by road, may soon be the same by air.

That, at least, is the viewpoint of the Mayor, Mr. G. E. Trood, who, at a meeting of the Town Council this week, spoke of the town's pride in their road accessibility to the county.

"Why," he asked, "should we not be similarly proud from an air standpoint?"

A committee was appointed to go into the matter immediately, and take whatever steps were possible to provide a suitable landing ground.

Councillors' Approval.

MEMBERS OF THE COUNCIL spoke favourably of the possibility of a site being found at Launceston to enable aeroplanes to land in connection with the air port at Plymouth.

SEARCH FOR SUITABLE FIELDS.

The question arose on the receipt of a letter from International Air Lines, Ltd., stating that it was their intention to provide facilities for passengers living in such towns at Launceston, etc., to be conveyed by air from the precincts of the town in question to the air port of Plymouth, where the regular services to London were in operation. They wished to ascertain what landing facilities in the shape of large suitable fields were available for such a purpose, and on what terms the company would be entitled to make use of them.

Exeter Western Mail
1933

The Scooter Comes Into Its Own.

Scooters of all shapes and sizes, each piloted by a youthful mechanic, were to be seen trundling their way along the streets around the West Ken. Super Cinema on Saturday night.

They were all making for the same goal—the stage door of the cinema—and all were entrants for the scooter competition staged by the management in connection with the film, "Broadway Thru' a Keyhole," which ran throughout the week. The film features the popular song, "When I was the girl on a scooter." And so the management asked all the little owners of scooters and miniature cycles in the district to compete in a competition for the most original vehicle.

Despite the rainy night there was a large entry, and the contest proved a novel innovation to the programme.

Prizes of scooters and a tricycle were awarded.

West London and Chelsea Gazette
1934

COLLISION-PROOF ROAD SIGNAL.

POSTS MADE OF RUBBER.

On four occasions yesterday a lorry crashed into an island refuge in Charles Street, Leicester and deliberately "charged" a post bearing one of the refuge lights.

The lorry swept over the post which, after the lorry had passed, sprang back into its normal position. The lorry and post were undamaged.

The post was made of rubber, and is said to be the first of its kind in the country. It is the invention of Mr. T. Wilkie, the Leicester public lighting engineer.

On an average five of the existing cast-iron posts on Leicester street refuges are damaged in a week. They cost £3 each.

The new post is hollow, and bears a red electric warning light. When it is struck there is no danger of short circuiting.

Further experiments are to be made.

Birmingham Mail 1934

HEARD—NOT SEEN.

The first woman B.B.C. announcer, Mrs. Giles Borrett, who has been appointed at Broadcasting House, London.

A Glimpse Of The B.B.C.'s New Voice.

SHE IS CHARMING— BUT SHY.

I have seen the B.B.C.'s New Voice (writes a "Sunday Express" representative).

She was wearing a vivid scarlet wrap over a river frock. In her hand was clasped the front door of a house in West Cromwell-road, Earl's Court.

It was only a glimpse that I got— through a one-inch gap between door and door-post.

A tall dark girl with deeply tanned bare arms stood there. Two large greyish eyes looked at me inquiringly. Above the jolliest of smiles was a mass of wavy hair.

* * *

I explained my mission.

"You must go to the B.B.C.," said the Voice.

It was an exquisite contralto. Again I spoke.

"You must go to the B.B.C.," said the Voice.

That was all. But the journey was repaid.

Gently but firmly the door closed.

* * *

The dullest weather forecast will be worth listening to if Mrs. Giles Borrett reads it. Mrs. Borrett is the B.B.C.'s first woman announcer, and broadcasting is going to be "different."

And she starts work to-morrow.

Sunday Express 1933

Protection from Car-Thieves. A clutchless gear-change for all models is the new feature of the 1934 Humber motor-cars. This, combined with synchro-mesh easy-changing gear-box, makes them as easy to control on the road as any novice could possibly desire. They are also protected against the car-thief by means of a steering safety lock which it would take considerable time and ingenuity to overcome, even by the most astute mechanic desirous of "borrowing" somebody else's vehicle. Practically every car in the exhibition is provided with direction indicators of the semaphore type, which automatically return to their hiding-places in the door-posts of the vehicles

A CAR WHICH LENDS ITSELF EQUALLY WELL TO FORMAL OR INFORMAL OCCASIONS : ONE OF THE LATEST DAIMLER 15-H.P. SALOON MODELS, OF WHICH ITS OWNERS ARE MAKING GOOD USE.

The "fifteen" is the smallest Daimler chassis—specially designed for those who hanker after luxurious motoring, but whose income limits them to a very moderate initial and annual outlay.

Illustrated London News 1933

when the steering-wheel is straightened after making the desired turn. This should add generally to the safety of our roads, because, in the past, many a driver has forgotten to replace or return the direction arm to its cover, so making following traffic wonder where he was going to turn on a perfectly straight road. All the Humber cars are fitted with these, as well as with self-closing radiator shutters and a built-in jacking system.

TRAFFIC LIGHTS PIONEER

FINED FOR PASSING

On being summoned at Croydon yesterday for passing the red traffic light, Mr. George Longfield Beasley, of Homefields, Merton, said he did not see them.

He added that he was the means of introducing automatic traffic lights into this country and America.

Asked for an opinion on what could be done to give them greater visibility, defendant said he thought they were too high, and should be brought down to the motorist's line of vision.

The Chairman (Sir Arthur Spurgeon) said he was impressed with the suggestion, and hoped some notice would be taken of it.

A fine of 20s. was imposed.

Sunday Times 1934

THRILL FOR TRAM PASSENGERS

Trolley-head and Wire Falls

Passengers on a Blackpool open circular tour tramcar, travelling along Lytham-road, South Shore, had an alarming experience when they were near the corner of Highfield-road, last night.

The trolley-head on the tramcar snapped off and fell into the roadway.

A section of the overhead wire also dropped to the ground. The wire fell clear of the tramcar, which was full of passengers at the time.

Tram traffic along Lytham-road was disorganised for more than half-an-hour, and great care had to be exercised by the tram officials in keeping people away from the wire which lay on the ground.

A breakdown gang arrived and normal traffic was presently resumed.

Blackpool Gazette and Herald 1934

ROAD TRAFFIC SIGNS.

ALL IN BRITAIN TO BE UNIFORM.

All road traffic signs throughout Britain are to be standardised as the result of new regulations now in force.

The regulations (which are provisional only until statutory rules have been made under the Road Traffic Act, 1930) came into force on December 22, 1933, but details were not issued by the Minister of Transport until last night. They are based on the recommendations of a Departmental Committee which reported last July.

In a circular letter to highway authorities the Minister urges that the review of existing traffic signs should be carried out without delay. Signs in existence at the date of the Committee's report which differ in form from those recommended need not be removed unless they conflict in principle with the Committee's recommendations, but as it becomes necessary to renew them, they should be replaced by standard signs of the types now authorised by the regulations.

The importance of avoiding the erection of unnecessary warning signs is emphasised, but it is added:

"There is, however, one warning sign,

SLOW, MAJOR ROAD AHEAD,

which should, as the Committee recommends, be freely used. The sign hitherto used to indicate the approach to a major road was open to the criticism that it did not state specifically the source of danger to which it was intended to draw attention. The new sign imposes upon a driver on the minor road a definite responsibility for avoiding a collision with a vehicle on the major road, and, as its meaning is clear and unmistakable, it should assist to reduce accidents at crossroads."

Birmingham Mail 1934

MERSEY TUNNEL OPENED

THE KING'S TRIBUTE

FROM OUR SPECIAL CORRESPONDENT
LIVERPOOL, JULY 18

When the King and Queen were about to enter the Royal train at Rock Ferry station at the end of their visit to Lancashire and Merseyside the King said to Lord Derby that he had never seen such a demonstration of affectionate loyalty as the Queen and he had encountered during their visit.

The King's words justify one's own impression of the scenes in Manchester yesterday and here in Liverpool to-day. The purpose of the Royal visit was to give Royal approval to great and notable works of public improvement in this part of the country, and this has been most generously expressed by the King in his four speeches; but the dominant feature of these two days' happenings has been the spontaneous outburst of popular affection for their Majesties. To-day it is estimated that 1,000,000 persons in Lancashire and Cheshire have turned out to see the King and Queen and express their loyalty and affection.

Times Educational Supplement 1934

CROSSINGS IN LONDON

60 JUNCTIONS TO BE MARKED

REGULATIONS IN FORCE ON MONDAY

Early in April particulars were published of proposals for pedestrian crossing places in London, and the Minister of Transport now announces that the marking of these experimental crossings at some 60 junctions will be completed in Westminster and Holborn on Monday next. The regulations provide that the markings may be made in paint or metal, and the use of paint is contemplated as a temporary expedient.

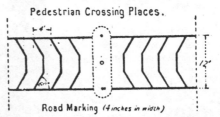

These crossings, it is stated, will fail in their purpose unless drivers and pedestrians alike recognize the obligations placed on them, and, on the advice of the London and Home Counties Traffic Advisory Committee, regulations (London Traffic (Pedestrian Crossing Places) Provisional Regulations, 1934) have been made which provide that at these points (1) pedestrians must not obstruct a vehicle proceeding in the general line of traffic movement—*i.e.*, straight ahead; but (2) vehicle traffic turning at right angles must give way to pedestrians using the marked crossings.

Drivers are required at all times to exercise due care, and if convicted of a breach of the Regulations are liable to a fine not exceeding £5; while in the case of pedestrians similarly convicted a maximum fine of 5s. is laid down.

These first experimental crossings are all at points where traffic is controlled by light signals or by police. In the near future further crossings are proposed to be marked in Poplar, St. Pancras, and Stepney. Some of these will be at

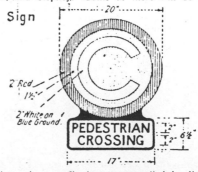

points where traffic is not controlled by light signals or police, and will be marked by the special sign "C" on a red and white ground in addition to the markings on the carriageway itself. At these points all vehicles must allow free passage to any pedestrian and must, if necessary, stop for that purpose.

The Times 1934

Reflector Studs.—Reflector studs of rubber, with tiny glass "eyes," have been laid down at a pedestrian crossing in Bradford; it is said that these are the first of this type in the country.

Autocar 1935

THE "ROAD"

One could hardly imagine to-day a word more generally and constantly in use than the word "road." It is continually on the lips of speakers, and must stand ready in type from day to day for the headlines of newspapers: The Road Traffic Act; The Toll of the Road; The State of the Roads; Road Deaths—all are daily headings. Numerous books have the word in their titles, "The New Road"; "The Broken Road"; "The Open Road"; "The Roadmender." To the ordinary speaker the word seems to be one that must have come down to us from early times with other familiar names of ordinary things. But this is not so; it is not what our Elizabethan grammarians call "an old-denizened" word; it first appeared with its present meaning in the reign of Queen Elizabeth.

As the King ended his speech the vast audience broke into cheers. The curtains over the tunnel entrance were swept upwards on their pivoted supports, disclosing the inscription over the Tunnel arch, "Merseyside welcomes your Majesties," and behind that the receding lines of lights in the Tunnel. These changes of scene engrossed the attention of all, and it was only when the transformation had been completed that the King again advanced to the microphone and said "I wish this new tunnel to be known as the Queensway." After a number of presentations had been made the King and Queen drove slowly down the slope and disappeared into the Tunnel on their passage under the Mersey to Birkenhead. The accessory ceremonies on the arterial road and at Birkenhead were carried out in the presence of enthusiastic crowds of onlookers. At Rock Ferry station the King and Queen entered the Royal train and left for the South.

Times Literary Supplement 1934

Aeroplane 1935

WITHOUT A TICKET

EDINBURGH MAN'S JOURNEY TO LONDON

Giving an address at Arthur Street, Edinburgh, James Moss (36), a labourer —who said he was a Birmingham man and had married in Edinburgh—was charged at Clerkenwell Police Court to-day with travelling on the London & North Eastern railway from Edinburgh to London without paying the fare and intending to avoid payment.

Moss, in the witness-box, said his home was now in Edinburgh, but he had decided to go back to Birmingham to look for work. He did not get a ticket to Birmingham, having no money, but got on the train by obtaining a platform ticket. A ticket collector on the train at Berwick accepted his story that he had lost the ticket and took his name and address. His sister in Birmingham would have paid the fare. He intended to change for Birmingham at York, but fell asleep.

In remanding the prisoner Mr Pope (the magistrate) said it always surprised him that the railway did not put out these people at some wayside post and leave them to "hop it."

Edinburgh Evening News 1934

FLYING SCOTSMAN

Two Train Records in One Day

97 M.P.H. ATTAINED

A DOUBLE railway record was set up yesterday on the London and North Eastern Railway line by the same locomotive—the Flying Scotsman (No. 4472), which was in charge of Driver Sparshatt.

The first record was achieved yesterday morning when the train left King's Cross, London, at 9.8 with a dynamometer car attached, containing instruments for recording speeds and reached Leeds at 11.39, thus completing the journey in two hours 31 mins., an average of 73.8 miles an hour for the 185¾ miles.

The return journey, which started at two o'clock from Leeds, was accomplished in 2 hours 37 mins. 17 secs., and although this was six minutes longer than the previous run, the train was half as heavy again, more coaches having been added. Both journeys are records.

At one point in the Leeds to London run a speed of 97½ m.p.h. was reached.

NOT A "STUNT"

Mr Barrington Ward, a superintendent of the London and North Eastern Railway, who was on the train, told a reporter that the speed of 97½ m.p.h., which was attained near Essendine, was a record for the London and North Eastern Railway. "There were six coaches on the train from Leeds to London," said Mr Barrington Ward, "and the total weight of these was 210 tons, apart from the engine. We averaged 90½ miles an hour for 15 minutes between Corby and Peterborough.

"The purpose of this run is not a 'stunt,' but an experiment. We made the timings in order to try it out as against the timings of a Diesel-electric unit. We have done better than a Diesel-electric unit and proved that a steam engine can do better than the Hamburger Flier (the German express), which burns oil.

"These are the two fastest runs ever made in Great Britain. For 155 miles our figures show that we averaged 80 miles an hour on the down journey. The Hamburger Flier does 178 miles in 138 minutes, an average of 77.4 miles per hour, and although we have not equalled that average, owing to the number of 'slacks' and greater weight and accommodation, we should have beaten it on a flat road."

PREVIOUS RECORD RUNS

Previous record train runs include that of the G.W.R. Cheltenham Flier on July 6, 1932, when it covered the 77¼ miles between Swindon and Paddington, which is much shorter than the Leeds to London run, in 56 mins. 47 secs., an average of 81.6 m.p.h.

The fastest speed ever recorded by a British train is 102 m.p.h. It was reached by a Great Western Ocean special from Plymouth to Paddington on the decline east of the Whitehall tunnel in 1905.

The Scotsman 1934

Driving Licence Examinations

By
A Special Correspondent

The Motorist 1935

THERE is still some confusion regarding the driving tests necessary before driving licences can be issued to new and comparatively new motorists.

Licences are granted at present without official test, the present procedure of filling up the appropriate form and making certain declarations remaining unaltered. This will apply until April 1, 1935. After that date, all drivers who have taken out a licence between April 1, 1934 and April 1, 1935, and all applicants for a first driving licence after April 1, 1935, will be required to pass the driving test. The method of procedure is to apply to the Supervising Examiners of the Traffic Area in which they reside, for a time and place to be fixed for the purpose of carrying out the driving test.

All those applying for a first licence after April 1, 1935, will be able to take out a provisional licence that entitles him or her to drive a car only when under the supervision of some person who has held a licence for not less than two years, and at the same time shall display on both the front and back of his car a plate 7 inches square with the capital letter "L" in red on a white ground.

When the driver, considered as the learner, is ready to be examined he makes application to the Supervising Examiner of his area and is later notified as to time and place. There is no specified time stated as to how long a learner should be under instruction before making application for a driving test. It is a matter for his own discretion as to whether he feels competent, or the advice any driving tuition school he may have been using. When he passes the test a certificate is issued to him and this certificate must be produced when application is made to the local licensing authorities for the driving licence.

OLYMPIA REVISITED—CONTINUED

BRITISH FOUR-DOOR SPORTS SALOONS
(From top to bottom.) 12 h.p. British Salmson close-coupled four-door saloon (£395). The new 11.98 h.p. 1½-litre S.S. Jaguar saloon (£285). The M.G. new model – the 15.96 h.p. six-cylinder 2-litre saloon (£375). 9 h.p. Riley Merlin saloon, which has a preselector gear box (£269).

Autocar 1935

Autocar 1935

TROLLEY BUSES AND WIRELESS.

COMPLAINTS OF INTERFERENCE.

The "Wireless and Gramophone Trade contains the following:—
"BOURNEMOUTH ACTION AGAINST TROLLEY BUS INTERFERENCE."
Interference with radio reception as a result, it is said, of trolley buses, is causing serious complaints in Bournemouth, where the trolley buses recently superseded the old tramway system. The local Radio Dealers' Association and the Corporation Transport Authority are in touch with the R.M.A., and it is hoped that something will soon be done to improve the present state of things. 'Interference is so bad that we do not demonstrate a set in the shop if we can avoid it,' stated Mr. S. S. Searell, chairman of the local Association. It is pointed out by the officials of the Corporation Transport Department that all possible steps have been taken to eliminate interference, and that all the vehicles have been fitted with chokes and condensers. In spite of these precautions the interference continues."

Dover Express 1935

THOUGHTLESS

The Story of a Cigarette End

[44634.]—The other afternoon I saw a young lady throw the lighted stump of a cigarette through the sunshine roof of a car travelling fast along a road which had a wood at the side.
The stump was carried rapidly along by the back draught and came to a stop in the dry grass at the road edge. This was ablaze before I reached it. I stamped it out, but— *don't do it!*
F. E. GOLDING.
Henbury, Macclesfield.

Driving Tests for Motorists.

34,000 Applicants For Posts.

A Self-Supporting Service.

Mr. Hore-Belisha, Minister of Transport, presenting to the House of Commons yesterday a token vote of £10 for the establishment of driving tests for motorists, stated the total cost would be £3,000, which would be received from the Road Fund. The new organisation would comprise a chief examiner, twelve supervising examiners in different areas, and 250 other examiners. There were 34,000 applicants for these posts. The test would consist of the demonstration of the capacity to manipulate a motor car and knowledge of the highway code. The fee would be 7s 6d, and at this figure the service would be self-supporting. It was estimated that there would be four hundred thousand new drivers to be examined annually. Every person who obtained a first driving licence after April, 1934, would be required to undergo the test.

"The establishment of this service," said the Minister, "is the earnest of the seriousness which which we regard road accidents, and should give protection to the public and greater convenience to other road users."

The vote was agreed to.

Londonderry Sentinel 1935

THE QUEEN MARY.

NO RECORD, BUT GREAT ACHIEVEMENT.

For two hemispheres the sustained interest and thrill of the week has been the maiden voyage across the Atlantic of the great ship Queen Mary. It has been a historic and epoch-making event in the march of progress. The eyes of all have been focussed on the magnificent new Queen of the Seas as she has cut her way majestically over the ocean from the Old World to the New. Such are the marvels of the modern age made possible by wireless communication that, mighty vessel as she is, she has been literally dwarfed in her passage into the likeness of a fine new toy boat speeding across from side to side of a pond surrounded and admired by a fascinated crowd of children. Vast though her journey is, she has never been a moment out of touch with either side of the "pond." By the wonders of wireless millions of people on both sides have all but in fact taken part in her crossing, have heard her life aboard, the roar of her engines and propellors racing her forward, the deep, vibrant warning signals of her sirens, and even the crash of the mid-Atlantic breakers on her hull; they have heard the details of her progress from her own voices from day to day and they have heard her captain address them from the bridge as his great ship sped on under his command. From her memorable and tumultuous send-off from Southampton, witnessed by a quarter of a million people on Wednesday afternoon till her arrival at New York yesterday afternoon amid an amazing demonstration of welcome, it has been a thrilling, auspicious and triumphant maiden voyage.

Banffshire Journal 1936

THE ELEVENTH COMMANDMENT

THOU SHALT NOT SPEED.

THIRTY MILES AND NO MORE.

On another page will be found an official statement by the Chief Constable of West Sussex (Mr. R. PATERSON WILSON) regarding the steps to be taken in this area for enforcing the thirty mile an hour speed limit. The wide publicity given to the matter elsewhere renders it unnecessary to deal with it at any length here, but an "Observer" representative did take steps, just a few up one of Chichester's main roads, to find out what the man in the street thought about it all.

Spotting a suitable victim, I (as the representative) pounced on him or her, with the question "What do you think of the new speed limit idea?"

Here are the answers:—

A retired Army man who drives his own car strangely enough: "I never drive at more than 15 miles an hour, and I regret that the limit imposed is more. You can tell everyone so, too."

The young blood with his supercharged car and super-attractive female companion: "It's all rather amusing: I propose disguising myself as a plain-clothes cop."

The lady: "It's too priceless for words, too awfully so."

Departure of pair, with every qualification for appearing at an early date, before the Magistrates.

A lady pedestrian: "How silly."

I was left in doubt as to whether she referred to me, the question, or the speed limit.

A bright young thing, also on foot, whispered in my ear. I blushed.

A lorry driver. Really unprintable but my vocabulary was improved.

Chichester Observer 1935

Aeroplane 1935

BACK TO FIRST PRINCIPLES.—The Hawker Monoplane Fighter, built on an all-metal skeleton. After all the complication of braced biplanes, we thus return to the simplest form of flying-machine.

The BBC Television Service

By Sir NOEL ASHBRIDGE, B.Sc., M.I.E.E.,
Controller (Engineering), BBC

ON Monday, November 2, at 3 o'clock, the new London Television Station at Alexandra Palace began transmitting regular programmes for the first time. It cannot be said, however, that television was seen for the first time by the public on this occasion, because during Radiolympia, in August, demonstrations from the Alexandra Palace were seen by some 100,000 visitors to the exhibition. Since October 1, the station has been transmitting on an experimental basis mainly for the benefit of the trade, but November 2 marked by far the most important step in the development of this interesting extension of our service, and the programmes will be planned for reception by the public as part of the BBC service, and not merely as demonstrations or experiments.

World Radio **1936**

The first BBC television broadcast. Louie Freear in the television studio

World Radio **1936**

Aeroplane **1936**

Mr. Mitchell's little Supermarine fighter, like a baby Schneider Racer which folds up its feet, is a sweet little job all over. But the other Vickers fighter's ugly square wing-tips spoil its looks, and I should like to know what they do to its flying.

Not-so-Golden Voice TIM

"Sunday Referee" Special

SEVENTY-FIVE THOUSAND people had dialled TIM between the inauguration of the time-clock with the "golden-voiced girl" in attendance and seven o'clock last night.

I was number 56,783—or thereabouts.

I found the "golden voice" less a romance than a carefully good - tempered schoolmistress making a virtue of her patience in answering me.

"At the third stroke," said the voice, "it will be three twenty four precisely." Pip. Pip. Pip.

It seemed to echo with its faint variations every ten seconds like the ceaseless drip of an inexhaustible ewer trickling over an unfathomable precipice. The voice was as monotonous, as relentless, as inexorable as the tick of an electric clock.

Almost should I have welcomed anger, irritation, gruffness, rudeness—anything but that soulless perfection.

"At the third stroke it will be three twenty-five precisely." Golden voice? It fell on my ears like lead.

Sunday Referee **1936**

£3 Fine for Defective Brakes

At Kesh Petty Sessions on Tuesday, before Major Dickie, R.M., Michael M'Elwiny, Donegal, was fined in all £3 and costs for driving a car with defective brakes. The case was the sequel to a collision at Letterkeen, on 17th August. Defendant admitted the offence. For a charge of driving without due care and attention defendant was discharged under Probation of Offenders Act.

John W. Moore, Maguiresbridge, was fined 10s and costs for conveying the carcases of 17 pigs not properly covered.

Impartial Reporter **1938**

FAMOUS EXPRESSES

THE FLYING SCOTSMAN

AT the New Year the thoughts of all good Scotsmen turn northwards and the Flying Scotsman, always a popular train, has been especially busy in the closing days of December. This winter she is timed to cover the 392¼ miles from King's Cross to Edinburgh in 7 hrs. 20 min., which is five minutes longer than the time scheduled for the journey last summer. But though spending these few more minutes on the way, the Flying Scotsman is a faster train now than ever she was.

That may seem paradoxical, but it is true, and the riddle is not hard to read. Last summer the journey was a non-stop performance, accomplished in 7¼ hours. Now, the time of 7 hrs. 20 min. includes stops at Grantham, York, Newcastle and Berwick totalling 13 minutes, so that the actual running time is only 7 hrs. 7 min. This means that while she is travelling she has to maintain an average speed of over 55 miles per hour. Such an average, maintained for nearly 400 miles, means much

more than a short, sharp burst of speed. Stiff gradients, sharp curves, speed restrictions through stations, delays due to repairs—all sorts of difficulties, normal and abnormal, crop up in the course of a long journey; and an average speed of 55 m.p.h. involves, in the case of the Flying Scotsman, covering long stretches at a mile a minute and at times accelerating to 75-80 m.p.h.

Improvements in railway travel are taken so much as a matter of course that it is sometimes forgotten how great has been the advance in " speeding up " the British main line " fliers " in the last few years. As I write I have before me a shilling booklet issued by the London & North Eastern Railway Company under the title " The Flying Scotsman: The World's Most Famous Train." It is dated 1931 and contains an illustrated history of the train, with a description of the journey to Edinburgh and beyond. It recalls that the Flying Scotsman has run—not always under that name, but as the " 10 o'clock " from

King's Cross—since 1862. The time occupied then by the journey was 10½ hrs., including half-an-hour for luncheon at York. Gradually accelerations reduced the time to 8¼ hrs. in 1888—an achievement which, owing to the competition between the various railway companies running from London to Scotland, led to the famous " Race " to the North in the summer of that year. It produced in the case of the Flying Scotsman a best performance of 7 hrs. 26¾ mins., and for a short time the journey was scheduled to be done in 7¾ hrs. But soon the old schedule of 8¼ hrs. was resumed, and in this connection the writer of the booklet states:

" Incidentally, the time of 7¾ hrs. has never since been repeated with this train, though for a long time it was done by one or two of the night expresses. But the day train had too much to do on the route to make such a fast time really practicable, particularly with the heavy loads always taken on the ' 10 o'clock,' and a time of 8¼ or 8½ hours has applied ever since."

Travellers Gazette 1936

OVER-RIDE: The new Vickers "geodetic" medium bomber with its twin Pegasus engines receiving over-ride boost, sails up like a fighter. This machine represents a new class of bomber, the development of which is receiving close attention in this country. (*Flight* photograph)

Flight 1937

CAMPBELL BEATS OWN RECORD

Daily Telegraph 1937

SPEED OF 129 M.P.H. CONFIRMED

Sir Malcolm Campbell, on Lake Maggiore, Switzerland, yesterday set up new figures for the world's water speed record, beating his own record time of the previous day by 3.18 m.p.h.

The official figures for the measured mile, received in London yesterday, were:

Wednesday .... 126.33 m.p.h.
Yesterday .... 129.50 m.p.h.

Yesterday's speed is 4.64 m.p.h. better than Commodore Gar Wood's best time, made when he beat the record in 1932, and more than 19 m.p.h. faster than the previous record for single-engined motor-boats.

When he took out Bluebird yesterday Sir Malcolm announced that he was merely making a trial run following repairs to the cooling apparatus.

There was a good number of spectators on the lakeside. When Sir Malcolm landed he was given a big ovation.

He stated that he was leaving Locarno to-day, although he was certain Bluebird was capable of greater speed. He attributed the better times to adjustments made overnight to the intake pipes.

Last night Sir Malcolm was entertained at a dinner party, when the hope was expressed that he would return to Locarno if he contemplated making attempts to improve his record speed.

A toast to "A great English sportsman" was drunk.

Club News 1937

——: o :——

THAT we heartily congratulate Mrs. Henrietta Girling, J.P., whose name appeared in the first list of honours conferred by King George VI., and who has been awarded the O.B.E. for public services in Shoreditch.

——: o :——

THAT in 1930 Mrs. Girling was accorded the distinction of being made the first woman Mayor of Shoreditch. She also takes a great interest in the work of the No. 2 Haggerston Division of St. John Ambulance Brigade, etc.

——: o :——

FAMOUS STATION 100 YEARS OLD

ONE of the most famous stations—Lime Street, Liverpool (London, Midland and Scottish Railway) has celebrated its one hundredth birthday.

Lime Street Station was built for the Liverpool and Manchester Railway, the first inter-city railway in Britain and the oldest section of the London, Midland and Scottish Railway system. From 1830 until the opening of Lime Street on August 15, 1836, the railway used another station at Crown Street, Liverpool, the inconvenient position of which was due to the railway company's fear of opposition to a more central site.

Lime Street station is approached from Edge Hill by a long gradient which was originally considered too steep for locomotives and trains were hauled up and let down on endless cables worked by steam winding-engines.

The present Lime Street station has eleven platforms and is used by 370 trains a day. Whereas the earliest trains between London and Liverpool or vice-versa took 9 hours on the journey, the fastest time is now 3 hours 20 minutes.

Home and Country 1936

Homefinder Small Property Guide 1937

CHEAM, Surrey

(Sutton and Cheam Borough Council).

Population—45,000 (estimated). Sutton and Cheam, 82,000 (estimated).

Altitude—120 to 250 ft. above sea level.

Subsoil—Mainly chalk.

Rates—9s. 6d. in the £ for the year.

Water—4½ per cent. on gross assessment

Gas—9.2d. per therm.

Electricity—Two-part Tariff : Fixed charge, according to area of house : September-March, charge per unit, ¾d. ; two summer seasons, ½d. per unit.

Cheam is a quiet residential district in the most charming part of Surrey. On the borders of Cheam Village is Nonsuch Park, once the Royal domain of Henry VIII. There are excellent schools, good shops, and a fast and regular service of trains to the City and West End. The sanitation is up to date, there is a pure water supply, and the roads are clean and well lighted. All kinds of indoor and outdoor amusement may be had, either in the village itself, or at Sutton, which is near by

TRANSPORT SERVICES.

There is a twenty-minute electric service from and to London Bridge and Victoria during the rush hours, and a thirty-minute service at other times. Season ticket rates ; Quarterly, third class, £4 4s. 9d. Return day tickets, 1s. 6d. Bus route 156, Morden-St. Helier-Sutton - Cheam - North Cheam - Morden

BROMLEY, Kent

(Bromley Borough Council).

Distance from London—10 miles.

Population—45,374. (58,000 estimated.)

Altitude—Approx. 250 ft. above sea level.

Subsoil—Gravel.

Birth Rate—13.3 per 1,000.

Death Rate—9.5 per 1,000.

Rates—9s. 5d. in the £ for the year.

Water—(Metropolitan Water Board) 6 per cent. on rateable value per annum.

Gas—(South Suburban Gas Co.) 9½d. per therm.

Electricity—(Bromley Corporation) Lighting, 4½d. per unit ; Heating and Cooking, 1¼d. per unit ; All-in tariff, 7 per cent. on rateable value of house and 1d. per unit.

Bromley is known to be very healthy, and is fortunate in possessing all the amenities which are essential to a popular residential district. There are many good shops, excellent schools, churches of every denomination, fine recreation grounds, and sports facilities of the very best. Hayes Common, Wickham Woods, Keston Lake and Common, Chislehurst Caves and Petts Wood are in the near neighbourhood, providing delightful country rambles amongst beautiful rural scenery.

TRANSPORT SERVICES.

There is a fast and frequent service of trains to and from Town.

Third class season tickets, quarterly—Bromley North to London Bridge, Cannon Street and Charing Cross, £3 14s. 6d. Cheap day returns, 1s. 6d. Workmen's tickets, 10d. Grove Park, £3 10s. Cheap day returns, 1s. 2d. Workmen's tickets, 9d. Also Bromley South, Southern Railway.

Buses No. 137 to Marble Arch, and No. 47 to Shoreditch. And many others (9 Services).

Green Line Coach Services, L and X.

R.A.F. LEADS THE WORLD

7,000 PILOTS ON THE STRENGTH

SPEED-UP IN NEW MACHINES

By OUR AIR CORRESPONDENT

The number of pilots in the Royal Air Force now exceeds 7,000, consisting of approximately 6,000 Regular and Auxiliary Air Force and 1,100 pilots in the R.A.F. Volunteer Reserve.

This achievement, which has not been equalled in any air service in the world, has exceeded even the expectations of the Air Ministry. Viscount Swinton, who created the R.A.F. Volunteer Reserve, originally estimated that the annual intake would be 800 pilots. His hopes have been more than realised, for before the end of the financial year, the first since its inauguration, the total should reach 1,200.

Owing to the fact that pilots in the Volunteer Reserve have their training during the evenings and at week-ends, the scheme has a purely local appeal, and as this success has been attained with the twenty local centres for training at present in operation, the Air Ministry can expect a still greater influx when, this year, the number of training centres is increased to thirty-three

BEST TYPE OF PILOT

In the future the R.A.F. Volunteer Reserve should be one of the most valuable sources of well-trained pilots and, with the short service commission scheme, should ensure that the R.A.F. will never be short of pilots in a national emergency.

Those who join the Volunteer Reserve are youths who are in employment and who, because of the need for adequate reserves, are willing to give up their evenings or week-ends to training for active service. They constitute the best type of war pilot.

Except for a few details the success attending the production of new machines has almost equalled that concerning personnel.

NEW MACHINES

As was disclosed in the SUNDAY TIMES at the beginning of the month, approximately one-quarter of the 123 squadrons were then equipped with the latest types. Before the end of March it can be estimated that only a little less than half the squadrons will be supplied with fast bomber and fighter machines. .

Although one or two squadrons have already been equipped with the Hawker Hurricane, one of the " 300 m.p.h. plus " machines, the greater number will consist of Blenheims, Wellesleys and Battles, all fast bombers.

Now that these machines are in large production and have been in use for a considerable time, the Air Ministry is satisfied that they have no particular vices, although initial orders for them were placed " off the drawing board."

Sunday Times 1938

THE KING'S MESSAGE

'BE OF GOOD CHEER'

CALL FOR STOUT HEARTS

When the Queen launched the Cunard-White Star liner *Queen Elizabeth* at Clydebank on Tuesday afternoon, she conveyed a message of encouragement from the King to the nation.

' I have a message for you from the King,' her Majesty said. ' He bids the people of this country to be of good cheer in spite of the dark clouds hanging over them and, indeed, over the whole world.

' He knows well that, as ever before in critical times, they will keep cool heads and brave hearts. He knows, too, that they will place entire confidence in their leaders who, under God's Providence, are striving their utmost to find a just and peaceful solution of the grave problems that confront them.'

Heard by Millions.

The Queen's words were heard over the wireless by millions of listeners in all parts of the Empire. She spoke with feeling of the fact that the launching ceremony ' must take place in circumstances far different from those for which they had hoped.'

Impartial Reporter 1938

PROTECTING THE LAKES

ALL who know the Lake District and appreciate its beauty must be appalled at the very real threat to its sanctity by an " opening up " policy. The policy of the Friends of the Lake District is as follows : " On secondary roads, to provide the bare minimum of safety for careful driving, since no sane person aims at record breaking through an area of great beauty : on the few through traffic routes of the real Lake District, to follow out in general the principles allowed by the Ministry of Transport merely as an exception ; and, in sum and substance, to prevent any further ' opening up ' of the Lake District."

Tourist 1939

Railway Electrification

The electrification of railways is proceeding steadily. The opening of the new length of railway from Tolworth to Chessington has provided additional facilities for an area in which great housing development is proceeding. The Motspur Park to Tolworth section of this new railway was opened last year, and although no announcement has been made of any immediate proposal the extension of the line from Chessington to Leatherhead is probable. Last month saw the completion of two important stages in the electrification of existing lines. Electric services have been inaugurated in Kent on 54 miles of track. Electric trains which previously were run only to Gravesend, Sevenoaks, and Swanley were extended last month from Otford to Maidstone East (16 miles), from Gravesend Central to Maidstone West, *via* Strood, and from Strood to Gillingham (19 miles), and from Swanley to Gillingham (19 miles).

PITT CLUB MAKES HISTORY

13½ Miles Backwards in 5½ Hours

BETS and manners maketh man as was proved yesterday afternoon by D. T. Greig, of Trinity, and W. P. Spens, of Pembroke, who for the sake of a wager walked the distance from Cambridge to Newmarket backwards in an incredibly short space of time.

The bet arose from the spectacle, seen from the august windows of the Pitt Club, of a dog, walking slowly backwards for reasons best known to itself. The feat appears to have aroused the sporting instincts of two of the spectators, who forthwith betted that neither could accomplish the journey from Cambridge to Newmarket in less than 12 hours.

The contest began from the steps of the Pitt at the grim hour of 6.30 a.m., and both competitors had finished strongly by midday. They were accompanied, picturesquely enough, by an open landau, drawn by a chesnut mare ; and other undergraduates followed them in motor cars. Betting during the journey was free, odds of 5 to 1 being offered against Greig, and even money on Spens.

Interviewed after the race, Mr. Spens is said to have declared : " I did it for the honour of the upper classes." Our reporter sought a further statement from Mr. Greig, but the latter was—naturally enough, after the exigencies of his arduous journey — incapable of giving a coherent comment on the proceedings.

It is to be hoped that both competitors have now fully recovered from their unnatural exercise.

Varsity Weekly 1938

Times Trade and Engineering 1939

ABNORMAL LOADS DEMAND
SCAMMELL SPECIAL VEHICLES

The English Steel Corporation Ltd., Sheffield, holds the record for the world's largest steel ingot. Here is the one-piece mould from which it was cast being delivered, on a special Scammell vehicle, to their Vickers Works, Sheffield.

Scammell make light work of the world's heaviest loads. Special type Scammell vehicles carry anything from 12 to 100 tons *economically*—without dismantling or trans-shipment. Each is individually designed for its job. Each has the easy manœuvrability of an articulated vehicle. Each has detachable carrier wheels, so that loading and off-loading may be speeded up. Whether you contract to carry abnormal loads, or have unusually large plant and equipment yourself, it will pay you to get in touch with Scammell.

SCAMMELL LORRIES LTD.
*Watford West, Herts. 'Phone: Watford 5231.
'Grams: Twelfton, Watford.*

Next we have, on B8856, Mackenzie-Rogan's arrangement of Hamm's *The Coldstream March* and J. H. Amers' arrangement of Walford Davies' *Royal Air Force March Past*. This is excellent. The latter always intrigues me by its folk-like characteristics.

The third new record by the **Coldstream Guards Band** contains *Light of Foot* and *The Whistler and his Dog* (B8844). The former is an old favourite of mine and is splendidly played. The latter inevitably invites comparison with the record made by **Arthur Pryor's Band** with the assistance of those two wonderful whistlers **Margaret McKee** and **Billy Murray**. This record was issued well over ten years ago and it has never been replaced in my collection and I shall still keep it now though this new record is the best alternative that I have heard and probably the superior recording will decide most people in its favour.

The Gramophone
1939

1940
1949

[Photo: C. U. R. Cavell.

The above pictures illustrate how the Dutch motor vessel, " Nora," carried out her work of destruction, the last showing her final position on the north side of the pier. Post card copies of the first three pictures may be obtained from Messrs. G. Stewart Dunn and Son,

Deal, Walmer, Sandwich and East Kent Mercury 1940

Home Guard Not to Pay Toll When On Duty

VEHICLES driven by members of the Home Guard when on duty and wearing the official armlet are to be allowed free passage through Penarth-road toll-gate for the duration of the war.

The joint proprietors of the Cardiff-Penarth road are Mountjoy, Ltd., and the Plymouth Estate, and their decision to waive the toll, as stated, was announced on Friday by Mr. W. J. G. Beach, manager, Mountjoy, Ltd., in a letter to the editor of the *Western Mail*. He wrote :—

Sir,—I am asked by the joint proprietors of the Cardiff and Penarth road to inform you that they have given instructions that during the present war vehicles driven by members of the Home Guard, when on duty and wearing the official armlet, will be allowed free passage through the toll-gate.

This follows a case at Penarth Police-court on Wednesday when Mr. Frank Morgan, company director, Plymouth-road, Penarth, was fined 10s. for evading the payment of 1s. toll at the toll-gate.

Mr. Morgan is a section leader of Penarth Home Guard. He told the court that at the time he was on an errand of national importance and maintained that he was not personally liable for the toll because he was on national duty.

Western Mail 1940

END OF FIRST-CLASS ON UNDERGROUND

ABOLITION ON THURSDAY

On Thursday the provision of separate accommodation for first-class passengers will come to an end on all London Transport trains except the through trains between the Aylesbury and Watford Joint Lines and the Metropolitan Line. All first-class labels will be removed from other trains, and 450 doors which separate first-class from third-class accommodation will be removed.

The history of the undertakings now grouped under the control of London Transport has been marked by the gradual removal of different classes of accommodation for their passengers. The Metropolitan Line, opened on January 10 1863, and the District Line, opened on December 24, 1868, both began with first, second, and third-class accommodation. In 1904 second-class accommodation was abandoned on the District Line, and the Metropolitan Line followed suit in the following year. In March, 1932, first-class tickets were abolished on the District Line to South Harrow in anticipation of running Piccadilly Line trains, which were of one class only, and four years later first-class was abolished on the Hammersmith and City Line on the introduction of through running between Hammersmith and Barking.

The Times 1940

SHOULD PASSENGERS BE LEFT BEHIND?

War-time Overloading of 'Bus

INSPECTOR FINED 5s.—CASE AGAINST CONDUCTOR DISMISSED

The alleged overcrowding of a Blue 'bus led to two of the Company's officials appearing at Stratford-on-Avon Borough police-court on Wednesday—William James Langford (conductor) for carrying passengers in excess of seating capacity, and Reginald Bert Careless (an inspector) for permitting the offence.

Mr. J. R. H. Baker appeared for the defence, and pleaded " Not guilty."

P.c. Child said that at 4.2 p.m. on February 16th, in consequence of a complaint, he went to Banbury-road and saw the 'bus proceeding towards Kineton. It was overcrowded, and he stopped the driver. Langford was the conductor, and together they counted the passengers.

19 PEOPLE STANDING

The vehicle was a 32-seater, and altogether there were 51 passengers, 32 seated and 19 standing, the corridor being absolutely blocked, while two men stood on the steps. There were 28 adults and 23 children. Witness invited an explanation, and the conductor said : " Inspector Careless loaded the 'bus." About 4.15 p.m. witness saw Careless at the station, and asked if he cared to say anything. He replied : " I am responsible, but we have to be careful with the petrol, and it is very difficult to turn people away." Fifteen minutes before the 'bus was due to leave the station was blocked, and witness suggested that it would have been easy to order a relief 'bus from across the road.

Mr. Baker: Counting two children as one adult, it would make 39½. What do you suggest the driver or conductor should have done ?

Witness: The law says a 'bus must not carry an excessive number of passengers.

Mr. Baker: We know what the law says, but this is not peace time. What should you have done if you had been conductor ?

Witness: I should have asked for a duplicate 'bus. The Manager told me the Inspector was in a position to order another 'bus if he thought one was necessary.

Stratford-upon-Avon Herald 1940

A single-decker express coach converted into an ambulance evacuating hospital patients during the Blitz. *Transport Goes to War.*

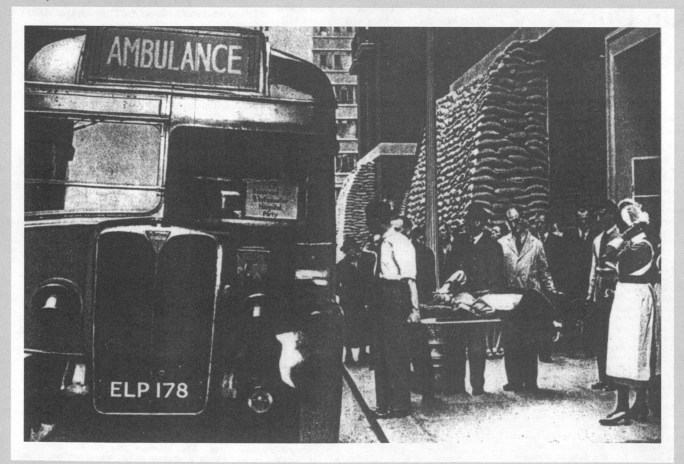

Balham, 1940: a bus dives into a bomb-crater.
Transport Goes to War.

ON PULLING TOGETHER

More than two years after the inauguration of the A.R.P. Service in the City of Salisbury a gesture of appreciation has been made to the volunteers in the form of a concession. They may now park their cars free when on duty. It would seem that such a concession was obvious, and a majority of the councillors who listened to the debate during the City Council meeting on Monday, and to a further discussion in committee afterwards, held that view. They felt, as no doubt any citizen will feel, that wardens have for a long time given many hours of willing service, and have spent many a sixpence, with the sole idea of serving their fellow townsmen. Of late their hours have been long and calls on their time frequent, but they do not desire, and indeed would resent, any offer of reward. This gesture, which recognises their services and also reduces delay at a time when speed may be vital, will be appreciated.

Not all our city fathers, however, were of the same mind. Incredible as it may seem, objections were raised upon the most unstable foundations. The proposal was stigmatised as "charity," and it was suggested that wardens should buy season parking tickets. It was implied that some would take advantage of the concession to park cars free at any time. A councillor threatened to resign from the A.R.P. organisation—not the Council—as a protest. There was, in short, vigorous opposition to a resolution which every citizen would approve.

The time of the Council was wasted to no good purpose, and the same delaying tactics were noticeable throughout the meeting. Since the outbreak of war the City Council has made a commendable attempt to deal with matters brought before it with despatch and efficiency, and in the main has been successful. That cannot be said of Monday's meeting. It is lamentable when councillors cannot pull together. It is deplorable that some do not distinguish between notoriety and fame.

Salisbury and Winchester Journal **1940**

HORSES REPLACING CARS

DRIVING CLUBS FORMED

Daily Telegraph Reporter.

Horses have come into their own again as a result of the war. Not for many years has there been so great a demand for their services in agriculture and in the town delivery of goods. Private citizens are also beginning to use horse-drawn vehicles instead of cars.

Mr. R. A. Brown, secretary of the National Horse Association, said yesterday that driving clubs in the country were increasing. "The members are all drivers of horse-drawn vehicles," he added, "and regularly hold meets at which they are able to obtain information from one another about equipment and the care of their horses."

It is calculated that there are about 40,000 horses in use in London. "There is an exceptionally strong demand for both vanners and heavy horses," said the manager of the Elephant and Castle Repository. "There is one disconcerting feature. Fodder, in some instances, is proving as difficult to obtain as petrol is for motor-cars."

Daily Telegraph **1940**

NEW CARS NOT FOR SALE

A new unregistered motor vehicle cannot now be purchased without a license from the Minister of Transport. Motor cycles not adapted for carrying goods and certain specialised vehicles such as tramcars, agricultural tractors and mowing machines are exempted, as are also vehicles for export.

For the present no licenses will be granted for the purchase of new private cars. The Board of Trade is in consultation with Mr. W. E. Rootes, president of the Society of Motor Manufacturers and Traders, with a view to creating machinery whereby new vehicles in stock can be diverted to overseas markets through the export group of the motor industry.

Forms of application for licenses to acquire new public service or goods vehicles can be obtained from the Ministry of Transport.

Financial Times **1940**

REQUISITIONING OF SHIPS

SUBSTANTIAL EARNINGS EXPECTED

FROM OUR SHIPPING CORRESPONDENT

Although British ships are now being freely requisitioned by the Ministry of Shipping the duties of management remain with the owners. These include arranging for the crews, the provisioning and bunkering of the vessels, the payment of disbursements at loading and discharging ports, meeting the cost of marine insurance, and, in fact, dealing with all the details of managing the ships which normally fall to the owners. The Ministry of Shipping directs the vessels to load particular cargoes homewards, but sometimes owners are permitted to find outward cargoes of coal for the ships. This policy of leaving the detailed management to the owners recognizes the fact that they know the capabilities of their various vessels in a thorough way that newcomers to the work could not hope to approach.

The belief in the industry is that by taking advantage of good outward freights, directing the ships to load homewards on remunerative terms, and by ensuring the continuance of efficient management, substantial earnings should be secured by the Ministry. The publication last week of a long list of members of Government Departments who have been transferred to the Ministry, excluding those who have joined it from the Marine Department of the Board of Trade, suggests that important establishment charges will need to be met. The formidable list includes, however, the members of the staff of the War Risks Insurance Office, who are not distinguished from the rest.

The terms of hire which owners are to obtain for the use of their ships are now the subject of negotiations. In its concern for fair terms the British shipping industry cannot ignore the large earnings which continue to accrue to neutral mercantile marines. These promise materially to influence the intensified competition which British shipping will have to face in future.

The Times 1940

44 DIE IN OPEN BOAT

An unnamed naval officer in a broadcast last night told of the ordeal of 82 people in sailing 1,00 miles in an open boat in the Tropics.

They were from a British liner sunk by an armed merchant cruiser in the South Atlantic.

In the lifeboat were 64 Indians and 18 Europeans, of whom 13 Europeans and 25 Indians survived when Brazil was reached 23 days later.

"We could have only about an egg-cup fll of water a day each, one biscuit and two tins of condensed milk divided among us," he said.

"After the second day most of us were unable to swallow our daily biscuit. Some of the Indians drank salt water, despite warnings, and died.

"We were soon all covered with sores and boils. It was impossible to sit, lie or even stand in comfort because of overcrowding."

Daily Telegraph 1941

SPITFIRE FUND JUMPS TO £1,041

MANY activities contributed to the amounts raised on Friday for the Cardiff "Spitfire" Fund. Even the German Air Force unwittingly did its bit.

On Thursday night Messrs. L. Way and Son gave a benefit night for the fund at the Fairground, Loudoun - square, and about 3,000 Docks folk took part, with the result that on Friday Mr. Way was able to hand £20 5s. to the fund. In addition he presented the fund with a copy of a Hitler's speech leaflet dropped "somewhere in Wales," and its sale realised £1 2s. 8d.

Street collections continued to pour in. Again from the Docks area, Henry, Patrick, Alice, and Hannah Streets (per Mrs. de Gabriel) sent in £2 14s. 6d. A collection among Ely residents (first instalment), per Mrs. F. Thomas, Penygarn-road, Ely, amounted to £5 14s. 1d. Partridge-road and Woodcock-street, Roath, forwarded £5 0s. 6d.

A bowling match by the Ladies' Social Union Bowling Club (organised by Mrs. D. G. Fletcher) realised £3 3s.

Western Mail 1940

Asleep in the cabin of a liner which was taking children to Canada last autumn, Robert Wilson, eleven, of Newton Mearns, near Glasgow, awoke to find himself alone on the abandoned ship. A torpedo had hit the liner and by some accident this lad was left behind. He went to bed. Next morning a British warship came alongside and the liner was towed to port.

Daily Mirror 1941

PRICE OF USED CARS IS HIGHER THAN EVER

Demand Cannot Be Met

"STAR" REPORTER

IN spite of the new petrol ration cuts, the demand for second-hand cars is still exceeding the supply, and prices have reached what is expected to be the limit.

Few new cars for use by civilians have been manufactured since 1939, and today's big demand is for cars made in that year which have done less than 20,000 miles.

Star 1942

"People are buying the miles still left in a car, and they assess the value at so much a mile," a leading London motor expert told me today.

Recognised trade price for 1939 cars of comparatively low mileage is 10 per cent. more than the original cost. Retail price is roughly 50 per cent. more than the cost of the car when new.

Here are typical examples of cars being offered for sale today:

1938-9 eight h.p. £200. Cost when new £145.

1938 ten h.p. £300. When new £185.

1938 12 h.p. £500. When new £325.

1937 14 h.p. £425. When new £350.

"It is difficult to sell cars of more than 14 horse power," the expert said. "But certain world famous makes can be sold at any time.

"Though these may be five or six years old, they still bring higher prices than they did when new because it is a known fact that they are perfect until they have done at least 100,000 miles.

"The average free-from-trouble life of a popular car is 20,000 miles."

Many people whose cars have been laid up for a year or more are refusing to sell because they think they will get an even better price after the war.

"This is a fallacy," a motor authority told me. "Prices will never be higher than they are to-day."

Vandals did this in one year

HERE is a list of the damage done by hooligans and vandals on British railways during the past 12 months:—

17,435 carriage windows broken,

115,000 electric light bulbs stolen,

12,400 black-out shades damaged,

31,328 window straps removed or damaged,

9,250 cushions and upholstery damaged.

These figures were given officially to the Sunday Express, and an official of the Railways Executive Committee said to a reporter:

"Cushions have been found on the line, having been deliberately thrown out of the window.

"Mirrors and toilet fittings are being removed; woodwork is being wilfully damaged, and cases are reported of seats being fouled by tar.

"Sufficient materials and labour cannot be found to repair the damage. The electric light bulbs operate only at 24 volts, and are useless in the home."

Sunday Express 1943

Prediction 1942

The Ghost-dog

Lastly, the strange case of Miss K——'s dog. Miss K——, a lady of my acquaintance, had a spaniel that was so attached to her fiancé, Flying Officer Kester, that it used sometimes to follow him to the aerodrome when he was on duty there. Dogs not being allowed there, he always sent it home. On one occasion, however, it got in without being noticed and was accidentally killed when a plane alighted. Since then a ghost dog, believed to be that of the spaniel, is said to have been seen frequently in different parts of the aerodrome.

On one occasion an airman seeing it near a shed apparently eyeing him, threw it a sweet biscuit, and as it took no notice of the biscuit but still seemingly stared at him, he threw it another. The same thing happened. Losing patience, the airman picked up a piece of stick, and exclaiming "Here, eat this, if biscuits aren't good enough for you," he threw it directly at the animal. The dog did not stir and the stick passed right through it. This so alarmed the airman that he promptly decamped.

AMY JOHNSON'S FRIEND MYSTERY

Four months after Amy Johnson's plane crashed in the Thames estuary, the identity of the companion who was seen with her in the water still remains a mystery.

Able Seaman Raymond Dean, of Chester-road, Worthing, of H.M.S. Trawler Haslemere, yesterday told the Chatham coroner, at the resumed inquest on Lieut.-Commander Walter Edmund Fletcher, 34, who died trying to rescue Miss Johnson, that he saw two people in the water. One was a young woman.

An officer said he saw Commander Fletcher reach one of the bodies, but he got into difficulties and had to let go.

Verdict: Death by misadventure.

Daily Mirror 1941

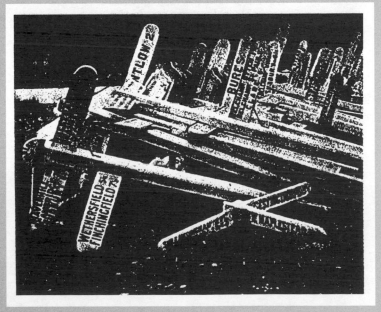

Signposts were removed during the war so as not to give any assistance to the enemy.
Transport Goes to War.

ALL EUROPE RESOUNDS TO V RHYTHM

"PORTENT OF NAZIS' FATE"
—Mr. Churchill

DAILY TELEGRAPH REPORTER

All Europe resounded yesterday to the rhythm of the V as Britain's Victory Campaign surged across the Continent to the fateful opening theme of Beethoven's Vth Symphony.

Rat-ta-ta-taat—"Fate knocks at the door."

Dot-dot-dot-dash—"V for Victory."

V-ictoire, V-rijheid, V-ictory.

Mobilised at midnight, Britain's V Army faced the Nazi occupiers when light broke over Europe yesterday, V-ingt Juillet. Its troops were disposed in every street of every city, town and village.

At midnight, zero hour of the campaign, Mr. Churchill sent a message to the oppressed people of Europe.

"The V sign is the symbol of the unconquerable will of the occupied territories and a portent of the fate awaiting the Nazi tyranny," he said.

Col. Britton, the broadcaster in charge of the campaign, in his final orders for the day said: "In a few minutes there will be millions of new Vs on walls and doors and pavements all over Europe.

"It's dark now. If you listen you may hear distant bugles sounding the V rhythm or drums tapping. Perhaps you'll hear a train whistle sounded by one of our comrades."

CAMPAIGN AT HOME

A few hours after he spoke a train whistle did blow a three-short-and-a-long blast. It was an electric train with the V symbol on its cab. Early travellers cheered as it drew up in Victoria Station, London.

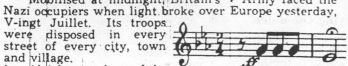

The opening notes of Beethoven's Fifth Symphony which form the "fate motif" and when tapped out are the same as the Morse for the V sign.

Daily Telegraph 1941

Dancing Stars

My daughter has seen, upon several occasions, bright stars on the floor in her bedroom. A few weeks ago my wife witnessed the same phenomenon while she was making a bed; the stars jumped from pillow to pillow. What could be the meaning of these stars?—F.L., Gravesend.

THEY are most probably a preliminary to some more concrete form of manifestation, which will follow in due course. In the proximity of a medium, and very likely a member of your family is one, the appearance of psychic lights of many kinds is quite common. Sir William Crookes attested that, under the strictest test conditions, "I have seen luminous points of light dancing about and settling on the heads of different persons . . . I have seen sparks of light rising from the table to the ceiling and again falling upon the table, striking it with an audible sound." Such dancing stars or sparks, it is reasonable to infer, may be caused by the forceful splitting up of the "astral light" in its utilisation for the production of psychic phenomena.

Prediction 1941

The Spectator 1941

The Ministry of Transport has issued detailed instructions regarding the immobilisation of cars in case of invasion. "The distribution head, magneto or fuel-injection pump," it says, "should be smashed with a hammer, and high-tension leads removed," adding thoughtfully, "If owners are in any doubt as to how to carry out these instructions they should go to the nearest garage at once to find out." They need not do that. I can tell them. Take a hammer or spanner of sufficient weight in the right hand (or if left-handed in the other one), raise it to a height of some eighteen inches above the distributor-head, magneto or fuel-injection pump, and bring it sharply down. Repeat till the state of smash seems up to Goering standards. I waive all copyright in this guide to action. JANUS.

Home and Country 1942

M IS FOR MERCHANTMEN

A is for Apples, Almonds and Apricots,
B is for Bacon and useful Bamboo,
C is for Coffee and Coconut products,
D is for Dates which are so good for you.
E is for Eggs and the Empire which sends them,
F is for Flour, for Fruit and for Fish,
G is for Ginger, Groundnuts and Grapefruit,
H is for Herrings, a nourishing dish.
I is for Indiarubber and Ivory,
J is for Jam and also for Jute,
K is for Kerosene Oil from America,
L is for Lemons, now very rare fruit.
M is for Mustard, Meat and Mahogany,
N is for Nutmegs and Nuts, every sort,
O is for Olive Oil, Onions and Oranges,
P is for Pumicestone, Pepper and Port.
Q is for Quicksilver in our thermometers,
R is for Raisins, so nice in a cake,
S is for Sugar, Sardines and Sultanas,
T is the drink that we nearly all take.
U is for Union Jack in the Red Ensign,
V is for Voyages made far and near,
W the World supplying the freight.
X is for Ten Times the things mentioned here.
Y is for the Yarns that our seamen can spin,
Z for the Zeal that brings the ships in.

D. COWARD, *Seaview W.I.*

Leslie Howard took his place

THE story of a Catholic priest's escape from death in the plane in which actor Leslie Howard lost his life was told to the Sunday Express yesterday.

The Rev. Arthur S. Holmes, vice-president of the English College in Lisbon, in a recent visit to this country described what happened to his friend the Rev. John Winder, of Burgess Hill, Sussex.

Father Winder said yesterday, "Father Holmes called at the English College on the way to Lisbon airport for the plane to England.

"A telephone call from the airport came through and he heard that Mr. Leslie Howard had arranged to travel to England with a party of four, but that one must remain behind as there was not room in the plane for all.

"Father Holmes was asked if, as a special favour to Mr. Howard, he would catch another plane, and readily agreed, thus most providentially being saved from the fate of the other passengers."

Father Holmes has since returned to Lisbon.

Sunday Express 1943

HALF SHIP GOT HOME

H.M.S. Wolfhound

HALF a destroyer, her back broken and her bows sunk, fought off an enemy air attack and got back to port safely.

She is H.M.S. Wolfhound, a veteran, 25 years old.

Months ago, while escorting a convoy on the east coast, she was attacked from the air.

Her back was broken and her main deck split open.

Bows dropped

Within three-quarters of an hour 100 feet of her bows had dropped off and sunk.

The boiler-room began flooding and steam pressure failed.

Engine-room Artificer Sydney Prickett tried to raise steam on an emergency boiler.

Veteran of 25 years.

All this time gunners on the upper deck were still engaging the enemy aircraft.

The situation became so perilous that most of the crew were sent to another ship.

The half-destroyer was taken in tow by a trawler, and the engine-room staff tried to get the engines going to assist the tow.

After six hours of pumping oil fuel by hand they were forced to give up.

Could not see

Then came a fog and the disabled destroyer at the end of the towing hawser could not see the trawler. For six hours volunteers remained on board the crippled ship.

Then the weather began to clear and towing began again. Twenty hours after the first air attack the Wolfhound reached harbour.

Workers at a naval dockyard in the south built on new bows, and made her ready for sea again.

Sunday Express **1943**

Look Both Ways

HAVE you noticed the way some mothers cross the road when pushing prams? It sounds incredible. I know, but quite a lot of them turn the pram, push it off the kerb and *then* look up to see if anything's coming.

Of course we know that what really makes them behave in this unmotherlike fashion is their anxiety to get the pram down from the pavement with the least jar possible—and also to avoid delay with the pram at an awkward angle on the pavement.

Almost all the road accidents to young children happen in families where the children would go to elementary schools, although the majority of accidents are to children of three, who are not generally at school.

But the point is that it is among the less affluent children that accidents happen the children who are likely to play in the streets, whose mothers are too tied up with other duties to be always with the children and who are not so likely to be in "go-carts," as we used to call them.

Daily Worker
1944

MEN WON'T BUY WOOD SOLED SHOES

Women are buying 200,000 pairs of wooden shoes a month: men will not have them.

Salvaged rubber is to be used on a larger scale for soling and heeling all kinds of boots and shoes.

Manufacturers and repairers of boots and shoes have been advised by the Board of Trade that in future two-fifths of their material will be rubber and three-fifths leather.

Sunday Express
1943

The Spirit of '44

A FLYING FORTRESS *which bombed Oschersleben in the great U.S. attack on the German fighter plant last Tuesday:—*

Shot down ten fighters;

Had two engines and the oxygen system knocked out over the target;

—Was chased from Germany to the coast by two twin-engined Messerschmitts, sometimes at less than tree-top height and

Reached Britain bullet-ridden, with its nose shot out and cannon shell holes gaping in the wings and fuselage. Yet none of the crew were injured.

Its name—"The Spirit of '44."

U.S. headquarters told the story last night.

Daily Worker
1944

SECRET ENGINE OF THE FUTURE

Sunday Express Reporter

DEEP in the heart of the English countryside, remote from town or village, and under the surface of the earth, a factory has recently been built which is unlike anything of its kind in this country and possibly anywhere in the world.

It was started two years ago and is now producing engines for one of our oldest firms of airplane engine constructors, whose aircraft have a world-wide reputation.

It is a novel experience to leave daylight and descend deep into the earth to find almost exactly similar conditions prevailing.

This factory bears not the smallest resemblance to any mine. Workshops and inter-connecting galleries hewn out of the solid white rock are scrupulously clean and are lit by artificial sunlight.

Keep our place

The air, which is blown into the factory by one set of fans and sucked out by another, is fresh and clean. There is no hint of stuffiness anywhere.

The engines being built are of a type which is on the secret list.

Each is remarkably compact. The power output from an engine of such a moderate size is amazing.

It has undoubtedly a great future. It will enable us not only to produce more effective war weapons, but also to help to keep for Britain that pride of place in civil air transport which her military aircraft have earned for her.

Girl supervisor

The factory covers a large area, but there is ample room to expand. Most of the machinery which it is intended to instal is already in operation. Many of the tools were designed by a Bristol firm and manufactured in America.

The manager said that the regularity with which these are being delivered bears witness to the success of our campaign against the U-boat.

Many of the tools are marvels of ingenuity. Parts which until recently took a highly skilled workman five days to make are now being produced in two and a half hours by a machine which can be supervised by a girl with only very limited tuition.

Sunday Express 1943

GROUP PRODUCTION OF HALIFAXES

Early in the war a number of firms, most of them without previous experience of aircraft production, joined forces to produce Halifax bombers under the guidance of the parent firm, Handley Page. The group, known as London Aircraft Production, consisted of the English Electric Company, L.P.T.B., Rootes Securities, Chrysler Motors, Express Motor and Body Works, Duple Bodies and Motors, Park Royal Coachworks, and the Fairey Aviation Company.

At a luncheon at the Dorchester yesterday SIR STAFFORD CRIPPS, Minister of Aircraft Production, paid tribute to their achievements. He said that the output of Halifaxes was ultimately built up to 200 a month. The group had accounted for something like two-fifths of the total heavy bomber output in the country—a fine record for a single group. Halifax bombers had dropped more than 200,000 tons of bombs.

SIR FREDERICK HANDLEY PAGE proposed the toast of the " daughter " firms, and presented silver models of the Halifax bomber to the heads of each and scrolls of commendation to representative workmen. LORD ASHFIELD, SIR GEORGE NELSON, and SIR WILLIAM ROOTES responded.

The Times 1945

London-Paris Service

Arrangements are being made by the Ministry of War Transport in co-operation with the French Authorities for opening a London-Paris sea-rail passenger service on January 15. Passages for civilians will be reserved solely for : *A*—Persons whose journeys are certified by a government department to be in the national interest ; and *B*—Compassionate cases where the journey is of immediate urgency.

Exit permits and French visas will be required. Passages will be allocated only through the certifying departments to persons in class *A* and through the Passport & Permit Office to persons in class *B*. Exit permits cannot be granted for travel to the military zones unless military entry permits are first obtained. Persons in class *A* should approach the Government Department interested in the object of their journey (*e.g.,* business men should approach the Department of Overseas Trade). Persons in class *B* should apply to the Passport & Permit Office.

Railway Gazette 1945

Teach children KERB DRILL

See that they always do it and set a good example by doing it yourself.

1 At the kerb HALT

2 EYES RIGHT

3 EYES LEFT

then if the road is clear

4 QUICK MARCH

Don't rush
Cross in an orderly manner

"REPAIR SQUAD, PLEASE!"

Yesterday . . . in the garage . . . repairing cars . . . "a little trouble with the plugs, sir ? Soon get that fixed !" Today a soldier—Right in the thick of it . . . shells bursting . . . snipers taking a crack at him. But he does it ! And repairs another tank — ready for action ! Salute his toughness — his endurance !

 Salute the Soldier — with more savings ! Let us all vow today to mobilize our money — by cutting spending and increasing lending. Let us lend to our country — and so lend practical help to "the boys out there !"

SALUTE THE SOLDIER

Issued by the National Savings Committee

'South Sea Bubble' In Used Cars?

By John Prioleau

IF some of the prices asked in advertisements are any indication, it looks as if we are in for a sort of South Sea Bubble in the used-car market. Indeed, the North Midland Regional Price Regulation Committee reports that fantastic prices are being obtained already on a wide scale. It gives these examples: 1939 Buick 30-6 (list price £615), £1,000; 1939 Rover Ten (list price £275), £600.

It is true, I suppose, for the moment, that the price of a car is what it will fetch, and the acute shortage of the more popular types is bound to send prices to uncomfortable heights, but however badly a man needs or wants a car of any sort, after five years' deprivation, he will be well advised to consider the difference between price and value.

Main Consideration

The engine and transmission of a car that has been properly laid up and cared for during the war will probably not have deteriorated much since it was last used. It will need a new battery and almost certainly new tyres, but the mechanism should be in good condition. The foundation will be sound. It is in the externals that it may add appreciably to its high price and these should be examined with scrupulous care. The five new tyres cannot as yet be priced, but we can be sure that they will cost more than they have done for many years

The upholstery may be in bad shape, body rattles may have developed, safety glass may be discolouring. These are serious considerations. It may be a long time before things can be put right, and when it is done the bill is likely to be heavy. Indeed, all repairs to the car as a whole will be at a premium and probably difficult of attainment. Manufacturers, coachbuilders and repairers will have lost skilled labour which they will not be able to replace, at any rate for a long time. All are likely to be overwhelmed with work.

From the mechanical point of view there must be very many excellent cars to be had, but it would be rash to buy them "blind."

Observer 1944

At eventide

"MANY of our resident birds have begun to nest, *and later our visitors from overseas will be nesting, too.*" (From a Government announcement.)

If I may say so, the above announcement has obviously been lost in his Majesty's mails for the past few years. I will go further, and point out that in the great forests of Hampstead and St. John's Wood ; throughout the verdant lowlands of Kensington, Westminster, Bayswater and Chelsea ; and along all the bridle-paths leading to and from Paddington Station, our overseas visitors have nested so thickly, so comfortably, so permanently, that there is left to us so-called "resident" birds not one solitary branch, bough or twig around which to hook our tired claws.

With patient scepticism we can but await the Great Migration.

FIRST BUS QUEUE
Londoner Started It

Mr. E. F Snellgrove, trolley-bus inspector, of Wanstead Park-road, Ilford, who has retired from London Transport after 40 years' service, claims that he was one of the first to start a tram or bus queue in the London area.

Mr. W. Back, of Coppermill-lane, Walthamstow, who has also retired, began work with the North Metropolitan Tramways Company as a horsekeeper and strapper in 1900. During the whole of his 45 years' service he has not lost a single day through sickness.

Evening News 1945

Daily Express 1945

Daily Sketch 1946

Kay Petre tries the "feel of the wheel" of the new 2.4 Litre Healey Sports Model.

New 100 m.p.h. British Car In Exports Race To U.S.

By KAY PETRE, 'Daily Sketch' Motoring Correspondent

FROM the quiet roads of Warwickshire to New York's car-thronged Broadway is going Britain's latest 100 m.p.h. streamlined car to bring back valuable dollars.

Filling that 3,000-mile gap is a threefold story of a car, a record and an ambition.

THE CAR, the Healey 2.4 litre (saloon and sports models), is made by a firm born during the war. Slick, streamlined, with remarkable acceleration—zero to 60 m.p.h. in 10 seconds—it is capable of 70 m.p.h. in third gear and over 100 m.p.h in top. It is designed to give an American performance with superb British road-holding qualities.

I was the first motoring correspondent to drive the new Healey, and I put it through its paces yesterday.

Sixty m.p.h. felt like a sedate 30. Corners were taken with armchair smoothness. Visibility — for my 5ft. 1in.—was perfect.

A fast, safe car was my verdict.

VOICE SAID 'WALK' — AND CRIPPLE DID

PARALYSED for ten years, without use of arms and legs, Mr. Sidney William Julian, aged 57, of Hanham-road, Kingswood, Gloucestershire, says a " voice " whispered to him:

" Get up and walk! "

Mr. Julian did so. Neighbours were astonished to see him walking about.

For a long time special prayers were offered for Mr. Julian in the local Congregational church, and the Minister, the Rev. W. J. Downes, visited him. Mr. Downes said:

" It is a sheer miracle—the result of answered prayers which many of us in the churches have made to God for Mr. Julian."

Mr. Julian was working in the garden when a DAILY SKETCH reporter called. He said:

" The other night, while I was sitting in my armchair, a voice said: ' Get up and walk.' I managed to rise from my seat, and for a quarter of an hour walked slowly up and down."

Daily Sketch 1946

RADAR WAS WAR-WINNING WEAPON

"GREATER THAN ATOM BOMB"

10-YEAR BRITISH SECRET

A 10-year secret is lifted to-day with the disclosure of the story of Britain's war-winning weapon, radar.

It is the invention which, as Sir STAFFORD CRIPPS, President of the Board of Trade and former Chairman of the Radio Board, said yesterday, contributed more than any other scientific factor to the victory over Germany.

" It has played a greater part in the war than the atom bomb." he said, " and holds far more immediate potentialities of service to the human race than the splitting of the atom."

Radar was entirely a British achievement. [Details, Pp 4 and 3.] Born about the time of Hitler's rise, it provided, by means of a radio " echo," a precise method of detecting and identifying objects up to 400 miles away.

Adapted to many different purposes it has entirely changed methods of war on land, at sea and in the air.

Daily Telegraph 1945

Wandsworth Borough News 1946

NEARLY 50 YEARS A CONDUCTOR

Earlsfield Man's Fine Record

Nearly half a century's service in London Transport has just been completed by ex-Sergeant Thomas Cheshire, of 23, Swanage-road, Earlsfield, who has retired as a conductor on trams and buses at the Wandsworth depot.

"I joined the old South London Tram Company in 1896, said Mr. Cheshire to a reporter, "when I went on reserve from the Oxford and Bucks Light Infantry.

"In my early days as a conductor," he continued, "we used to work seven days a week for 28s., doing 14 hours, 10 hours, and 8 hours duty in rotation. Incidentally, a few of us formed a penny-a-week union of our own quite early, before there was any Transport and General Workers' Union, and I have been a keen union man ever since."

In October, 1899, Mr. Cheshire was recalled to his old regiment and served through the South African war, until he returned to the trams in 1902.

He volunteered for active service again in 1914, and served in France with the 25th Division, being wounded in the foot during the Somme battle, in September, 1916. He finally completed his military service in April, 1919, with the rank of sergeant.

"I have been a conductor on every type of vehicle," he said. "Horse trams, electric trams, horse buses, motor-buses, and trolleybuses. Sometimes I have found it very hard work but I am thankful to say that I have never taken a day off for sickness. Is this a record for the L.P.T.B., I wonder?

During his Army career, Mr. Cheshire was a notable athlete, winning the regimental mile championship three years in succession, and finishing second in the Irish mile championship at the Curragh, in 1896. He was also successful in the regimental 440 yards.

"My last journey as a conductor," continued Mr. Cheshire, "was from Wandsworth to the Hop Exchange, which was the route I was on at the time of Queen Victoria's Diamond Jubilee in 1897."

SOUTHERN RAILWAY

MORE REFRESHMENT CARS

from Monday, 7th January, 1946

The Southern Railway will restore Refreshment Cars in *certain* additional main line services. The routes on which these Refreshment Cars will be provided are :—

- Certain steam trains (morning and evening) between London, Faversham, Folkestone, Dover, Deal, Tunbridge Wells and Hastings.

- Fast electric trains between Waterloo and Portsmouth.

- Electric trains between London, Horsham and Bognor.

- Electric trains between London, Eastbourne, Brighton, Worthing and Littlehampton.

- Certain steam trains between Waterloo and Bournemouth and an additional service between Waterloo and Exeter.

Details at S.R. Stations and Enquiry Offices.

SURPLUS LORRIES BY AUCTION ONLY

The Ministry of Supply has decided that all Government surplus commercial vehicles will be sold by auction in future. Auction sales were begun this year to supplement the scheme under which vehicles were disposed of through trade channels after reconditioning and at fixed prices. The change announced affects only commercial vehicles, and the trade scheme will still apply to passenger cars.

In a statement yesterday, the Society of Motor Manufacturers and Traders and the Motor Agents' Association said the Ministry had decided that the trade scheme for commercial vehicles had outlived its usefulness. The Society and the Association would have preferred to continue the complete scheme, on the ground that "the orderly disposal of vehicles in sound condition at reasonable prices is preferable to their being offered for sale by auction and would enable vehicles to be made available at controlled prices."

They had raised the question of vehicles sold by auction being put on the road in an unsafe condition, but the Ministry replied that steps they had taken to impress on purchasers at auctions the provisions of the Road Traffic Acts, coupled with the good sense of the purchasers themselves, gave a sufficient safeguard.

Sunday Times 1946

Sunday Times 1946

EXPRESSES POSTPONED

From Our Own Representative

BERNE, Saturday.

Departure of the first post-war Engadine express to St. Moritz, and the Bernese Oberland express to Interlaken, scheduled to leave London and Calais on Monday, has been postponed for a week, the Swiss Railways announced. The reason given is the electricity shortage following the unprecedented nine-week drought in Switzerland.

Flight 1946

R.Ae.C. CERTIFICATES

DURING 1945 the Royal Aero Club issued 444 Certificates. Incidentally, the cost of these is now 15s., with the addition of a further 5s. if the oral examination is held at the Club. After the issue of a Certificate, the Club applies to the Ministry of Civil Aviation for an "A" licence at a cost of 5s.

In order to assist the A.T.C., the Royal Aero Club has, during the war, been issuing Gliding Certificates at a figure well below cost price. These wartime fees have now been cancelled, and all such Certificates will now cost 5s. for each category, with a reduction of 50 per cent. in the case of A.T.C. cadets. The British Gliding Association has been forced to increase the price of their gliding badges. Except for the "A" type these, however, are not at present available.

CIVIL AVIATION

Empire and Atlantic

Details of Future B.O.A.C. Services : Three New Main Lines : Increased Frequency and Speed

Flight 1946

In brief, the proposals covering the coming six to twelve months are as follows: (1) the re-introduction of a service to Australia and New Zealand by way of India, which will be operated at first four times a week to Australia and once to New Zealand, with an eventual frequency increase to seven and two respectively. (2) A service to India by way of the Middle East, with an immediate frequency of seven a week from the start and an ultimate frequency of ten services each way. (3) An increase in the frequency of the now weekly service to South Africa to six a week. (4) Two daily Atlantic services across the Atlantic from Heathrow—one to New York and another to Montreal; the frequency on these runs will be doubled as soon as possible—making a total of 28 services weekly from the United Kingdom to the North American continent. (5) Three services a week, with a possible increase to four, to Accra and Lagos in West Africa, via Algiers. (6) A 9,000-mile service to Hanoi (Indo-China), Hong Kong, Shanghai and Tokio, by way of Vienna and the Middle East.

The European Set-up

During last week-end the European Division of B.O.A.C. officially accepted responsibility for services to Paris, Brussels and Amsterdam, but the change-over was necessarily more academic than real, and for some time to come these services will be run by R.A.F. crews and aircraft, while the maintenance work and traffic operations will be the responsibility of B.O.A.C. personnel who have been "shipped" for this purpose to the paraphenalia of Works and Bricks which is the present Northolt during the enlargement and reconstructive stage.

The European services are now being run from this terminal, where temporary buildings have been erected for traffic purposes, and where equally tentative arrangements have been made for the accommodation of maintenance crews. Towards the end of this month the present services to Madrid, Lisbon and Stockholm, which are at the moment being run from Croydon, will be re-based at Northolt. Empire and Atlantic services will continue to be operated from Hurn and Hythe until Heathrow and any new flying-boat base may be ready. Internal services, which are still being operated by the Associated Airways Joint Committee, will probably be running from Croydon for some time to come.

So far as the aircraft are concerned, austerity Dakotas will be used for the European services until the Vickers Vikings come into use in the summer. The priority system for passengers must necessarily remain, but this will gradually become less and less troublesome from the traffic point of view.

Flight 1946

The Sketch 1946

The men who beat the Air Speed Record in Gloster Meteor IV. jet-propelled fighters—GROUP CAPTAIN E. M. DONALDSON, D.S.O., A.F.C. (second from left), and SQUADRON LEADER W. A. WATERTON, A.F.C. (second from right), are hearing from AIR MARSHAL SIR JAMES ROBB, C.-in-C., Fighter Command, exactly how fast they went! He is reading out the official lap times to the members of the High Speed Group at Tangmere. On September 7, in conditions which were far from ideal, Group Captain Donaldson averaged 616 m.p.h. and Squadron Leader Waterton 614 m.p.h.

British Jets Being Made In U.S.

By E. COLSTON SHEPHERD, The Sunday Times Air Correspondent

British jet engines are now being manufactured in the United States, but deliveries to customers will not begin until the end of next year, and in the meantime Rolls-Royce gas turbines required for use there will be imported from England.

Two Derwent (3,400-lb. static thrust) and two Nene (5,000-lb. static thrust) gas turbines have been supplied to the Taylor Turbine Corporation, and have been handed over by it to the Navy and the Army for official tests. There is thus a good chance that gas turbines of British design will shortly be in use in the United States Air Forces.

Orders for military purposes are evidently the main prospect, and these would mean using the British gas turbines for jet propulsion. The United States are less interested in the use of turbines to drive airscrews, the tendency, even in commercial aircraft, being to go direct from the piston engine to jet propulsion. In Britain the intention is to apply the high power of the gas turbine to airscrews in commercial aircraft up to a speed of about 450 m.p.h.

There are new liners in the United States at present which would benefit from similar treatment. One is the Constitution, which has started its flying trials, but is under-powered with its four 3,500-h.p. piston engines. It could have nearly double the power from British gas turbines, but it is not designed for speeds high enough to use them to advantage for jet propulsion.

United States designers have great need of British gas turbines at present. Their own turbines are behind the British in output and in length of life. There has also been neglect of the design of gears for the 10 to one reduction for use with airscrews. Britain can supply what they want in both classes.

Sunday Times 1946

The Short "Shetland," largest of the flying-boats to be constructed by Short Bros., is a four-engined aircraft of 150ft 4in span, with accommodation for 40 day or 24 night passengers, and a crew of eleven. Its first prototype, a military version, was delivered in 1945 to the Marine Experimental Station, but the civil version prototype is now nearing completion at Rochester for delivery to B.O.A.C. It differs slightly in the design of the nose, hull and tail from the first prototype which we illustrate. The all-up weight of this machine is 130,000 lb and with Bristol "Centaurus" engines of 2500 h.p. each, it has a maximum speed of 267 m.p.h. and a range of 4230 miles.

The Engineer 1947

SHORT "SHETLAND" FOUR-ENGINED FLYING BOAT

A New Era of Motoring Refinement
Introduction of the Austin "A40" Saloons

If ever there was an example of sustained and painstaking endeavour being crowned with the success it deserves, such an example is surely to be seen in the new "A-40" saloons which are Austin's contribution to better motoring for the home and overseas market.

It is confidently expected that the A-40 model will establish a new era of motoring refinement, for the method of construction employed has enabled the designers to offer a car with an unusual power to weight ratio combined with all round strength.

The saving in weight effected together with the provision of a powerful 1,200c.c. four-cylinder overhead valve engine developing 40 b.h.p. at 4,300 r.p.m.

The Austin "A40" Devon 4-Door Saloon

(maximum torque 59 lbs. ft. at 3,000 r.p.m. and compression rates 7.2 to 1.) Forged steel crankshaft supported by three detachable "Thinwall" bearings split skirt pistons in aluminium alloy with anodised finish, with synchromesh engagement for second, third and top, and independent suspension ensures an extremely economical car of great durability with first class road holding characteristics and remarkable power of acceleration, yet capable of sustained high-speed cruising in luxurious comfort.

Irish Motoring 1947

STYLED FOR TOMORROW IN *Sheerline*

The new AUSTIN '110' six cylinder

The new Austin '110' is the finest car we have yet produced. We're proud of its handsome lines, luxurious equipment, high performance, and above all, its comfort and lithe grace. Ask your local Austin Dealer and he will confirm its excellence with more detailed information.

· '110' Sheerline Saloon £1,000
plus £278. 10. 6. Purchase Tax
· '120' Princess Sports Saloon £1,350
plus £375. 15. 0. Purchase Tax

AUSTIN — you can depend on it!

THE AUSTIN MOTOR CO LTD · LONGBRIDGE · BIRMINGHAM

Aeroplane 1947

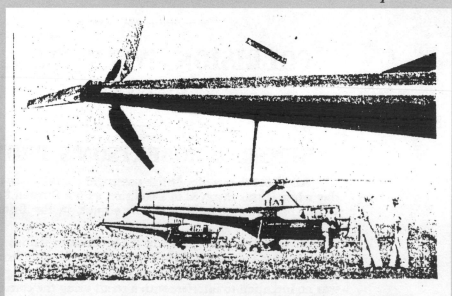

HELICOPTER SERVICE.—Three of the S-51 Sikorskys of the Helicopter Air Transport Inc. operated by Norman Edgar from New York. A licence to build aircraft of this type in England has been acquired by Westland Aircraft Ltd.

The Leader 1947

TRAVEL SICKNESS

Maybe there are legitimate reasons prevailing conditions in British way travel these days, but, from public health point of view, the te of the various toilets on the vast ority of trains is a constant source danger.

To be quite truthful—they make me quite sick!—Harry Double, 16 Walnut Tree Walk, Stowmarket, Suf-

Flight 1948

(Top, right) E. A. Swiss (Bristol 171 pilot) hands over the message to "Bill" Waterton on the Gloster Meteor at Biggin Hill. (Bottom, right) the scene at Orly, near Paris, where the Meteor landed and the message was taken over by the Westland-Sikorsky, piloted by A. Bristow. (Left) the end of the journey. Bristow landing at the Place des Invalides in Paris. In the background is the Grand Palais, the scene of many aero shows.

COMBINING the fastest type of aircraft with the slowest, a jet-propelled fighter trainer and two helicopters, produced a "record" on September 30th, when a message from the Lord Mayor of London, Sir Frederick Wells, was delivered in Paris to the representative of M. Pierre de Gaulle, President of the Municipality of Paris, in a lapsed time of 46 minutes 29 seconds, city centre to city centre.

The demonstration had for its purpose to show how full advantage of very fast aircraft on the air routes could be achieved by speeding-up the airport-to-city part of the route by the use of the helicopter. Three West-of-England firms collaborated: The Bristol Aeroplane Co., Ltd., the Gloster Aircraft Co., Ltd., and Westland Aircraft, Ltd., and the event was sponsored by *The Aeroplane*.

A Bristol 171, piloted by Mr. E. A. Swiss, was used for taking the message from the National Car Park behind St. Paul's to Biggin Hill, where the Gloster Meteor 7 two-seater was waiting. Piloted by Mr. W. A. Waterton it left immediately for Orly, near Paris, where Mr. Alan Bristow was

waiting with a Westland-Sikorsky S.51. He delivered the message on the Place des Invalides to the Deputy President of the Paris Municipal Council, M. de Gaulle being away.

The demonstration was spoilt somewhat by the fact that the take-off from St. Paul's had to be postponed several times on account of poor visibility over France. The original intention was that Mr. Swiss should have taken off at 8.30 a.m., but actually he did not get away until about 12.30.

This was not, of course, the first flight between the centres of the two cities. In 1921 a number of flights were made with a Vickers Viking amphibian flying-boat piloted by Mr. Stanley Cockerell. The first of these was made on April 29th, and the experiment was continued for some time. On one occasion Mr. Cockerell brought to London as a passenger in the Viking M. Laurent Eynac, who was French Air Minister at the time. The fastest trip during the series of tests took only a little over two hours, from the Seine in the centre of Paris to the Thames at Westminster. And that was 27 years ago! A modern amphibian could reduce this time considerably.

The Times 1948

BRITISH AIRCRAFT DOWN NEAR BERLIN

---◆---

COLLISION WITH RUSSIAN FIGHTER

GENERAL ROBERTSON'S PROTEST

All 14 occupants of a British passenger aircraft were killed yesterday when it was involved in a collision with a Russian fighter just as it was preparing to land at Gatow airport, in the British sector of Berlin.

A serious view was taken of the incident in British quarters and a protest was lodged with the Russian authorities in Germany. This brought an assurance from Marshal Sokolovsky last night that there was no intention to interfere with aircraft using the corridor. Orders for the provision of fighter protection for British transport were subsequently cancelled.

SHIPBUILDING OUTPUT IN 1948

Of the 11 vessels launched by Swan, Hunter and Wigham Richardson in 1948, totalling 77,257 tons, five of 51,600 tons are motor ships.

R. and W. Hawthorn, Leslie and Co. launched five ships of 50,565 tons gross, with machinery of 39,300 h.p., and of these, four were motor vessels of 39,000 tons gross. The tonnage launched is nearly double that in 1947.

Three motor ships and one steamer were launched by Sir James Laing and Sons; they aggregated 37,685 tons gross.

At S. P. Austin and Son's yard, four colliers were launched, with a total deadweight capacity of 12,090 tons. Orders on the books will occupy the building berths until about 1951.

The Furness S.B. Co., Ltd., have launched 10 ships of 57,348 tons and, of these, nine are motor vessels of 46,400 tons.

All of the five vessels launched at Bartram and Sons' yard were motor ships for Portuguese owners, totalling 26,673 tons gross.

At Smith's Dock Co.'s yard, 15 vessels of 18,044 tons gross were launched, mostly steamers.

Vickers-Armstrongs, Barrow, launched two ships of 43,000 tons, and the Walker yard four vessels of 36,831 tons gross, three being motor ships.

Propelling machinery for four additional motor ships was built at Hawthorn, Leslie's St. Peter's Works, totalling 16,700 b.h.p.

At the Wallsend works of the North Eastern Marine Engineering Co. the machinery of nine motor ships was built, totalling 54,148 i.h.p., and at the Sunderland works the propelling plant for 12 steamers totalling 18,565 i.h.p.

Richardsons, Westgarth and Co., Ltd., have built at Hartlepool the machinery for three motor ships and one steamer totalling 17,334 i.h.p.

Propelling machinery totalling 33,700 i.h.p. for four motor ships and one steamer was built by the Wallsend Slipway and Engineering Co.

Seven motor vessels of 43,505 tons gross were launched by Wm. Doxford and Sons, Ltd., and 10 engines constructed of 44,060 i.h.p.

Three of the five ships of 38,975 tons gross launched by Alexander Stephen and Sons, Ltd., were oil-engined vessels and Diesel engines totalling 28,000 b.h.p. were built. David Rowan and Co., Ltd., Glasgow, manufactured marine machinery of 21,420 i.h.p., including the 4,000 i.h.p. Rowan-Doxford engine for the M.S. "Scottish Trader."

Two turbo-electric and two Diesel-engined ships of 22,662 tons gross were launched at the Fairfield yard at Govan, the machinery totalling 34,200 h.p., in addition to which two Fairfield-Doxford engines of 11,300 h.p. were constructed for other yards.

Henry Robb, Ltd., launched five self-propelled vessels and four non-propelled craft totalling 10,455 tons gross.

Four ships of 38,125 tons gross were built by Barclay, Curle and Co., Ltd., and the machinery of five other vessels was manufactured, the total power of the machinery being 45,810 i.h.p. All of the engines were of the Barclay, Curle-Doxford type, in addition to which 17 boilers of 11,990 i.h.p. and five B.W. turbines of 4,480 i.h.p. were manufactured.

Harland and Wolff launched 16 ocean-going ships at their Belfast and Glasgow shipyards, totalling 125,922 tons gross, and the machinery built, including engines for four vessels not constructed by Harland and Wolff, totalled 146,500 i.h.p. Diesel machinery of 64,500 i.h.p. was also completed for land installations and auxiliary purposes.

Electric propulsion machinery for three turbo-electric ships and one Diesel-electrically propelled vessel was built by the British Thomson-Houston Co., the total power being 47,750 s.h.p. Electro-magnetic couplings for use with the geared Diesel drive were constructed for five ships.

The Burntisland S.B. Co. launched seven vessels (all oil-engined) of 18,786 tons gross, with machinery of 15,860 b.h.p.

Six motor ships were completed at the same yard, totalling 21,401 tons gross, with machinery of 17,300 b.h.p.

Motor Ship **1949**

Christening *Windmill Girl,* a Percival Proctor light plane bought second-hand by Captain Arthur Mansfield (far right) in 1948 for an attempt on the 'Circuit of the Earth' record.

The Brabazon

The Brabazon I paid a visit of courtesy during one of the days of the Flying Display and impressed all present by its size. I have heard the opinion expressed that it looked more like a large ship sailing past than an aeroplane. From an engineering point of view the Brabazon is a most magnificent achievement and the wealth of experience its development will yield will be invaluable. Whether it will ever be a great success as an airliner can only be hoped for; personally I am inclined to doubt that aircraft of this size can be operated economically. There is, of course, little doubt that on a basis of ton/miles per gallon a large aircraft will be very efficient, but if its carrying capacity proves to be too great for the traffic volume offered it will rapidly become inefficient. The Stratocruiser has been alleged to have the ability to lose money faster than any other type if its load factor falls below a certain value. With the Brabazon this will be even more pronounced. With such large aircraft flexibility of operations will decrease and this flexibility is one of the main assets by which to avoid heavy losses.

Aircraft Engineering 1949

Training and Status

An encouraging beginning, in the form of the new specialized post-graduate courses in production engineering at Birmingham University and at the Cranfield College of Aeronautics, has now been made in amending shortcomings in specialized training but much remains to be done. The Birmingham course is more general in character than that at Cranfield which specializes in aircraft production and economics—and the aircraft industry is, indeed, particularly fortunate in having available a course the curriculum of which is conceived in the most liberal terms. Both of these courses are open to entrants from industry as well as to external- and internal-degree men from the universities—though the entry for each is highly selective and the Birmingham course might almost be described as post-post-graduate, as it requires industrial experience in addition to a degree from a university entrant.

Aircraft Production 1949

STRIKE ACTION AS CHALLENGE

ARBITRATION SYSTEM DISREGARDED

VEHICLE BUILDERS OUT

From Our Labour Correspondent

The strike called by the National Union of Vehicle Builders and the Amalgamated Society of Woodcutting Machinists was generally effective yesterday, according to first reports received in London by the United Kingdom joint wages board of employers for the vehicle building industry. It affects about 20,000 workers, including those employed by the principal builders of public transport vehicles. Technically it began last Friday, but as most of the workers have a five-day week it was not until yesterday that its extent was known.

The strike is a serious problem for the Government because it appears to be a direct challenge to the authority of the system of compulsory arbitration, which has been continued by the Government since the war, with the concurrence of the Trades Union Congress, whose approval was reaffirmed at the last congress. The unions concerned are all affiliated to the T.U.C.

There have been other strikes since the war which have had the backing of unions, some inside and some outside the T.U.C., but almost invariably there have been considerations of jurisdiction or recognition not easily settled by arbitration. There is nothing of the sort here. It is a straightforward wage claim which has not been granted.

The Times 1948

Now! Daily! DOUBLE DECKED Clippers to New York!

● Now you can fly between London and New York in the world's largest, most luxurious airliners — the new double-decked Clippers! It is the *fastest* service, and offers you a spacious club lounge, more comfortable seats, oversize berths (only a nominal additional charge), a steadier ride high above the weather. For reservations, call your Travel Agent, or Pan American, 193-4, Piccadilly, W.1 (REG 7292). Clipper Cargo (WHI 3311).

Also, Sundays only !
Fly THE PRESIDENT special de luxe service

PAN AMERICAN WORLD AIRWAYS

British Manufacturers Lead the World

Among the outstanding achievements of British industry during the post-war period the remarkable progress made in the production of bicycles and motor cycles is particularly noteworthy. The transition from wartime to peacetime conditions showed in a striking manner the vitality and resourcefulness of these two industries and the advance made has been such that all previous production records were broken so far as complete machines were concerned. This progress has been particularly welcome in connection with the nation's export drive because the conversion value of bicycles and motor cycles is very high, British labour rather than raw material making its contribution to the value of the finished article.

Record of Progress

Some idea of the progress of the industry can be gained from some interesting figures on the export trade. These show that since 1945 when cycles were exported to the number of 272,722, valued at £1¼m., which trade was itself more than double that in the previous year, shipments have jumped to 1,449,662 units, valued at over £10m., in 1947 ; while exports of motor cycles have risen in the same period from 3,948 units, or nearly four times the number shipped in 1944, to 55,367, valued at £4·4m., in 1947. For 1948 exports of both bicycles and motor cycles have exceeded those for the previous year, and it is expected that when total figures are available the very creditable figure of about £25m. will have been attained.

In addition there is a large production of, and trade in, components. The British production of these goods is of great importance and has played a large part in the export drive of the industry, for it is called upon to assist manufacturers and assemblers in all parts of the world as well as to supply spare and replacement parts for the millions of U.K. bicycles that have been exported. Like the cycle trade, shipments of parts has grown phenomenally, and at £4·3m. (bicycle parts) and £642,000 (motor cycle parts) for 1947 was, respectively, four times and fifteen times what it was in 1945.

Britain's Dominant Position

The dominant position occupied to-day by the United Kingdom in the world market for bicycles is emphasized by the fact that France, the second most important world exporter of bicycles, exported only 191,876 units in 1947, or less than one-seventh the British total, while the United States as the third supplier of importance sent abroad only 93,984 units. In the motor-cycle trade the United Kingdom in 1947 exported four times the number of machines shipped by Czechoslovakia, the second largest world exporter, and more than five times the number of American motor-cycles. The chief markets for British bicycles are, within the Empire, India and South Africa, and among foreign countries, Argentina and the Netherlands. The largest buyers of motor-cycles are Australia, the United States, India, Switzerland, Belgium, Sweden and Canada.

Chamber of Commerce Journal 1949

Pomp and Circumstance

Grace and character distinguished the Dunkley perambulator of yesteryear, when life was serene and unhurried. Through subsequent difficult years the Dunkley retained its character though straight-jacketed with restrictions. Now, new models appear. The "Duchess" once more reveals unhampered craftsmanship, and with all its gracious line, keeps ahead of modern demands for generous proportions and ease of handling (with its bed-length of 34¼" and width 14¼" ; its large ball-bearing wheels). The "Duchess" is a worthy upholder of Dunkley tradition which prompts the proud parent to proclaim that

ONLY A

WILL DO

Fashioned with the same craftsmanship are — the Dunkley Polyplay Chair, the Nursery Cot and the Electric Nursery Airing Cabinet. Ask your Dealer for leaflets, or write to Dunkleys (London) Ltd., National Works, Bath Road, Hounslow, Middlesex.

APPOINTMENT

Standing for three hackney carriages at Oxford Street (Argyll Street), W.

The standing shall be in the centre of the roadway, commencing at a point three yards east of the refuge east of Argyll Street, extending eastward as far as necessary for three cabs.

Cabs shall be ranked facing westward.

The Order and Regulations dated 23rd November, 1932, with regard to the standing for eight hackney carriages at Oxford Street, W. (Argyll Street), in two portions, are hereby revoked.

HAROLD SCOTT,
Commissioner of Police of the Metropolis.

Metropolitan Police Office,
New Scotland Yard, S.W.1.

24th September, 1948.

Owner Driver 1948

HONEYMAN

Above: An arrow of a car for the young and sports-minded : the Jaguar XK120, beneath whose bonnet lurk 120 m.p.h.—and more. It has space to accommodate sports gear, or luggage, in the boot. Worn here (left), a classic camel-coloured cashmere and wool fleece sports coat—cosiest of coats for an open car : by Aquascutum. Small matching fur-felt hat, safe against the wind : by Rodolf. Right : a leopard-skin sports coat, warm and windproof : by Maxwell Croft. Well pulled-down bronze-green velours hat : by Erik

Vogue 1949

BONUS IF BUSMEN COLLECT FARES UPSTAIRS

"DAILY MIRROR" REPORTER

A TOWN may offer its bus conductors a 5s.-a-week bonus—to encourage them to climb the stairs and collect fares on the upper deck.

Drivers, too, would get the bonus—if they pulled up at every stop to pick up passengers.

Rochdale (Lancs) Council are waiting to see what their new transport manager thinks about the scheme which, it is hoped, will lead to greater all-round efficiency in the department.

Transport employees would qualify for the bonus by being at work regularly, by punctuality, and by doing "a complete job" while at work

Daily Mirror 1951

Tough bred 2-seater

ALTHOUGH raised in the tough school of motor racing, the new 1½-litre Jowett Jupiter, now in production, is an extremely comfortable little two-three seater touring car.

While retaining the rugged essentials of a fast competition car, like the rigid tubular chassis which makes the car hold the road like a leech, the body is designed to suit every-day motorists who want a practical two-seater model.

The bench type seat, adjustable, is wide enough for three adults, or three small children and a driver.

And again the four forward speed gear lever, mounted on the steering column (remote control gear lever on the floor is optional) is a cunning compromise between a racing box and the modern type lever.

The car would idle along lazily in top gear, its 1,485 c.c. engine ticking over quietly, at 20 m.p.h. in town driving, or it would accelerate snappily by using the gears.

Another item that appealed to me was the good weather protection. A wide-vision V-screen and side windows with ventilators, and a good solid canvas top made it a rainy-day car

TECHNICAL DATA: 4 cylinder o.h.v. 1½-litre engine. Petrol 33 miles per gallon. 0 to 50 m.p.h., 11 seconds. Maximum speed 88 m.p.h

DOUBTFUL DEPT.: Pedals too far away for small drivers. Under-dashboard hand brake difficult to reach.

PRICE: £850 plus £236 17s. 3d. purchase tax

Kay Petre

Daily Graphic 1950

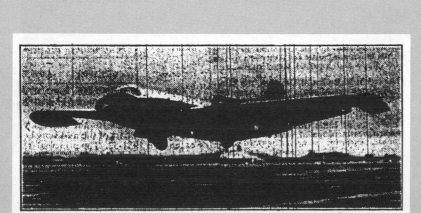

The jet bomber Canberra leaving Aldergrove, Northern Ireland, for its record-breaking transatlantic flight to Gander, Newfoundland, yesterday.

The Times 1951

Chilworth **MIDGET**

Just the thing for your summer holidays. It has three berths and can be towed by an 8 H.P. car Price **£285**

The

CHILWORTH CARAVANS

48 THE AVENUE SOUTHAMPTON

MY POINT OF VIEW

GILBERT HARDING

One last grouse—why can't women get into those special compartments labelled "Ladies Only"—especially on crowded suburban trains? Is there anything particularly attractive in the company of grim-faced post-breakfast belching men all smoking like chimneys, when the harem-like seclusion of a "Ladies Only" compartment is used perhaps by just one or two?

Did I say that that was the final grouse? There is one more. Why, oh why, is it always women who ask for a ticket in a busy queue and only when the ticket has been slid towards them do they begin to open their bags, look for their purses and never find the right change?

I am not saying that men are any better: they are just different, I suppose.

Shopping 1951

ALL TRAINS FREE-FOR-ALL FOR 5s. A WEEK

Reveille 1951

AS railway fares rise still higher the plan formulated by a Surrey man for free travel for all in return for weekly contributions similar to those payable under the National Health Scheme seems an attractive idea.

He estimates that a weekly levy of 5s. from every wage earner. in the country would produce about £5,000,000 against the present income of British Railways of about £2,500,000 a week. Under his scheme tremendous economies could be effected.

The 20,000 ticket-issuing clerks and the 10,000 men who collect them at our journey's end could be dispensed with.

H.M.S. TRUCULENT

THE LOSS OF A BRITISH SUBMARINE IN THE THAMES ESTUARY

THE BRITISH SUBMARINE "TRUCULENT," A PATROL VESSEL OF THE "T" CLASS, WHICH WAS SUNK IN NINE FATHOMS OF WATER IN THE THAMES ESTUARY WITH SEVENTY-NINE MEN ON BOARD : News of the accident did not reach the Admiralty until eighty minutes after the Swedish motor-tanker *Divina* had collided with the *Truculent*, and questions have now been asked about the *Divina's* wireless equipment. The 1,000-ton *Truculent*, completed in 1942, recently had an extensive refit and was in reserve. During the war, while on service in the Pacific, the *Truculent*, with prisoners on board, attacked a Japanese convoy. Submarine chasers made her dive quickly. She hit the sea bottom. Depth charges exploded all around. But she escaped. The *Truculent* was in the same class as the *Thetis*, which sank in Liverpool Bay on June 1, 1939 Out of 103 in *Thetis*, only four survived

Sphere 1950

SPEEDWAY ENTHUSIASTS

This badge set with beautiful stones in YOUR TEAM'S COLOURS had a wonderful reception when advertised at the latter end of last season.

The silver badge is made with fob pin for wearing on coat lapels or with pin only as a brooch.

The Chrome badge is only available in brooch style.

CHROME FINISH & STONES	REAL SILVER & STONES
10/- (pin)	15/- (fob or pin)
delivered post free	*delivered post free*

REGISTERED DESIGN No. 860254
SPEEDWAY TEAMS' COLOURS IN STOCK
Birmingham, Sheffield, Glasgow, Hanley, Tamworth, Wimbledon, Bristol, Fleetwood, Newcastle, Wembley, Belle Vue, Exeter, Edinburgh, Harringay, West Ham, Hull, Plymouth, Middlesbro', New Cross, Cradley Heath, Coventry, Norwich, Bradford, Walthamstow, Liverpool, Poole, Yarmouth, Hastings, Wombwell, Rayleigh, Swindon, Southampton.

Send Cheque, P/Order or cash, stating chrome or silver, your name and address, your team, and whether fob or pin brooch required to:—

E. F. LEVITT, Unitas House, Livery Street, BIRMINGHAM, 3
Inspection invited at above address or at offices of Echo

Nuffield and Austin Amalgamation

UNIFIED CONTROL PROPOSED FOR MORE EFFICIENT AND ECONOMIC PRODUCTION AND TO FURTHER THE EXPORT DRIVE

by the Midland Editor

AMALGAMATION of Morris Motors, Ltd. and the Austin Motor Co., Ltd. is proposed by the two boards.

This announcement was made at a hurriedly convened Press conference at the Austin works at Longbridge, Birmingham, shortly before 5 p.m. on Friday last; that is, after the Stock Exchange had closed. The announcement was made jointly by Mr. J. F. Bramley, managing director of the Austin Motor Export Corporation, Ltd., Mr. Alan Hess, Austin P.R.O., and Mr. R. A. Bishop, Nuffield Organization publicity and sales promotion manager, who issued the following notice:

For some time past the boards of Morris Motors, Ltd., and the Austin Motor Co., Ltd., have had under consideration the desirability of amalgamating the two companies. In the result they have arrived at the conclusion that unified control would not only lead to more efficient and economic production, but would also further the export drive, and be particularly beneficial to manufacturing and assembly abroad. They have formed the opinion, therefore, that amalgamation would be both in the national interest and to the advantage of the shareholders of both companies. Accordingly they propose a merger of interests.

Autocar 1951

Swamped By Telephone Calls
City Exchange Was Overloaded

There were so many telephone calls in the Liverpool area after the news of the King's death that unprecedented congestion was caused at the nerve centre of the city's automatic system in Lancaster House, Old Hall Street, for about an hour this morning.

Soon after the news had been put out by the *Echo* in a special Stop Press announcement, it seemed that every other person in the city wanted to talk to someone else about it.

At one time, demands on the automatic system were seven to eight times more than the normal peak—and more than the system could cope with.

When subscribers failed to get numbers by dialling, many called the operator on the "O" signal, but the traffic was so great that overtaxed operators found it extremely difficult to meet the demand.

EXCEPTIONAL CASES

"All we could do in such cases," said an official, "was to connect what appeared to be the exceptional cases; otherwise it would have merely increased the difficulties in the automatic system.

"Here we normally pride ourselves on a four-seconds' speed of answering. In to-day's busy period the time went up to six seconds.

"As it was we did very well and handled double the normal amount of telephone traffic between 11 and 12."

Liverpool Echo 1952

THE PEDESTRIAN CROSSINGS [LONDON] REGULATIONS, 1951

As from 31st October, 1951, **NEW REGULATIONS** governing the use and observance of PEDESTRIAN CROSSINGS will be in force.

It is, obviously, most important that all road-users should understand the effects of these Regulations which are summarised below:—

PEDESTRIANS....

⊙ You have priority over vehicular traffic at crossings which are marked by **BLACK & WHITE ("ZEBRA") STRIPES**, in addition to the usual beacons and studs.

(Before starting to cross, you should, of course, make sure that the driver of any approaching vehicle has time to stop for you).

⊙ You must not remain on a "ZEBRA" Crossing longer than is necessary to cross the road.

⊙ Crossings where traffic is controlled by Light Signals are **NOT** marked by "ZEBRA" Stripes and you have **NO** priority over vehicular traffic at these Crossings.

(So you should take great care and cross the road only when the Lights indicate that it is safe to do so).

DRIVERS &' CYCLISTS....

You **MUST** allow free passage to a ⊙ Pedestrian using a Crossing marked by **BLACK & WHITE ("ZEBRA") STRIPES**, in addition to the usual beacon and studs.

Pedestrians have no priority over ⊙ vehicular traffic on Crossings controlled by Light Signals or Policemen.

(You should, however, drive with great care at these crossings—particularly if you are "filtering" round a corner).

Unless it is unavoidable, you must not ⊙ halt your vehicle on any Pedestrian Crossing.

"Waiting" within 45 ft. of certain ⊙ Crossings is prohibited and, in such cases, the limit of the prohibition area is indicated by two yellow semi-circles painted on the kerb.

⊙ N.B. At any "ZEBRA" Crossing, traffic may be ⊙ temporarily controlled by a Policeman. In these circumstances, Pedestrians have **NO** priority and all road-users must obey the policeman's signals.

Daily Express 1952

Power steering is coming to stay

by
PHILIP TURNER

A REVOLUTION in steering was initiated by the Chrysler Corporation last year when at the Brussels Show they revealed in public for the first time a car with power steering. This new development may well become almost universal for big cars not only in America but throughout the world in the next five years or so.

The reasons for this are three in number. To begin with, the current fashion for engines mounted as far forward as possible in order to bring the rear passengers ahead of the rear axle has meant that an unduly high proportion of a car's weight is now carried by the front wheels.

Not so long ago, at least 50 per cent. and often 55 or 60 per cent. of the weight of a car was carried by the rear wheels of the average saloon, but today, the exact opposite is the case for it is usually the front wheels that are carrying 60 per cent. of the load.

Car and Car Topics 1952

BRINGING BACK A BREATH OF " EMETT " TO THE RAILWAYS OF THIS ISLAND : THE TAL-Y-LLYN RAILWAY RUNS AGAIN FROM TOWYN, ON THE COAST, TO ABERGYNOLWYN.

Amateurs of railways will be delighted to learn that the famous Tal-y-llyn Railway, that ancient steam-hauled, narrow-gauged railway which runs from Towyn, on the Merioneth coast, to Abergynolwyn, is once more alive, thanks to the activities of a society which has put the line in running order again.

Illustrated London News 1951

Tom Thumb's trike

DENNIS MAY dissects the Bond Minicar (80 m.p.g) in the second instalment of his serial on economy cars

Car and Car Topics 1952

U NLESS a great many respected economists have been getting their sums wrong, Europe, Britain included, stands today on the threshold of the Minicar Age. And, when that epoch comes upon us, there seems every reason to believe the featherweight three-wheeler will command a sizeable cut from the over-all sales.

NAVY'S SECRET CRUISER RUNS AGROUND

By Daily Mail Reporter

T HE 10,000-ton British cruiser Cumberland, try-out warship for guided missiles and other modern weapons, ran aground while leaving Plymouth Sound. Yesterday she was in dry dock at Devonport.

Her departure for Portsmouth and the Mediterranean, scheduled for today, has been postponed indefinitely pending survey and repairs—expected to take several weeks. Plymouth Naval H.Q. said : " The damage is being investigated."

The Cumberland was leaving by the shallower, narrower eastern entrance to Plymouth because midget submarines were exercising in the western entrance. She grounded on a rocky plateau. She freed herself and went into dock for examination. The C.-in-C. ordered a board of inquiry.

The Cumberland was converted into the Navy's first trials A.A. cruiser after the war. She is used for secret experimental work.

Daily Mail 1952

Comet's farewell party

BEFORE taking off on the first leg of the 6,724-mile flight to Johannesburg this afternoon, the 500 m.p.h. De Havilland Comet was given "prima donna" treatment.

She was posed for pictures; her pilots and crew were photographed and interviewed, and the passengers on this first-ever all-jet route were feted and photographed.

Brighton Evening Argus 1952

THE PRINCESS—MILES ABOVE BORDEAUX

TEST-PILOT JOHN CUNNINGHAM yesterday took the Queen Mother and Princess Margaret on a lightning whisk around Europe in a Comet jet-liner—by way of the Alps, the Italian and French Rivieras, the Pyrenees, Bordeaux, and the Normandy beaches.

No queen, no princess ever flew so fast or so high before.

Maximum speed reached: 510 miles an hour. Said Sir Miles Thomas, chairman of B.O.A.C., who made the 1,850-mile trip and also took these pictures: "It was a perfect flight.

"The Queen Mother and the Princess said they were delighted with the smoothness, comfort, and fatigue-free travel of the Comet."

Princess Margaret, here, holds a lighted cigarette.

Daily Express 1952

And in London to-night—
MIDNIGHT FAREWELL TO THE TRAMS

London's last tramcars will disappear from the streets shortly after midnight to-night.

Their disappearance marks the completion of London Transport's £9,000,000 post-war scheme to replace all remaining tramcar routes by buses.

To-night, Lord Latham, chairman of London Transport, is to welcome at New Cross tramcar depot the very last passenger tramcar to run in London.

From Woolwich

It will be car No. 1951, on Route 40, leaving Perrott Street, Woolwich, at 11.57 p.m. and arriving at New Cross, via Greenwich and Deptford, at 12.29 a.m.

At the controls of the last tramcar will be Mr. John Cliff, deputy chairman of London Transport, who himself started his 52 years' career in transport as a tramwayman in Leeds.

The last tramcar from the Embankment and Central London, will be a route 40 tramcar, leaving Savoy Street at 11.38 p.m. and arriving at New Cross at 12.11 a.m.

Several farewell tramcar rides will be made by parties who have hired special tramcars, during the afternoon and early evening to-day.

London's tramcars — which were first introduced by an American, George Francis Train, in 1861—when the American Civil War was being fought—have served London for 91 years. They were electrified in the early 1900's.

Evening Standard 1952

Non-stop Jaguar breaks 9 records

The British Jaguar XK coupé which has been circling the Montlhéry track near Paris for more than four days, has now brought its tally of records to nine, and is still running. Four are world records and five are in the international "C" class (for cars with a capacity between 3,000 and 5,000 c.c.).

The car is being driven for three-hour periods each by Leslie Johnson, Stirling Moss, Jack Fairman, and Bert Hadley. At 7.5 last night it gained the 10,000-mile world record in 99 hrs. 28 mins. 21.87 secs. at an average speed of 100.66 m.p.h.

The Jaguar's average for 15,000 kilometres was 101.95, despite torrential rain. It also set up a four-day world record of 9,713.1 miles at 101.17 m.p.h.

OUR MOTORING CORRESPONDENT writes:
This achievement has done much to regain British prestige in motoring events and is a fine tribute, not only to the power and stamina of the car as a whole, but also to its comfort and road holding.

The very long distance high-speed test is the crowning achievement of a car that has been developed over the years by its sponsor, Mr. William Lyons, who started as the builder of sidecar bodies and has now become the maker of one of the outstanding British cars in quality—a modern example of private enterprise.

Daily Express 1952

TRACTOR GIRL

She beats the men

A 21-YEAR-OLD farmer's daughter won two tractor-driving competitions yesterday, beating 14 men in the first and 26 men in the second.

It was at the Royal Agricultural Show at Newton Abbot, Devon—so some of England's best tractor-drivers were there.

But Miss Lydia Rowe, of Ideford, near Newton Abbot, has years of experience behind her. "I have been driving one particular type of tractor for the past eight years," she said, "and I drove one or two other makes before that."

Sunday Times 1952

World's fastest jet flying-wing bomber makes first flight

Dramatic leap in progress of British aviation, says Minister

By E. COLSTON SHEPHERD,
The Sunday Times Air Correspondent

THE world's first four-engined operational delta-winged jet bomber, the Avro A.698, which has been on the secret list, made a 35-minute maiden flight from Woodford Airfield, Cheshire, yesterday.

This revolutionary "flying-wing," with a speed approaching that of sound—

Can fly faster, higher and farther with a bigger load more economically than any other aircraft;

Can carry a large bomb load over great distances;

And is designed to fly at heights giving it considerable immunity from ground defences.

Yesterday's flight is important from a civil as well as a military point of view. According to one authority, it presages the day when transcontinental air travellers, instead of being seated in a long tubular cabin formed by a conventional fuselage, will be in a spacious compartment in the thick wing-roots of a delta civil air liner.

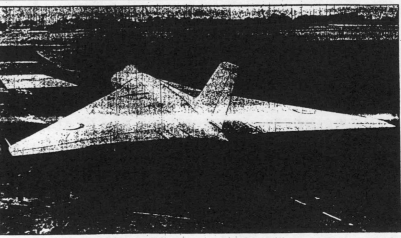

Britain's new revolutionary flying-wing bomber before its flight.

Sunday Times 1952

LOOK! Now we can give the kiddies a

GRESHAM *Flyer*

THE SAFEST TRICYCLE IN THE WORLD

AT **£9.19.0**
(INCLUDING P.T.)

TELESCOPIC CONTROL HANDLE!

SPACIOUS CAR-TYPE LUGGAGE BOOT!

BUILT FOR HARD WEAR!

RANGE OF ATTRACTIVE COLOURS!

IT'S ONE OF THE
NEW 'ROCKET RANGE'
OF TRICYCLES
UP IN VALUE! DOWN IN PRICE

Sturdy girder type frame, precision built. Exclusive built-in roomy luggage boot. Safety telescopic control handle that stows away neatly behind the boot. Comfortable spring mattress saddle. Safety roller lever handlebars with rim brakes. Full rubber pedals. 14" wide-section cushion tyres.

ROCKET Mk I
As illustrated, *less luggage boot and control handle.*
£7.12.6 (INCLUDING P.T.)

ROCKET Mk II
As Mk I but with 16" wide-section cushion tyres.
£7.15.0 (INCLUDING P.T.)
* Mk's I & II available with control handle: 15/- extra.

ROCKET Mk III
As illustrated.
£9.19.0 (INCLUDING P.T.)

ROCKET Mk IV
As illustrated, but with Dunlop 14" x 1½" pneumatic tyres.
£11.2.6 (INCLUDING P.T.)

Write for illustrated leaflets and name and address of your nearest dealer who will be only too happy to demonstrate these and other GRESHAM FLYER models.

ABERDALE CYCLE COMPANY LIMITED

Manufactured under one or more of the following Patent Nos. 628991, 628992. Registered Design Nos. 848809, 857480, 857481, 857482, 857483, 857484, 857485, 857486.

GENEROUS HIRE PURCHASE TERMS on application to your local dealer.

Daily Express
1952

SO-CHEAP-TO-RUN PLANE IS READY

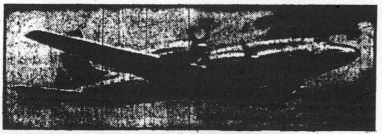

By Group Captain HUGH DUNDAS

A NEW British airliner, the prop-jet Bristol Britannia, is due to make its first flight today, if weather permits. The plane is designed to carry 85 passengers at nearly 400 miles an hour for 5,000 miles.

Sir Miles Thomas, chairman of B.O.A.C., told me this week that it will be even more important than the Comet to British civil aviation.

It is expected to be the most economical airliner ever built, with a vital part in the planned extension of B.O.A.C. high-speed, all-weather tourist-class services to all parts of the world.

The importance of the Britannia is closely linked with the success of the tourist-class air travel introduced ex-

perimentally on the North Atlantic route last May.

Statistics show that between May 1 and July 19 a profit of £128,328 was made by B.O.A.C. on tourist services to the U.S. and Canada. Six planes weekly flew each way between London and New York, and three each way between London and Montreal.

Up to the end of July 6,049 tourist passengers travelled on the B.O.A.C.'s New York service, and 2,968 on the Montreal flights—a total of 9,017 "new" TransAtlantic air passengers.

Yet the first-class or "standard" services did almost as much business as last year. Altogether 21,500 passengers flew British over the Atlantic in May and July, compared with 14,577 in 1951—an increase of about 50 per cent.

Birth of a Station

by FRANCES COLLINGWOOD

O**N OCTOBER** 14 this year King's Cross Station is celebrating its one hundredth birthday. Many of you probably know this famous terminus and will be interested to know that when it was built in 1852 the shareholders of the old Great Northern Railway grumbled because they said it was so far away from London that nobody would use it!

Old prints of that part of London show the Small Pox Hospital, which had to be pulled down to make way for the station, standing in the midst of fields; and the first trains to draw out of the new terminus were in the depths of the country within a mile of their start.

Arrivals and Departures

The original idea of the architect, Lewis Cubitt, was very simple. He designed two immense sheds, divided from one another by a wall formed of piers and arches. One shed was for arrivals, and the other for departures. They each measured 800 feet in length, 105 feet in width, and were 71 feet high. Into each was placed one long platform served by a number of trackways. And over the whole was set what was then the largest arched roof in the world.

This consisted of bundles of planks, bent like the wood of a bow, and was a copy of the roof of the riding-school at Moscow that had been built for the Czar of Russia. Unfortunately it wasn't strong enough to stand the strain, and in 1869 the 'arrival' half had to be replaced by iron girders, while 17 years later the same thing was done to the other half. Altogether King's Cross Station covered 59 acres, 49 of which were detailed for goods traffic and coal.

The very first train to leave King's Cross that morning in October one hundred years ago was the 7 a.m. to York. It went puffing triumphantly out on its way north drawn by one of Crampton's engines. In all six fast and twenty slow trains used the new station that day.

Collins Magazine **1952**

Nowadays we talk of building 'space platforms.' Yet only 100 years ago they were building the London railway stations

King's Cross 1852

Opened only a year after the Great Exhibition, it isn't surprising that King's Cross Station looks rather like a crystal palace

King's Cross to-day

A century has brought a number of changes, but basically the station looks the same. In fact, we're so used to our stations being Victorian in appearance that a modern terminus would probably look 'funny'

Daily Graphic
1952

COBB WON BEFORE HE HIT THE RIPPLE OF DEATH

By Daily Graphic Reporter

JOHN COBB, the fastest man on land, became the fastest man on water yesterday—just a few minutes before he died.

Big, shy Cobb, who spent £100,000 to keep Britain first in the world of speed, was clocked at 206 m.p.h. over the measured mile on grey Loch Ness in his red and white jet boat Crusader.

His peak speed must have been 240 m.p.h., said Commander Peter Du Kane, who helped to build the boat.

Then a tiny ripple spread over the glassy surface; it crossed Crusader's path.

And John Rhodes Cobb, who had given so much for British prestige, gave his life.

The £15,000 boat, with the same engine as a Comet jetliner, smacked the ripple. She whined into the air, bounced on a second ripple —and nose-dived into the loch 100 yards beyond the measured mile.

Daily Graphic 1952

Nortons sell out to AJS

Herald Reporter

NORTON MOTORS, LTD., Birmingham makers of the world-famous motor-cycle, have sold out to rivals in a £1,000,000 deal.

Controlling interest in the firm has been sold to Associated Motor Cycles, Ltd., of London, who build the Matchless and A.J.S. machines.

But that does not mean the end of Nortons, a leading name in motor-cycle racing all over the world for 40 years.

The company, previously a family concern, will continue to make the machines—and race them—under the old name.

28 TT FIRSTS

Norton's record of 28 firsts in the Isle of Man T T races is never likely to be equalled. The names of those who rode them read like a motor-cycling roll of honour: Stanley Woods, Jimmy Guthrie, Harold Daniell and Geoff Duke.

Mr. O. Gilbert Smith, managing director, who joined the firm as a boy 39 years ago, said: "We shall continue as a separate manufacturing unit. The management will remain the same and we shall continue the same fierce competition in international racing."

Daily Herald 1953

Petrol-saving car for three

Production of the petrol-saving Workers' Playtime car is expected to start soon at Totnes, South Devon.

It is a three-wheeled hard-top saloon with a bench-type seat which will take two adults and a child comfortably, or three adults with little discomfort on short journeys.

Petrol consumption is 50 miles per gallon. The price will be £280 plus tax.

The car is 5ft. high, 8ft. 9in. long, 4ft. wide and weighs 5¼ cwt.

★

FOOTNOTE: Makers of the £465 60 m.p.h. German People's Car said yesterday: "German customers can get delivery at once without affecting exports."

Nose of the car hinges down to form the door. The 2½-h.p. engine is at the rear.

This three-wheeled Workers' Playtime car is designed to enable a man to run to and from his work or take his wife and child out for an afternoon spin.

A fourth wheel could be fitted if it is desired. The car's cruising speed is 37 m.p.h. in hilly districts and higher in flat country.

Inquiries about it have come from South Africa, Australia and the U.S.

Daily Graphic 1952

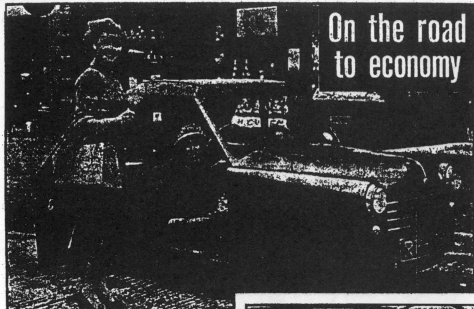

On the road to economy

The Petite three-wheeler. It seats two adults and provides 1½d.-a-mile motoring. Engine is at back.

Inside the Petite. Two-spoke steering-wheel and steering-column gear-lever give the modern look.

BRITAIN HAS ANSWER TO VOLKSWAGEN

By L. J. SMITH, Daily Graphic Reporter

A REVOLUTIONARY British car — the answer to the German volkswagen — is taking shape in a Thames-side workshop.

This light car will be a full four-seater with a 75 m.p.h. top speed. It will be able to outstrip the volkswagen in performance and economy and is designed to sell at a lower price.

Secret of the car's performance lies in the extensive use of light metals

1½d. A MILE

The 500 c.c. engine is a horizontally-opposed twin-cylinder with the capacity of an average size motor-cycle.

The designers expect the new car to do 60 miles per gallon.

Yesterday its manufacturers—A.C. Cars Ltd., of Thames Ditton, Surrey, who after 50 years of building some of the world's fastest sports cars are turning their attention to the needs of the not-so-wealthy motorist — demonstrated an interim 'economy-car.'

The new A.C. Petite economy car is a three-wheeler with a motor-cycle type two-stroke engine. It brings 1½d.-a-mile motoring-for-two to Britain.

So far this small, rear-engined car has been tested over 7,000 miles of roads of all kinds. It will cruise at 35 m.p.h. and has a comfortable maximum speed of 45 m.p.h.

Mr. William Hurlock, managing director of the A.C. Company, said:

"The Petite will cost us just over £200 to produce, but purchase tax and agents' profits will bring the price up to £398 10s.

"Next year's car will be a four-wheeler."

Taking your Pram by Train

THE farther you travel the cheaper it relatively becomes to take your pram too, as the charge made is worked out on a tapering scale. Also, it is the same amount for a return journey as for a single one, providing you yourself hold a return ticket. This would almost certainly apply on a holiday journey. Folding prams are carried free, so this concerns only larger coach-built models. Supposing you were travelling 50 miles, then the cost for a single or return journey would be 5s. 7d., but for six times that distance and more it would be just under four times that amount—20s. 11d. Perhaps this is a relief to parents who like to go a long way for their holidays! Even so, it does seem quite a lot for what may be a very necessary part of one's luggage. We have seen the charge compared with that for a bicycle; apparently the two items are worked out on separate scales, and, of course, a pram does take up quite a big space in the luggage van—more than a bicycle.

Nursery World 1953

The world comes to Britain for fine cars

thanks to Free Enterprise

● The Free Enterprise Campaign, 51 Palace Street, Westminster, London, S.W.1.
161.

News Chronicle 1953

Yes sir, she's my baby

BRITAIN GETS ITS FIRST PEOPLE'S CAR

HERE SHE IS—the new Standard "baby." Charles Fothergill, the News Chronicle Motoring Correspondent, is seen testing its loading capacity

by CHARLES FOTHERGILL

COVENTRY, Monday.

YOU have all wanted a people's car—the four- or five-seater, with a minimum of maintenance charges and cheap to run with petrol costing over 4s. per gallon.

And by you I mean the overalled factory worker as well as the wife of the wealthy industrialist who demands her own shopping car as an addition to her husband's limousine.

Like you, I had given up the idea of any British manufacturer ever getting to terms with his continental rivals in providing something so much better than a motor-cycle-sidecar outfit and yet almost as cheap to run—until last week-end.

A try-out

On Thursday Sir John Black, deputy chairman and managing director of the Standard Motor Company, telephoned me and said his company would be producing in quantity a new Standard eight - horse - power saloon car the following Tues-

The two rear seats fold up, giving extra luggage space—enough room, in fact, to carry two basket-chairs

day. Would I like to try it out?

I would and I did.

During the week-end I gave the new Standard eight "the works." I had a national motor-cycle rally to report in Yorkshire. This new Standard "baby" was hammered flat out up the Great North Road followed by all night motoring on the by-roads of the North and East Ridings of Yorkshire.

On Saturday afternoon I tried to blow up the car on Rosedale Chimney, a one-in-five trials climb off the Eskdale Road, on the one-in-three Summer Lodge climb made famous by the London to Edinburgh classic and Park Rash, the one-in-four climb near Kettlewell. In the words of the friend who accompanied me—"There was no trouble at all."

45 m.p.h.

The O.H.V. engine is extremely lively. In the 500 miles covered in the week-end test I had no difficulty in putting 45 miles in the hour.

The family man, looking for a people's car, probably could not care less about hill climbs and high average speeds. What does he get?

It is a good-looking car, with smooth lines, easy to keep clean and polished. It is austere in some respects and very light—but one can buy wheel discs and other extras if so desired.

The driving position is ideal. The car sits sturdily on the road and corners like many a sports model. Its handling at speed is extraordinary for a small car.

The arrangement in the rear seats is original. The two single seats can be folded up, providing luggage space of exceptional size. To test the car I carried two large basket chairs in the back. Two children could even sleep there.

At set out speeds my petrol consumption worked out at 38 miles per gallon. Over a special test at an average speed of 30 miles per hour I got a petrol consumption of 49.5 m.p.g.

With all this performance and economy we are getting very near to the people's car. The man who demands a people's car likes to tinker with the engine. There can hardly be a more accessible engine unit than the new Standard—the battery, carburettor, sparking plugs and all the bits and pieces can be dealt with without burnt or torn fingers.

The price? £481 including purchase tax, £36 dearer than Britain's cheapest car, the 8h.p. Ford Anglia, but still the cheapest four-cylinder, four-speed, four-seater, four-door car in the world.

Before the end of the year Standards will be producing 1,000 of the new eight a week. Early next year this will be speeded up to 2,000 a week—60 per cent. for export.

The three transport entries in the 1953 London to New Zealand air race lined up on the tarmac at London Airport.

Be first with the last word!

The

Hillman
Californian

Style-setter
for the future...
can be yours

Looked at, or looked out of, the view is superb. Its beautiful
lines and dual-colour scheme are only the beginning. Built into this
exciting car are all the qualities that have made Hillman famous
throughout the world . . . performance, safety, and comfort. Yes, it's the last
word in looks . . . the last word, too, in big-car luxury at light-car cost.

£510 plus Purchase Tax

THE PERFECT
ALL-THE-YEAR-ROUND CAR

The pillarless side-windows all slide out of sight for
fresh-air touring and seal snugly into hard-top for winter
car comfort. Note the all-round unobstructed view.
White wall tyres, over-riders and chromium wingshields,
optional extras.

HILLMAN CALIFORNIAN
A PRODUCT OF THE ROOTES GROUP

Consult your Hillman distributor or dealer today!

HILLMAN MOTOR CAR CO. LTD. COVENTRY   LONDON SHOWROOM AND EXPORT DIVISION: ROOTES LTD. DEVONSHIRE HOUSE PICCADILLY

Look out for space visitors, warns rector

'IT IS NOTHING TO SMILE AT'

By Daily Mail Reporter

THE Rev. Ronald Cartmel, who watches stars from his rectory, is warning his 9,000 parishioners to watch for visitors from Outer Space. Further, to help his parishioners prepare for any such visitors, he is recommending them to read two books on flying saucers.

"Don't smile," writes Mr. Cartmel in his Aldridge, Staffordshire, parish magazine. "It is nothing to smile at.

"Although thousands of sane, ordinary folk have seen them we are told they are mirages and spots in front of the eyes."

Mr. Cartmel, who is 54, believes that people from another planet are watching us from flying saucers. They may well land here within 50 years, he said yesterday.

Several reports

In his magazine he accuses the authorities of concealing information about Outer Space visitors. He adds: "Experts can tell us nothing about life on other worlds : ... But the much despised Bible has always spoken of principalities and powers in the Heavenlies."

Mr. Cartmel is a Fellow of the Royal Astronomical Society. He is building a 9in. lens telescope to study reports of atomic explosions on Mars and flashing lights on the moon.

He said yesterday : "If a space craft landed here I would, as Rector of Aldridge, welcome the visitors to our world. They seem friendly enough."

Daily Mail 1954

Illustrated London News
1953

EVENTS ABROAD: THE MACLEAN MYSTERY

(LEFT.) THE CENTRAL FIGURE IN A MYSTERY: MRS. MELINDA MACLEAN, WIFE OF A MISSING DIPLOMAT, WHO DISAPPEARED FROM GENEVA WITH HER FAMILY RECENTLY.

Mrs. Melinda Maclean, wife of Donald Maclean who with Guy Burgess disappeared on the Continent in 1951 and has never been traced, left Geneva on September 11 with her three children to spend a week-end in the Montreux area and did not return. It is believed that Mrs. Maclean went by train to Vienna and a ticket inspector remembers seeing a woman with three children in the train travelling from Zurich to Buchs, on the Austrian frontier, on the night of September 11-12.

Cheap off-peak fares 'won't pay'

A SCHEME for cheaper bus fares in London at "off peak" hours was dropped because it was thought it would not pay.

This was revealed by Sir Reginald Wilson, financial chief of the British Transport Commission, when he resumed his evidence before the Transport Tribunal in London yesterday.

The Commission is applying to increase London rail and bus fares by £6,000,000 and certain main line fares outside the area by £800,000.

An off-peak fares concession, said Sir Reginald, might increase off-peak traffic, but not enough to make up for losses on the services generally.

All the signs were that the Commission would have a " very small surplus " for 1952, he said, but added—

" I urge that it should be a cardinal point of financial policy to see that we do not slip back into the red in 1953, however difficult conditions may be."

The Tribunal goes on today.

Daily Herald
1953

News Chronicle
1953

Twice he smashes the record

MRS. D: LET'S DANCE

By COMER CLARKE

WELL done, Duke! Thumbs up, Britain! For today we secure supremacy in the air and wrest from America the proud title to the fastest level flight on earth.

Yesterday afternoon Squadron-Leader Neville Duke screamed his scarlet Hawker Hunter swept-wing jet over three kilometres of Sussex beaches at 12 miles a minute to capture the world air speed record.

Then, last night, he took his plane up again—and beat his own record. Shortly before midnight the Royal Aero Club announced his official speeds : average over the four runs, 727.6 : maximum 738.8 m.p.h.

This bettered by a big margin not only the existing 698 m.p.h. record set up by Captain James Nash in a U.S. Sabre, but also the 715 m.p.h claim (not yet confirmed) of another American, Colonel Barnes.

Daily Herald 1954

Now it goes even higher

By GILBERT CARTER

THE world's most unusual aircraft, Britain's " Flying Bedstead," has beaten its original test height record by 15ft. In subsequent tests the " Bedstead " has reached 25ft. with ease.

And all that this fabulous machine consists of is two powerful jet engines lashed together by tubular steel with a platform for the pilot on top.

On its first free flight at Hucknall, Notts, in August, the Rolls Royce men who invented it saw it remain airborne for 10 minutes.

At that time its existence was a secret, but early this month the Supply Minister, Mr. Duncan Sandys, told the world.

The " Bedstead " is kept aloft by the downward thrust of the jet blast.

Daily Herald
1953

£12 will fly you to U.S.

BRITAIN will have a 600-m.p.h., 100-seat, transatlantic jet passenger plane in regular service by 1958.

A model of the machine, to be called the " Atlantic," was shown in London yesterday by its makers, the A. V. Roe company.

The " Atlantic " is still on the drawing-board. But the machine from which it is descended, the Avro " Vulcan " bomber, is already well into the production stage for the R.A.F.

When the " Atlantic " is in service it will increase Britain's already long lead in air transport.

It will be able to fly non-stop from London to New York and then back again in a day. Air fares will be about a penny a mile —roughly £12 for the single trip.

Sir Roy Dobson, head of A. V. Roe, who gave these details of the plane, said deliveries could be promised by 1958 if reasonable production orders were placed.

B O A O chairman, Sir Miles Thomas, said the machine would be considered with others now being developed.

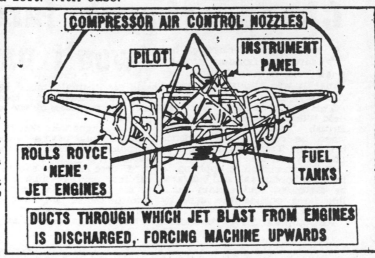

A MAKER OF MAPS

News Chronicle
1954

LONDONERS travelling along Gray's Inn Road in the early days of December may have seen a slender, distinguished-looking woman sketching one of the tall buildings near the Holborn end of the road. The result of her labours is seen in the enchanting little sketch on the right—her impression, as an artist, of the new premises of her map-making business.

Mrs. Pearsall, F.R.G.S.—seen with some of her draughtsmen in the photograph below—is the only woman map-maker in the British Isles or, for that matter, in the United States of America, where she has a controlling interest in a similar undertaking. Her London business, in which she is director, instructor and confidante of her staff, produces maps of all kinds, including the well-known *Geographers' Atlas of Greater London*, and the recently published smaller volume, *Geographers' Atlas of Central London*.

Map-makers are made, not born, and Mrs. Pearsall personally instructs her draughtsmen and supervises their work—a dying craft, she says sadly, attracting too few young artists.

A FIVE years' apprenticeship has to be fitted in with each young man's National Service, in which he asks to be given ordnance survey work. One member of Mrs. Pearsall's staff, posted to Crete and engaged on field work there, reported that his work has been made useless by the recent earthquake which altered the contours of the island. It is a significant comment on the care which is devoted to map-making that on his return he was required by Mrs. Pearsall to undertake two hours' practice a day to polish up his lettering, neglected during his service in the Army.

In setting out to make entirely new maps, instead of new issues based on old plates, Mrs. Pearsall embarked on a hazardous venture which might as easily have led to failure and heavy loss as to the success which they proved to be. One new map can take as long as four years to complete; details must be checked and re-checked, and new building developments included.

CUTTY SARK GOES TO HER LAST BERTH

By Vernon Brown

THE ghosts of Captain Dick Woodget, who drove the Cutty Sark 360 miles in a day, and of "Old White Hat" Willis, for whom the Cutty Sark was built, must have been aboard her yesterday as the most famous of all sailing ships set out on her last voyage.

The teak-built windjammer of 963 tons, which used to race home with cargoes from Australia and the Far East, left the East India Docks to be towed by tugs to a permanent dry dock near the Royal Naval College at Greenwich.

He remembered

One man aboard remembered her past. He was 83-year-old Captain C. E Irving, now living in Westminster, who joined the Cutty Sark as an apprentice under Captain Woodget in 1885 at the age of 13

He looked up, almost expecting to see the two-acre spread of sail once carried by the ship. "We used to load 921 tons of tea then," he told me, "and how we strove to get it to London. Cutty Sark was the wettest ship in the world, and when we were rounding Cape Horn we often had to go without hot food for three days because the galley was under water."

The Lady 1954

Reward for good luck

Almost two years ago, when one of them was fined for a motoring offence, 16 lorry drivers at West Wylam Colliery, Northumberland, opened a shilling-a-week fund from which they could draw if they got into trouble with the law.

None did, so the drivers decided to devote the money instead to sickness and injury.

There wasn't any. So, with more than £60 saved, the drivers are throwing a party for 56 at Hexham, Northumberland Among the guests will be Coal Board officials

Cruiser's farewell

Ships' sirens and Royal Marine buglers sounded a final salute to the 25-year-old cruiser H.M.S. Devonshire as she left Devonport yesterday. She is to be broken up.

News Chronicle 1954

Parliament Approves The New Highway Code

HOPE THAT COPIES WILL BE ON SALE TO PUBLIC NEXT FEBRUARY

THE new Highway Code has now received the approval of both Houses of Parliament. It was approved by the House of Commons on November 8, while just as we were going to press came the news that the House of Lords had given its approval on November 24. The Code will have a first edition of 10 million and it is hoped that copies will be on sale in February.

When the question was considered by the House of Commons, the Minister of Transport (Mr. John Boyd-Carpenter) said that the Government Committee on Road Safety had by a majority recommended an alteration in the legal status of the Code, with a view to giving certain of its precepts a higher legal status. That recommendation has not been accepted by the Government and the proposal before the House was that it should be approved on the same legal basis as were its three predecessors.

The Minister added "It is proposed subject to Parliament to print about 10 million copies, at any rate of the first issue. Of those, about 500,000 will be required for the holders of provisional driving licences. It is proposed to issue a copy to each driver when he applies for the renewal of his driving licence—that is a holder's ordinary licence—and that will absorb in all about six million copies."

"One million will be distributed to the older children in the schools. About two million will be on sale to the general public at the price of 1d. and the balance will go to the Armed Forces, the Police, the Royal Society for the Prevention of Accidents, road safety committees and other official and semi-official bodies, where it has its obvious use by way of persuasion and advice."

He summed up the Code by saying that for "vague exhortation" there had been substituted "crisp advice."

Safety News 1954

ODIHAM PILOT'S DEATH

INQUEST ADJOURNED

ONE of eighteen Hawker Hunters taking part in the fly-past at the Royal Aircraft Establishment at Farnborough, failed to make height, and crashed and broke-up in Chinnocks Wood, Crookham, on July 7. The incident was seen from the R.A.E. display which was attended by Princess Margaret.

The pilot, Flying-Officer Charles George Price, a member of 247 Squadron, R.A.F. Odiham, had baled out, but was found in the ejector seat and died on the way to hospital. F/O. Price was 20 years of age and his home was at Maidenhead.

Hants and Berks Gazette 1955

ROAD SIGNS WITH PUNCH ARE PLANNED

This new sign means "Children playing."

DAILY MIRROR MOTORING CORRESPONDENT

EYE-CATCHING, "Continental-style" road signs are planned for Britain by the Transport Minister. The use of the torch symbol on "School" and "Children" signs will be scrapped. Instead two pictures will be used.

ONE — for "School" — shows children with satchels walking into a road. The OTHER—for "Children"—shows children playing with a ball.

The changes cannot come into force until Parliament has approved them.

The Minister, Mr. John Boyd-Carpenter, is sending illustrations of the signs to police and road organisations. They are given until November 30 to comment.

Other proposed signs:
CROSS ROADS: Showing the road lay-out.
BEND: Showing the sharpness and direction of the bend.

MAJOR ROAD AHEAD: To be placed at "T" junctions. It shows a narrow, upright line joining a wide horizontal line.

Also planned:

A new system of CARRIAGEWAY markings.

STOP LINES used with "Halt" signs to be increased in width from 5in. to 8in.-10in.

Wider use of REFLECTORS on signs to aid visibility at night.

● An R.A.C. spokesman said: "We welcome the fact that the new signs are simpler."

● An A.A. official said: "The pictorial type of sign has undoubted advantages."

The PRESENT sign for a school—a torch—is pictured at top. Below it is the proposed NEW, more dramatic sign. Two children wearing satchels are walking into a road. This is a Continental-style "picture" sign.

Daily Mirror 1955

Britain's first day-trip across the Atlantic: Pilot Captain J.W. Hackett and navigator P. Moneypenny are seen here with their wives at London Airport after completing a round trip to New York in 14 hours and 21 minutes in August 1955.

SUPERSONIC INTERCEPTER

Twin-Sapphire English Electric P.1 Flies at Boscombe Down

Flight
1954

DESIGNED to be easily capable of supersonic speed in level flight, the English Electric P.1 single-seat intercepter fighter prototype WG760, powered with two Armstrong Siddeley Sapphire turbojets, made its first flight at the Aeroplane and Armament Experimental Establishment, Boscombe Down, on August 4th. The pilot was W/C. R. P. Beamont, D.S.O., O.B.E., D.F.C., who reported that the flight had been "remarkably pleasant and free from incident." He is also on record as having said, "It's a peach. Many people have thought that the super-sonic design might make the fighter hard to handle at low speeds. In fact, it handled beautifully and gave no trouble at all."

Getting there sooner

IF you cannot keep a horse—and who can, nowadays?—there can be no better way of travelling through the countryside than on a motor-cycle.

Every week more and more people are discovering the mental and physical stimulation of motor-cycling.

These handy machines can nip through heavy traffic on our badly-congested roads, and are simple to park. The greatly-improved reliability and weather protection of the modern product now draw customers from a far wider field.

In these credit-squeeze days motor-cycles have the advantage over cars in lower original cost and, of course, cheapness of maintenance. Most owners can carry out minor repairs themselves, and two-wheelers can be pushed into a small shed if you haven't a garage. When the gay bachelor finally lands a wife and family, he can add a "chair" and still enjoy cheap travel.

News Chronicle 1956

A THRILL for engine spotters the Royal Scot makes its first visit to Banbury.

All this week this powerful 4-6-2, Pacific type Royal Scot engine, No. 46237 "City of Bristol" has been calling at Banbury Station at 10.40 a.m. while hauling the 9.10 a.m. Paddington Birkenhead train.

Instead of its usual daily dash from London to Perth the engine is being used experimentally on special inter-city trials to determine the best type for the route.

Banbury Guardian 1955

we're saving ALL WAYS with the unbeatable Bantam

Save time, save fares. Save on initial costs and on running costs, too. No wonder more people ride the B.S.A. Bantam than ride any other motorcycle anywhere.

✳ Up to 140 miles on a gallon of petrol, up to 2,500 miles on a gallon of oil.

✳ Road Tax only 17/6 a year.

✳ Low insurance rates.

✳ Speeds up to 50 m.p.h.

✳ Weight only 180 lbs. for ease of handling.

(above figures for 125 c.c. model)

Model D1 125 c.c.
£94.4.10 (including tax)
Model D3 150 c.c.
£104.3.3 (including tax)

BSA
The most popular Motor Cycle in the World.

RAIL "THIRD CLASS" ABOLISHED

FIRST AND SECOND ONLY

Third class travel was abolished by British Railways yesterday, and all passengers will now be either " first " or " second."

This action has been taken to conform to Continental practice, and the change is simply on tickets and at booking offices. Prices and accommodation remain the same, and carriages will have the figure three painted out as they go in for maintenance and repair.

In the early days of railway travel the term " third class " was synonymous with discomfort and inconvenience, the " poorer classes " travelling in open trucks with hard wooden seats. In 1875 one of the railway companies abolished " second class," and called it " third," and the other companies gradually improved the standard of comfort of their own third class. Finally only the Continental boat trains to and from the United Kingdom ports gave second class facilities to enable through bookings to be made with Continental railways, although north-east London suburban services retained the class until a few years before the last war.

The Times 1956

'ATOMIC' ELECTRICITY NOW IN THE GRID

The Queen Opens First Nuclear Power Station

The Queen spent an hour and a half learning something of the secrets of Britain's first atomic power station when she inaugurated the £16,500,000 Calder Hall plant, West Cumberland, yesterday. At the opening ceremony she pulled a lever which switched electric power generated from nuclear energy into the national grid of the Central Electricity Authority.

The Queen said: "To-day, as power from Calder Hall begins to flow into the national grid, all of us here know that we are present at the making of history.

"For many years now we have been aware that atomic scientists, by a series of brilliant discoveries, have brought us to the threshold of a new age. We have also known that on that threshold mankind has reached a point of crisis.

"To-day we are in a sense seeing a solution of that crisis as this new power, which has proved itself to be such a terrifying weapon of destruction, is harnessed for the first time for the common good of our community.

"As new fields open before us, we become conscious that a grave responsibility is placed upon all of us to see that man adds as much to his stature by the application of this new power as he has by its discovery."

Two More Stations Next Year

Mr. R. A. Butler, the Lord Privy Seal, said it might be that soon after 1965 every new power station built would be atomic powered. By 1975 the total output of atomic power would certainly be more—and might possibly be double—the total electricity output of all the power stations supplying our needs to-day

Birmingham Post 1956

Windermere Treble For "NARNIE"

A feature of the Windermere Motor Boat Racing Club's meeting on Saturday, July 18. was the success of Major H. Coop, who piloted his speedboat. "Narnie" to victory in all three races to win Sir Lindsay Parkinson's Cup, the Bersey Cup and Sir Lindsay Parkinson's Coronation Cup

Westmorland Gazette 1959

And The Beer Flowed—Down The Drains

ONE signature on a piece of paper headed "Navy, Army and Air Force Institutes" has sent the contents of 43,200 cans of beer flowing down the drains of the Central Depot, Eastern Road, Portsmouth.

Workmen winced as a steamroller crushed the cans, and the brown beer spurted on to the dusty road. Nearby stood a Customs and Excise official, seeing no-one sneaked off with a can.

This was the scene that greeted a reporter yesterday. Today the operation finished.

The history of the ill-fated beer started when it was loaded into H.M.S. Warrior, for a round-trip to the Christmas Islands in the South Pacific — the scene of Britain's recent atomic tests.

FOR SIX MONTHS

On the cans, in small lettering, was a recommendation that the beer should not be left undrunk for more than six months.

H.M.S. Warrior was out of port for more than six months.

So the NAAFI decided that the beer should be destroyed. Ideas were mooted as to how this should be done. One was that the whole lot should be thrown overboard.

But economy prevailed, and it was decided to crush them, so the cardboard cartons and the can could be sold.

Reckoning on a shilling a can, the NAAFI have destroyed £2,160 of beer.

Said a NAAFI spokesman: "We might get some duty back on the beer. We thought it was best to destroy the beer having regard to its stay in Warrior, and that the ship has been in the neighbourhood of an atomic explosion."

Portsmouth Evening News 1957

JAGUAR WINS AGAIN AT LE MANS

British Cars Overwhelm Foreign Opposition

From Our Motoring Correspondent

LE MANS, Sunday Night

A 3½-litre British Jaguar entered by the Ecurie Ecosse won the 24-hour Le Mans endurance race to-day, over-whelming all the foreign opposition. Driven by N. Sanderson, of Scotland, and R. Flockhart, of Wolverhampton, it ran for 24 hours at an average speed of 104.48 m.p.h. over a distance of 2,507.25 miles.

One of the three works Jaguars—that driven by Mike Hawthorn, who shared the car with I. Bueb—had the fastest lap at 116 m.p.h. Hawthorn lost 1½ hours shortly after the beginning of the race because of a leak in the car's fuel system.

An Aston Martin driven by Stirling Moss and Peter Collins came second in the general classification and also won the class for cars up to 3,000 c.c. This works-entered car was the main rival to the Jaguar throughout the race.

Lotus Successful

The class for cars up to 1,000 c.c. was won by a British Lotus with a Coventry Climax engine, driven by Bicknell and Jopp. Second in this class was a Cooper, also with a Coventry Climax engine, driven by Hugus and Bentley.

This British victory, popular though it is in France, may mean an alteration to the Le Mans race next year. British cars now dominate the race to such an extent that the organisers fear the thrill of competition has been destroyed.

German cars were completely overshadowed this year and the Italians admitted before the race that they could not hope to catch the British cars. So it was a race between Jaguars and Aston Martins.

Birmingham Post 1956

'Design Cars for Safety Now'

Mr. R. Graham Page, M.P., chairman of the Pedestrians' Association for Road Safety, told the association's autumn meeting in London last night that at this time of the Motor Show the industry should concentrate on greater safety.

He said: "I would say you have reached something like a state of perfection in comfort, convenience, handling and speed; and so switch your minds to safety and refuse to submit to the proposition that the toll of death on the roads is an inevitable adjunct to the pleasure and convenience of motoring."

Birmingham Post 1956

So Simple, So Helpful.

A short time ago a friend told me that his young daughter was a very bad traveller; she was always sick if they travelled any distance by car. He consulted a doctor about the matter and was told that this was quite common among young people. The doctor explained the sickness was probably caused by the presence of static electricity in the bodywork of the car. My friend was advised to make his daughter sit upon a piece of newspaper the next time she had to travel—the newspaper would act as an insulator. She has done this ever since, and to his amazement it has worked wonderfully well. Other readers who are bad travellers may find this helpful, too.

Mrs E. M. K., Hamilton, has won a dress length.

My Weekly 1956

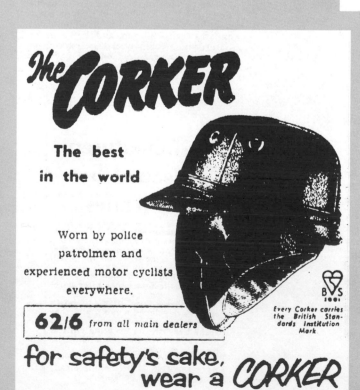

The CORKER

The best in the world

Worn by police patrolmen and experienced motor cyclists everywhere.

62/6 *from all main dealers*

Every Corker carries the British Standards Institution Mark

for safety's sake, wear a CORKER

NEW FROM LEEDS: The 197 c.c. Villiers-engined Scootacar with plastic saloon body seating two in tandem. Steering is by handlebar, but car-type pedals are used. Its compact dimensions enable it to fit into the most improbable of spaces.

Motoring News 1958

ONE PINT PLEASE

Airport Post 1957

I THOUGHT, while I was road testing the Austin A 35 that there was only one fair description that I could write. I would simply extract all the flattering adjectives from the glossy brochure and reprint them with a few compliments of my own thrown in.

But I find that in the most vital matter of petrol consumption I cannot, in the interests of accuracy quote the official literature.

BMC claim that, under normal driving conditions, the A 35 will do 53.7 miles to the gallon. But under fairly tough conditions, three heavy passengers up Ducks Hill and Rickmansworth-road for example—the car I had averaged over 56 m.p.g.

With a specially fitted one pint test tank I averaged 40 m.p.h. and with no soft pedalling, unnecessary gear changes and free-wheeling, and the bounding baby took me seven miles 200 yards. I have never been a small car enthusiast, and I would not like to have to travel too far in the back of this one, but for the driver and front seat passenger there is comfort and room aplenty.

I was convinced that here was the slickest little car that ever set wheels on the road. For the man of modest means, for the solo driver, for the small family, for the about town motorist this is just the job.

In the compact little buggy one finds a top speed of about 70 m.p.h., with crisp acceleration, smooth riding, easy handling to match. The visibility is splendid and the controls are sensibly situated with central controls and a deep, full width parcel shelf.

Yes sir—that's my baby. Despite the £181 7s. purchase tax that is added to the cost of £360.

Mr. Jack Inwards fills the special one pint test tank fitted above the Austin A 35 dashboard for my road test. After the test I could feign no surprise that Inwards Garages, the Ruislip Main Austin Distributors, have a waiting list for these bonny babies.

Star Quest

STARS, in our particular workaday world, tend to be people with agents, and success stories, and temperaments, and talents, and a certain unpredictability that can make them either tiresome or fascinating. But when we talked to Patrick Moore the other day about this month's stars, we found ourselves in a very different world. 'People tend to think,' he told us, ' that astronomy is a difficult, expensive, and unrewarding subject that has become the prerogative of old men with long white beards. It is in fact none of these things, and anyone can find interest and excitement in the night sky, if he knows what to look for.'

This is to be the theme of his new series which begins on Wednesday, and which will introduce each month the highlights of the current astronomical news.

Radio Times 1957

Autocar 1958

Parking by Meter

YESTERDAY, at a formal ceremony in Grosvenor Square, the first parking meters came into operation in the north-west area of Mayfair, London. The area involved is that bounded by Park Lane, Oxford Street, New Bond Street, Grosvenor Street, the south side of Grosvenor Square, and Upper Grosvenor Street. It contains parking places for approximately 80 vehicles.

As already stated, the charges are 6d for an hour, or 1s for two hours, with a ten shillings fee for staying up to two hours at a run-out meter. After that time the motorist is liable to prosecution.

Several new particulars have been released by the authorities, of which the most important is the rule that a motorist must pay the full charge even though time remains unexpired on the meter's indicator. However, it is difficult to see how —unless there happens to be a parking attendant on the spot—this rule can be enforced.

It will not be permissible to extend parking time after two hours simply by inserting another 6d or shilling in the slot; the car must be moved to another bay. On leaving one particular parking bay the motorist may not return to it until one hour has elapsed, though he may, of course, park immediately at any other bay. This is another rule for which enforcement will depend on the vigilance and number of attendants placed in charge of the parking zone.

Cars must be parked facing in the direction of the traffic flow, and must be wholly within the bay, which is marked by white lines on the road. Vehicles may stop without charge anywhere in the zone to take up or set down passengers, and for loading and unloading they may stop free of charge for up to 20 minutes, or longer if authorized by a police constable. If a parking meter is marked "out of order" parking is permitted in its bay without charge until two hours after it has been repaired.

The parking meter scheme is in operation from 8.30 a.m./to 6.30 p.m. on Mondays to Fridays (excluding bank holidays), and between 8.30 a.m. and 1.30 p.m. on Saturdays. As on weekdays, parking on Saturdays is permitted only at bays, but no payment is required.

Lifeboatmen rescued by comrades

THE crew of seven of a Padstow, Cornwall, lifeboat were rescued by their comrades in another lifeboat from a lee shore off the North Cornwall coast in to-day's gale.

They had been out all night searching in heavy seas after flares had been reported.

This morning the lifeboat's engines developed a fault, and they were only a mile off the treacherous rocks beneath the towering cliffs at Boscastle when the second lifeboat took them in tow.

This afternoon the two lifeboats were reported to be making steady progress back to Padstow.

Belfast Telegraph 1958

Longer talk could have saved young husband's life

By B.N. Staff Reporters

A Catford woman is a widow today because she did not keep her husband talking on the telephone for a few more minutes. Mr. Derek Rose of 89, Ardgowan-road—the proud owner of a Morris Minor car—had, because of the bad weather, gone to his job as a tailor's buyer in the Strand by train on the Day of Disaster, December 4.

Mrs. Jean Rose told me shortly after the Lewisham train crash that she had spoken to her husband on the telephone a few moments before he caught the train from Charing Cross.

"If I had talked to him just a few moments longer he might have missed the train," she said.

The most dreadful thought in Mrs. Rose's mind is that they talked only long enough for Mr. Rose to dash from the telephone to catch the train with seconds to spare. "He got into the last carriage," she sobbed. "Normally, he gets in the train at the front end."

Lewisham Borough News 1957

Westmorland Gazette 1959

Air-cushion Transportation

Aeroplane 1959

AS all the World knows, the Cockerell Hovercraft, built for Hovercraft Development, Ltd., a subsidiary of the National Research Development Corporation, has successfully levitated itself and achieved translational movement. It has not "flown" and never will. Neither is it saucer-shaped. But to the B.B.C. and most of Fleet Street it is "Britain's first flying saucer."

What a lot of illusions are going to be shattered when it is found that the "flying saucer" cannot lift itself more than a few feet above the ground and is quite incapable of making a steep or vertical climb to great heights. And its designer never intended that it should.

On June 11, after a successful and convincing demonstration over concrete, the craft was taken to the water and showed its ability to move at low speeds under full control. In these early stages, clearly an important problem is that of the large curtain of spray thrown up by the jets.

The whole object of the invention is to produce an

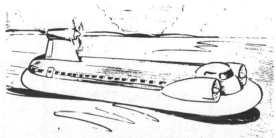

A projected 100-ton 300-passenger ferry.

amphibious vehicle which, having neither the water resistance of a hull nor the frictional resistance of wheels, shall be able to achieve economically very high speeds. The question of lift either by wings or propellers, fans or rotors, does not arise.

MOTORWAY TRAFFIC SIGNS

When the Prime Minister opened the Preston by-pass motorway motorists had their first view of the traffic signs for motorways which are to be tested on this road before being approved or modified for use on the longer motorways now under construction. The signs are designed for traffic travelling at speeds of up to 70 miles per hour and are large enough to be seen and read from a distance of not less than 600 ft. They also differ from signs on existing roads in many other ways. Lower case letters, i.e., small letters, are used instead of capitals, but these letters are 12 ins. high and stand out in white against a blue background. For night use all signs will either be lighted, where practical, or treated with reflective material.

The system of signposting is based on the interim report of the Advisory Committee on Traffic Signs for Motorways which was set up by the Minister of Transport and Civil Aviation, Mr. Harold Watkinson, under the chairmanship of Sir Colin Anderson a year ago. All the Committee's proposals are provisional. Final recommendations will not be made until experience has been gained.

Roads and Road Construction **1959**

An Inquest

After recording in our last issue that the Preston By-pass Motorway had been opened by the Prime Minister on December 5 last year, it is disappointing to have to record that on January 20 it was found that frost damage had affected the carriageway surface and that it was considered necessary to close the road while repairs were being carried out. We publish elsewhere in this issue the technical report presented to Parliament by the Minister of Transport and Civil Aviation, which is similar to that presented to the Lancashire County Council, who acted as agents for the Ministry in the design and building of this by-pass. We also publish much of the cross-examination of Mr. Watkinson in the House of Commons, from which it will be seen that the majority of the criticism has come from members of the Opposition, who are naturally only too pleased to have an opportunity of criticising the Government. Much of the criticism which also appeared in the national Press was also similarly motivated. We hope that this will explain to our readers, particularly those overseas, why so much fuss appears to have been made.

Roads and Road Construction 1959

Rural Transport (Mandate 1956)

Reports continue to come in of worsening conditions: further closures of branch lines and further cuts in bus services. Some of you may have seen the programme in Woman's Hour Television, *Come and Join Us* on September 1, 1958, which was introduced by our Chairman, Lady Dyer, and in which Women's Institute members fired off questions about bus services to a team of experts. It was clear from that programme how keenly our members felt about this question and how dissatisfied they were with the answers.

After correspondence with the Central Transport Consultative Committee, the N.F.W.I. Committee wrote to the Minister of Transport in April to urge that he should hold an enquiry. Since then he announced his intention to set up a small Committee "to enquire into trends in rural bus services". The Budget concession to bus operators will help a little. It amounts to a two-thirds reduction in the licence fee, subject to a minimum fee of £12 per annum.

Home and Country **1959**

FARES GO UP IN OCTOBER

By GORDON JEFFERY

RAILWAY fares and London Transport bus and Underground fares are to go up, it was announced yesterday.

The Transport Tribunal—the body which considers fare increase applications—said it had given permission to the British Transport Commission to raise fares from August 1.

BUT a Commission spokesman said that they would put off most of the increases until October " to save holidaymakers additional travelling expenses this year."

The Commission spokesman emphasised that the new rates approved by the Tribunal were MAXIMUM rates.

He said: " This does not mean the Commission will automatically impose them.

" It may well be that they will raise fares only by perhaps half the permissible amount."

How Much?

On RAIL fares the Tribunal approved new maximum charges of 3d. a mile second class (present maximum—charge is 2d.) and 4½d. a mile first class (3d.).

★ Examples of the increase authorised for second-class day return fares—present charges are not necessarily the maximum permitted—are :

Victoria-Sutton: New maximum, 4s. 6d. (present charge 4s. 2d.);

Euston-Watford: 5s. 10d. (5s. 4d.);

London Bridge-Bexley: 4s. 6d. (3s. 10d.);

★ Examples of the new maximum permissible rates for MONTHLY season tickets are : Ten miles:

Dearer by bus and rail

£3 0s. 6d. (present charge £2 13s.);

Twenty miles: £4 15s. 6d. (£4 3s.);

Fifty miles: £8 11s. 9d. (£6 16s. 9d.).

These new maximum rates will also apply to London Transport Underground season tickets.

On day-to-day travel by BUS AND UNDERGROUND, the present 3d., 4d. and 5d. fares for short distances will remain unchanged.

For longer distances fares will be allowed to go up by 1d. a mile up to twelve miles and by about 2d. a mile for more than twelve miles.

'One Only'

A London Transport spokesman said last night that the 6d. bus and Underground fare would go up to 7d. ON AUGUST 23.

" This is the only increase which will be made at this time." he added.

● The Tribunal confirmed its previous decision to allow cheap early morning train and bus fares to be abolished by the end of next year and to allow these fares to go up meanwhile.

Daily Mirror 1959

Barnet Press and News 1959

Rolls V-eight is revealed at last

IT may sound incredible, but the 1960 Rolls-Royces and Bentleys will be smoother and more discreet than ever. They will also be more powerful, thanks to the development of a new aluminium eight-cylinder 6,230 c.c. engine.

Motoring News 1959

1960 MODELS

B.M.C. BABY

Austin Seven and Morris Mini-Minor

versions with 848 c.c. four-cylinder, transverse engine

four-speed gear box, front-wheel drive,

and rubber suspension

WHEN Sir William Morris, as he then was, introduced the £100 open two-seater Morris in 1931 it was a sensation. Now the British Motor Corporation introduces a new model into its range which, on basic price, is relatively as cheap, but there are many important differences. The early Morris was an economy version of an existing car, cut down in price and specification in an effort to stimulate sales during a world-wide depression; it had little technical merit. These new 850 models, available as either an Austin Seven or a Morris Mini-Minor (each in standard and de luxe forms), are ample four-seaters of outstanding technical ingenuity and designed to compete in world markets at a time when sales are still climbing— although becoming increasingly competitive. They represent a noteworthy break-through in small-car design by the B.M.C. team of engineers led by Alec Issigonis.

Autocar 1959

RECORD ENTRIES

for

SUFFOLK HUNT

POINT-TO-POINT

at

MOULTON

TO-DAY (SATURDAY)

FIRST RACE: 1.30 p.m.

Seven Races, five of which have 20 entries each.

BE SURE TO COME.

'Red Rory' does it by motorcycle, helicopter and jet —then back in an hour

Evening Standard Reporter

Captain Roderick "Red Rory" Walker, of the Special Air Service, is the fastest so far in the Bleriot 50th anniversary race.

He reached the Arc de Triomphe, Paris, today 57min. 48sec. after leaving Marble Arch, London, 214 miles away.

After two glasses of wine in a Champs Elysees cafe the 28-year-old captain returned to Marble Arch in 1hr. 15sec.

8 a.m. start

On both trips he used motorcycles, helicopters and a jet aircraft.

Evening Standard 1959

1960 ★ 1970

Fears Over Town's Big Increase In Traffic By M1

THE STEADY INCREASE in the number of vehicles passing through the centre of Lutterworth, which has caused the parish council concern, was on Tuesday the subject of a long discussion at the South Leicestershire Accident Prevention committee meeting at Lutterworth.

It is feared that during the summer traffic will be even heavier and the situation in the town centre may become chaotic.

One of the chief reasons for the larger number of vehicles passing through the town was stated to be the M1, and the meeting felt that more rapid progress should be achieved in carrying out improvements to The Narrows and widening this entrance to High Street.

The area surveyor pointed out that the main Leicester Road had been reconstructed for the greater part of its length north of Lutterworth and that it was as wide as one lane of the M1.

One suggestion was that there should be signs at the approach to the town's centre, but the meeting felt that it was highly improbable that the Ministry would give approval, and one comment was that there were already too many signs in the locality.

The Committee were told that a Lutterworth parish council application for a halt sign at the top of Bank Street had been submitted to the Ministry of Transport and was receiving police support.

The committee were also told of the danger at the Dunton Bassett cross roads on the main Leicester road near Lutterworth, and a letter is to be sent to the County Council suggesting a staggered approach to the main road.

Peatling Magna Parish Council drew the Committee's attention to the danger in the village caused by parked vehicles near a blind double bend in the road and also to the need for speed restrictions.

The committee felt there was little hope in achieving success with an application for restriction signs. Similar applications had been turned down by the Ministry on Class A roads and consequently there seemed little hope where Class C roads were concerned.

Leicester Advertiser **1960**

MISSING GEESE

SIR. On Sunday, June 19, my flock of 13 Canada geese, accompanied by four greylags, flew off from their home here and have not been heard of since. Some of these geese have been with me for about ten years and the youngest are three of last year's breeding. Most carry coloured chicken rings, yellow and green. I should be grateful for any information your readers may have as to the birds' whereabouts. Although they have often been absent for a few hours this is a different matter and I am at a loss to account for their sudden decision to leave. They were last seen flying north-west on the London side of Sevenoaks.—GRAHAM L. REID, *Ringle Oast, Sandhurst, Hawkhurst, Kent.*

Country Life **1960**

Best selling small saloon, the Ford Anglia, firmly established after a year's production. It was the first small Ford to have an o.h.v. engine and four-speed gear-box.

Louth Standard **1960**

Motor Cycle **1960**

Wet Motorway

HAVE you yet ridden the length of M1 on a wet and windy day? Should you do so, and should the fast lane be full of folk inclined to press on regardless whatever the weather, then you will learn two lessons—and learn them unwillingly, wetly and in a manner that sticks. The first is the amazing speed and distance of the wet back-fling of a fast-moving large car. I dare not print my estimated figures for I doubt if you would believe them, but have a try yourself and you will ever after give the 80-m.p.h. gentry as wide a berth as possible. The second lesson is on the same subject and relates to lateral fling—which can be as much as two lanes wide and impacts upon you with a very solid kind of sensation. There is no possible protection from either aggression except sheer distance; and on certain days M1 hardly seems to furnish enough of that. I do not know how or why it was that the back-fling I experienced one recent day felt so solid and contained so much granulated matter. Dirty water I had expected, but neither so thick nor so far-flung.

Meccano
Magazine
1960

A GIANT OF THE SEAS

Innovations on the Canberra

By K. Slader

The launch of the 45,000–ton P. & O. passenger liner "Canberra" at the Belfast yard of Harland and Wolff, Ltd. Photograph: P. & O. S. N. Co.

A SYMBOLIC NAME

Giving their reason for choosing the name Canberra for the new ship, her owners say, "The name Canberra was chosen because it symbolises the part which the P. & O. Lines have played in the development of Australian trade, and commerce overseas, for the last century, and the growing importance in world affairs both of Australia and her capital city Canberra. Happily the name means 'The Meeting Place' in the language of Australia's Aborigines, and this ship will be the meeting place of the peoples of the world."

Motor Cycle
1960

SECRECY is usually tinged with excitement. Even more exciting is working against time on an advanced prototype of what may well be tomorrow's personal transport. We had our share, and more, last weekend as we slaved on the first hovercraft-type scooter seen outside the United States.

The Hover Scooter principle is simple. The prop forces air through the body and between outer and inner skins to an annular outlet below the rim of the plinth. At the outlet are over 100 vanes, coupled Venetian-blind fashion, which can be moved through 45 degrees by the handlebar. The thrust of air on the ground makes a cushion on which the craft "floats." Steering is by altering, with the vanes, the angle at which the air hits the ground and by the pilot moving his weight delicately, rather like a trials rider does as he poises on the footrests.

they are on the promenade deck, three decks nearer the water.

On the upper decks, the twin streamlined smoke stacks, an outstanding characteristic of the ship, will be placed well aft so that any smuts from the oil burners are thrown clear of the deck.

Passengers will be able to sit at ease on the upper deck, snugly screened from the wind as the ship moves swiftly along at 27½ knots.

There is ample space for deck games and there are four swimming baths on board,

Launch of H.M.S. "Dreadnought"

Marine Engineer 1960

Europe's first nuclear-powered submarine is being built by Vickers-Armstrongs (Shipbuilders) Ltd. and fitted with propelling machinery by Westinghouse Electric Corporation

The Barrow-in-Furness shipyard of Vickers-Armstrongs (Shipbuilders) Ltd. was the scene of perhaps the most significant launch since the war, when on October 21, Her Majesty the Queen named H.M.S. *Dreadnought* the first nuclear-powered submarine for the Royal Navy, and indeed for any European power. Some 12,000 people attended the ceremony. The platform party included Vice-admiral Hyman G. Rickover, U.S.N., head of nuclear Propulsion Division Bureau of Ships, Washington.

The *Dreadnought* has a length of 266 ft., a beam of 32 ft. and a surface displacement of about 3,500 tons. The hull is of British design as regards structural strength and the hydrodynamic features from amidships to aft are based on the U.S. Navy's *Albacore*-class conventionally-propelled submarine and the later *Skipjack*-class nuclear-powered submarines. The forward end of the boat is wholly British in concept. The *Dreadnought* was launched from one of the two open-air submarine slipways at Barrow, and we noted that the older covered submarine slipways are in course of demolition.

One of the Northern General's new London-pattern Routemasters. The prime difference is the fitting of front entrance electrically-operated Deans doors instead of the rear platform of the L.T. buses. 50 of these buses in all have been ordered by Northern General and the first 18 were handed over at a special ceremony at the end of last month

Evening Standard 1961
Modern Transport 1961

The Queen asks Yuri to lunch

PRINCESS MARGARET WAVES TO HIM FROM GARDEN

Evening Standard Reporters

Yuri Gagarin is to lunch with the Queen and Prince Philip at Buckingham Palace on Friday, it was officially announced this afternoon.

Thus did the Palace combine with Londoners to give official Whitehall the smartest rebuff it has had in years . . . After all the stuffy dithering about protocol and what level civil servant should welcome the first man into space.

Led by Princess Margaret, who waited 30 minutes in her garden at Kensington Palace to wave to Yuri as he passed by, and Sarah Churchill, who stood in the crowd near the Russian Embassy, Londoners turned out in their thousands to cheer the Russian astronaut.

As first citizen of London, the Lord Mayor, Sir Bernard Waley-Cohen, this afternoon invited Yuri Gagarin to be his guest at the Mansion House.

The cheering crowds, the civic chiefs and the Royal Family have managed between them to wipe out the grudging, ungenerous impression created by Whitehall and Downing Street.

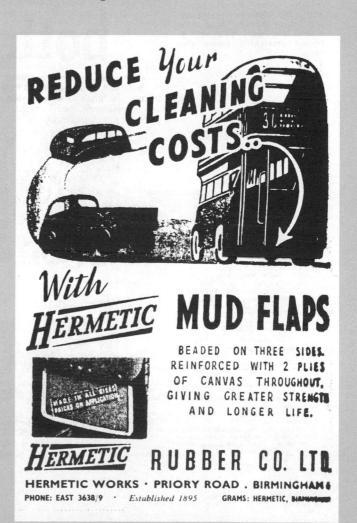

Two towns plan to celebrate bridge opening joyfully

THE full programme for the official opening of the Runcorn-Widnes Bridge has been drawn up by the various authorities concerned, and now the Weekly News publishes a complete guide to the day's events.

Princess Alexandra will arrive at Hawarden Airport, Flintshire, during the morning, and will travel by car to Runcorn. The car will go via the Queensferry by-pass and will then pick up the Chester - Warrington Road travelling through Helsby and Frodsham.

Widnes Weekly News and District Reporter 1961

It will turn left at the swing bridge at Sutton Weaver and travel through Runcorn via Clifton Road, Moughland Lane, arriving at the Greenway Road roundabout at 12-5 p.m. Greenway Road from the junction with Shaw Street will be closed from 11 a.m.

At Greenway Road roundabout a number of people will be presented to Princess Alexandra, including civic representatives from Widnes. Following this, the official opening of the bridge will take place.

The Princess will ascend a small dais and the Chairman of the Joint Bridge Committee, Sir Thomas Hargreaves, will invite her to open the bridge. She will then cut a ribbon stretching across the road.

PLAN TO HALT JAYWALKING

Express Staff Reporter

EXPERIMENTAL pedestrian regulations which will make jaywalking an offence are to be tried out in London soon, Miss M. Hall, of the Ministry of Transport's road safety division, said yesterday.

Miss Hall said the experiment would be tried out in busy shopping streets. There would be frequent light-controlled crossing places and when all traffic was brought to a standstill pedestrians would be able to cross.

"It will be an offence for a pedestrian to be on the road at other times," she said. "In other words, it will be an offence to jaywalk.

"We shall study the effects of this experiment in London before deciding whether to extend it."

Express Motoring Reporter writes: Mr. Marples, the Transport Minister, has asked 70 local authorities in and around London to try out pilot schemes investigating the benefit of no-waiting restrictions near important road junctions.

For the Ministry says experience with meter parking schemes, peak-hour clearways, and major one-way schemes has shown that restriction on waiting at major junctions have improved traffic flow.

Daily Express 1962

PCs' cars are towed away

POLICEMEN who took part in an angling competition off Southend yesterday were all at sea about parking regulations in the town.

Altogether 140 of them, from 13 different East Anglian police forces, took part. And six of them had turned up in cars.

While they faced bitter winds and heavy seas in the Thames estuary, their hosts—Southend police force—pounced.

Surprised

All six cars were towed away to police headquarters. And that was not all. They each had a warden's pink ticket stuck on.

The anglers got a shock when they reported the cars missing at the police station and learned what had happened.

An officer said his men had no choice as the cars had been left in a meter zone but not at meters.

However, the offenders did not have to go far to collect the vehicles. They were guests at an anglers' dinner at police headquarters.

Daily Herald 1962

Daily Herald 1962

Dive to disaster at bottom of the sea

SURVIVOR TELLS OF DRAMA 1,000 FT. DOWN

From JOHN SHERLOCK LONG BEACH, California, Tuesday

FROGMAN Hannes Keller told tonight how he came back alive from a deep-sea diving experiment in which two Britons died.

Keller, a Swiss scientist, went down in a diving bell 20 miles off the Californian coast with journalist Peter Small to test a secret breathing gas.

Small, aged 35, collapsed when they were 1,000 feet under the sea—a record for frogmen — and died after being hauled to the surface.

Another British frogman, 22-year-old Christopher Whittaker, went down to seal a leaking hatch on the diving bell as it surfaced. He vanished on his second dive.

NOT FAILED

Keller, aged 28, who blended the gas he and Small breathed in their record dive, said: "Our venture was not a failure.

"Peter died after I planted Swiss and American flags on the ocean floor."

He added: "After I climbed out on the bottom the flags caught in the air-hold and cut off my supply of oxygen. I went back into the chamber.

"There I saw Peter was in trouble. I took off his face mask to enable him to breathe some of the surface air and gases which half-filled the chamber.

"I knew it would be dangerous and he would lose consciousness. But I felt it was the only way to save his life."

Whittaker surfaces, is offered a rope, but turns again to dive. He was not seen again.

RAILWAYS CUT BY A QUARTER

Dr. Beeching's plan to shut 2,128 stations

LONDON FARES RISE OF 10 p.c. FORECAST

By RONALD STEVENS,
Daily Telegraph Industrial Correspondent

THE size of the railways will be cut by more than a quarter and 2,128 stations closed if the Railways Board report, published yesterday, is implemented in full. Provisions of the report, much of it written by Dr. Beeching, include:

Withdrawal of passenger services from Scotland north of Inverness, from much of North and Central Wales, and most of the West Country.

Abolition of 290 stopping train services in all parts of the country and " modification " of 71 others.

Elimination by the end of 1965 of extra trains during summer and public holidays.

Introduction of goods " liner trains," consisting of permanently coupled wagons, carrying large containers, running between major centres and combining with road vehicles.

Daily Telegraph 1963

£65 Million Line Will Be Most Modern In World

WALTHAMSTOW'S long, long wait for a Tube tie-up with town will only last for six more years. By then the long-planned Victoria line will be in action.

Work on the line will begin in the next few weeks following the Government's go-ahead for the project, given in a surprise Ministerial announcement on Monday.

The 11-mile line—Vic—will be the most modern in the world, taking in 12 stations from Walthamstow to Victoria.

Delighted London Transport chiefs, who have been pressing for the construction of the line since it was originally mooted in 1948, released full details at a hastily called headquarters Press conference on Tuesday.

Walthamstow Guardian 1962

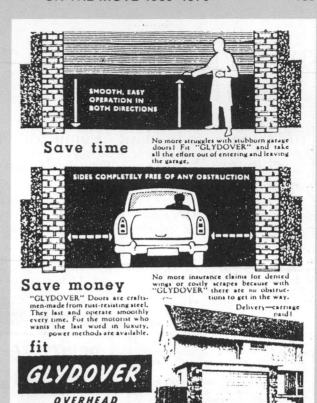

THE MILLIONTH MORRIS MINOR

FIRST BRITISH CAR TO REACH SEVEN FIGURES

The millionth Morris Minor to come off the assembly lines at Morris Motors, Ltd., Cowley, made its first public appearance this week, and it was announced that production of the phenomenally successful small car would continue.

Mr. J. R. Woodcock, deputy managing director of Morris Motors, gave the news at a reception for journalists in Grosvenor House, London, on Tuesday at which executives of BMC were present, together with the millionth Minor, in lilac finish.

Mr. Woodcock said that the occasion was historic.

" The Morris Minor is the first British car ever to achieve a production run of 1m. This achievement needs to be viewed in the perspective of the complete activities of BMC and its range of products.

" When the car was produced as a two-door saloon in 1948, its list price was £280, but even with the unfortunate fall in the value of the pound, to-day's price of £416 is equivalent to a price of only £254 12 years ago," he said.

" It follows, therefore, that the public is getting more for its money than ever before.

Oxford Times 1961

DR. BEECHING WANTS TO SHUT 2,128 STATIONS

67,700 men redundant : Compensation scheme: "Liner" goods trains

THE British Railways Board in its report on the future of the railways confidently forecasts that if its proposals are implemented "with vigour" a large part, though not necessarily all, of the industry's financial deficit, will be eliminated by 1970.

The most drastic suggestion in the report, "The Reshaping of British Railways," published yesterday, is that uneconomic passenger services covering 5,000 route miles should be withdrawn. This will mean the closing of 2,128 stations and halts.

On other lines only fast and semi-fast trains will run. In addition some services will be rearranged so that uneconomic portions are cut out and little-used stations are closed.

Among the well-known stations named for closure are Glasgow (St. Enoch), Edinburgh (Princes Street), Liverpool (Central) and Nottingham (Victoria).

LINER TRAINS
Freight traffic

In an attempt to win more profitable freight traffic, the report proposes the introduction of long-distance "liner trains." These would travel at top speeds of 75 miles an hour between the main industrial centres.

"By this combination of speed, reliability in all weathers, freedom from damage or pilferage, and convenience of service, liner trains will surpass anything known by rail or road," the report says.

Modern locomotives and rolling stock now in use on lines due to be closed will replace steam locomotives on services which are to continue. On the express inter-city passenger services, there will be "selective improvements and rationalisation of routes."

Daily Telegraph 1963

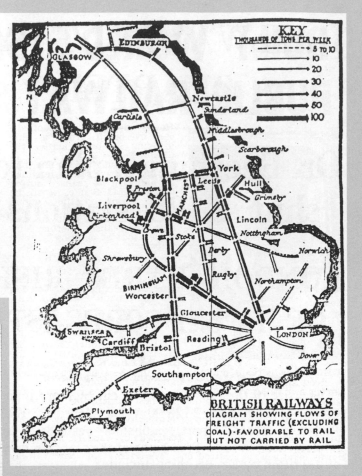

BRITISH RAILWAYS DIAGRAM SHOWING FLOWS OF FREIGHT TRAFFIC (EXCLUDING COAL)-FAVOURABLE TO RAIL BUT NOT CARRIED BY RAIL

POINTS TO REMEMBER

WITH the withdrawal of the "Isle of Thanet," only two British Railways ships, the "Canterbury" and the "Maid of Orleans" will be left to operate services from Folkestone. In addition, of course, there is the French "Cote d'Azur."

Already people are reading into the proposed plan a strong indication that there WILL BE a Channel Tunnel and that it will be operating within seven years.

It must be assumed that British Railways have been told: "Don't go to the expense of building any more ships because there is going to be a new Channel link."

It was reported a few days ago that early action on the Channel Tunnel is to be pressed on the Government by M.P.s.

The Anglo-French governmental report on the project is due to be published about the middle of this month.

As long ago as 1916 one of the leading Canadian newspapers published a scheme for a Channel Tunnel, which would have its terminus in the Sandling area.

Folkestone and Hythe Gazette 1963

Ideal Home 1963

Happy marriage

Finally, there are two instances of well-established firms introducing entirely new luxury cars. The V-8 engine, of 2½ litre capacity, which has proved its excellence in the Daimler sports car (another one with winding windows and an occasional seat) is happily married to the Jaguar Mark II and it fulfils two functions. It replaces the 2·4 Jaguar and it provides a medium-sized saloon in the Daimler range which has been lacking for several years.

The other entirely new car is the Jensen C-V8. To get its fantastic performance (maximum speed is over 140 m.p.h.) the Jensen uses a Chrysler engine and the whole car is built to a very high standard.

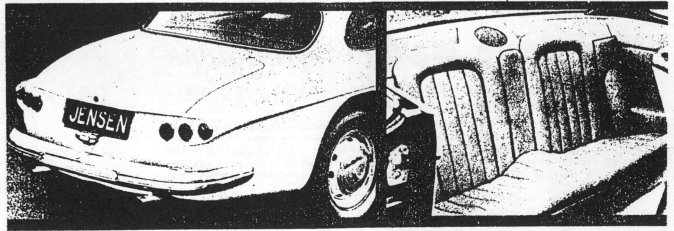

The Jensen C-V8: "to get its fantastic performance (maximum speed is over 140 m.p.h.) this new Jensen uses a Chrysler engine"

The back seats of the Ford Capri: "interiors are becoming more comfortable, more practical, less ornate; more attention is shown to colour schemes"

BUILT WORLD'S SMALLEST PUBLIC RAILWAY

*Folkestone and
Hythe Gazette*
1963

THE man who realised a child-hood ambition to build and run his own railway, Capt. John Edward Presgrave Howey, died on Sunday at his home over-looking New Romney station of the Romney, Hythe and Dymchurch Light Railway.

The life of Capt. "Jack" Howey, who was 76, centred on cars and trains. In his youth he was a successful racing-car driver, as well as a model railway enthusiast. In later years he lived for the light railway which he built 37 years ago.

Born at Coleshill, Warwickshire, Capt. Howey was educated at Eton. He spent much of his early life in Scotland, where he developed into a fine shot and fisherman.

A few years after he married he joined the Army to serve with the Inniskilling Dragoons in Cairo during World War 1. Later in the war he transferred to the Royal Flying Corps.

REMARKABLE FEAT

Acting as observer in one of the small two-seater fighter 'planes flying over Germany his pilot was shot dead. Capt. Howey climbed out of his cockpit and crawled along the fuselage into the pilot's seat and landed the aircraft safely behind German lines, where he was taken prisoner. He was repatriated before the end of the war.

During the 'twenties Capt. Howey achieved fame racing cars at Brooklands. He drove a Leyland-Thomas straight-8, one of two that were built. A third one, constructed of spare parts, is now in Lord Montagu's museum at Beaulieu. He also drove a Lagonda-12 across Australia from Alice Springs to Darwen, a 1,000-mile journey.

Evidence of his success is a glass cabinet full of silver trophies in the dining-room of his home, Red Tiles, Warren Road, New Romney.

He gave up racing in 1926, when his younger brother was killed in a hill-climb in France. It is well-known that Capt.

Howey dropped his brother's car overboard from a ship bringing it back across the Channel.

Throughout his life he had wanted to drive railway engines, an ambition he realised during the General Strike, when he drove trains on the London North-Eastern Railway. It was about this time that he was able to realise another ambition, that of building his own railway.

FIRST STRETCH

The first stretch, from Hythe to New Romney, was opened by Earl Beauchamp, Lord Warden of the Cinque Ports, in July, 1927. Present at the ceremony were Miss Betty Baldwin, daughter of the Prime Minister, the Mayors of New Romney, Hythe, Folkestone, Dover and Hastings, representatives of the L.N.E.R. and Southern Railway, and members of local councils and organisations.

The railway, using the smallest practicable gauge of 15in., was expected to bring prosperity to Romney Marsh, which, for the first time, was crossed by modern means of land transport.

The fame of the railway quickly spread all over the world, and today it is visited every year by well over 250,000 people, who travel along its $13\frac{3}{4}$ miles of track between Hythe and Dungeness.

Flapping hoods and whistling draughts are things of the past. Today, the modern convertible, though pricey, combines the joys of open-air motoring with all the snugness of a saloon

ROLLS ROYCE DROPHEAD COUPE

DARTFORD TUNNEL WILL BE OPEN ON MONDAY

*Dartford, Crayford,
Swanley Chronicle
and Kentish Times*
1963

—But breakdowns will be expensive

THE long-awaited £11,000,000 Dartford Tunnel opens at noon on Monday, bringing Essex within minutes reach of Kent, the Minister of Transport, Mr. Ernest Marples, announced on Wednesday. The news was given at a Press conference at the tunnel administration building on Wednesday morning.

After outlining plans for the new " under the Thames " tunnel, the concept of which was first mooted late in the 18th century, the general manager, Captain F. L. Millns, gave the 50 or so journalists present a conducted tour of the administration buildings, the toll area, and the tunnel itself.

London Transport tests an automatic train driver

TRIALS WITH EXPERIMENTAL equipment have been started by London Transport to decide the feasibility of driving trains automatically, and the equipment was demonstrated to the press on March 21.

A District Line train has been specially equipped and the first tests are being carried out along a one-mile stretch of track between South Ealing and Acton Town.

Later, if the trials are satisfactory, the special equipment required for automatic driving will be installed alongside the existing signals over a section of the District Line, west of Hammersmith. The special train can then be used for normal service and switched over by the motorman to automatic driving over this section of its journey.

London Transport is also studying the possibility of carrying out full-scale trials of automatic train operation possibly on the Hainault-Woodford shuttle service on the Central Line.

The system, which has been designed by London Transport engineers, envisages that there will be a train operator in the motorman's cab who will push a starting button. He will be able to take over the driving of the train in the event of a failure of any part of the automatic system.

Railway Gazette **1963**

STANSTED IS THE CHOICE

Noise problem will be closely studied

STANSTED AIRPORT is to become the third international airport for London. Mr. Julian Amery, Minister of Aviation, said at a Press conference in London on Tuesday, that the Government had approved this recommendation of a Ministry of Aviation committee. Work on it will start in two years' time.

The committee unanimously recommended Stansted as the third international airport for London, and Mr. Amery said at the Press conference, "There is nowhere better."

Herts and Essex Observer **1964**

In 1962, 48 per cent of the Scottish Bus Group's route mileage was unremunerative, and 26 per cent of the vehicle miles operated did not cover costs. About 25 per cent of David MacBrayne's routes were unprofitable on an individual route costing basis. This is a very serious situation, especially in the territories of Highland Omnibuses, where 88 per cent of the route miles were unremunerative, and in Fife where Alexander's operate nearly 70 per cent of their route miles at less than cost. It is well known that very few of the independent operators are making much money from stage services and certainly not from country services. Except for the owner-driver, who is satisfied with a living wage as his profit, the stage operations of the independents are being subsidised by school contracts, private-hire work or by other businesses, such as garages or hotels.

What does it cost to run a bus? Last year the average costs of the Scottish Group were about 2s. 3d. per mile, but costs of the independent operators can fall as low as 1s. per mile. With a fare level of 3d. per mile, the same as British Railways, it means that an average load of between four and nine passengers is needed to cover costs. However, even in rural areas, bus fares are generally well below railway level, and a load of seven to 14 passengers would be nearer the mark.

Passenger Transport **1964**

Strongavalterie, the terminus of one of the Alexander (Midland) company's least remunerative services. The houses at the north shore of Loch Katrine are linked with Callander by two return journeys on Saturdays only.

BUCHANAN BLUEPRINT FOR TOWN TRAFFIC

Expanding public transport services to combat urban congestion

THE need for cheap and convenient public transport in the "motor age" of the future is emphasised in the report of the Buchanan study group to the Minister of Transport*. Pointing out the probable need to limit the use of private cars in large towns and cities, the report says that the importance of this for public transport cannot be exaggerated. It foreshadows a city of the future, developed on two, or even three levels to allow free traffic circulation, but concludes "that in the long run the most potent factor in maintaining a ceiling on optional traffic is likely to be the provision of good, cheap, public transport coupled with the commonsense of the public".

Traffic on the ground; pedestrians above

Passenger Transport 1964

'Primrose' arrives

For the formal opening on July 9 the operating staff were all dressed in Victorian style, and the guests, many of whom were also dressed in period costumes, included two ladies who had witnessed the opening of the line 78 years before. The Brighton 'Terrier' had its original name of 'Stepney' painted on its tank sides, and the 'P' class tank had been christened 'Bluebell'. Press and television were present, and the two termini of the line must indeed have been reminiscent of the graceful Victorian days. The season that followed saw a total number of 15,000 passengers, among them the then Prime Minister and Lady Dorothy Macmillan.

Efforts were directed towards securing a second 'Terrier' locomotive to act as a spare engine. This did not unfortunately materialise since the S.R. had no intentions of withdrawing any members of the class at that time, and instead a second S.E.C.R. 'P' class locomotive was obtained. No. 31027 arrived in March and was promptly named 'Primrose' in readiness for the new season. In addition four Metropolitan Railway coaches of 1898 vintage from the Chesham branch were acquired. The President of the Society, Bishop Geoffrey Warde, inaugurated the 1961 season, and the first train was double headed out of the station by 'Stepney' and 'Primrose', with 'Bluebell' at the trailing end—a combination that was repeated on many subsequent occasions.

The whole beauty of the 'Bluebell' line lies in its ability to re-create the Victorian railway scene. Locomotives are undoubtedly the greatest single asset in achieving this, and every effort was made to locate and save remaining examples of historic locomotive types. A special fund was, therefore, set up for two engines of great historic value. The first of these, an Adams 4-4-2 'Radial' tank No. 488, reached the line in July, and the second, East Kent Railway No. 5, followed. This one had been associated with the Lyme Regis branch for 45 years.

'Stepney' had by now appeared in its final condition—a magnificent restoration job by the staff of the railway. The original L.B.S.C.R. livery was faithfully reproduced, and the locomotive now makes a splendid sight in its Stroudley Yellow livery. Another historic locomotive which arrived at Sheffield Park was North London Railway 0-6-0T No. 76, B.R. No. 58850.

Although the line to Horsted Keynes is now closed, the traffic on the Bluebell line has increased, it now carrying many thousands of passengers every year. The figure had increased to 91,000 journeys in 1961, and is growing larger every year.

Driver Mr. J. Hart of Surbiton and Porter/Ticket Collector, etc. Brian Thomas of Crawley with 'Primrose'

Meccano Magazine 1966

BOAT TRIP OFF AGAIN

TWO young Plymouth men who plan to cross the channel to Cherbourg and back in a nine-foot home-made, paraffin-driven boat, again postponed the trip last night.

Peter Charles, of Alvington Street, Cattedown, and John Coles, of St. Peter's Road, Manadon, both 24, originally intended to leave Dartmouth on August 20 but could not get a cover boat to escort them.

Mr. John Weir, managing director of Dart Services, who has been organising the venture, said strong winds prevented them leaving last night.

Plymouth Independent 1966

STANSTED AIRPORT
MINISTRY OF AVIATION

Herts and Essex Observer 1964

L.T.B. BARRIER-CONTROL SYSTEM

AN ELECTRONIC TICKET-SCANNING MACHINE, coupled to an electro-mechanical entrance gate was brought into use on January 5 at Stamford Brook Station, on the London Transport Board District Line as the first stage of the development of an entry and exit electronic barrier system.

The experimental installation controls only entrance to the platforms; a complete installation will comprise both entrance and exit barriers.

The scanning-machine and gate are installed in the booking hall of the station. The gate is waist-high and stands between slightly higher plastic walls. The right-hand wall houses the scanning-machine, and the top of the left-hand wall is fitted with rollers for carrying luggage.

Passengers from Stamford Brook Station are issued with a yellow ticket printed with the name of the station and the code number of the station, printed in ternary code. The ticket is inserted in the scanning-machine which takes less than half a second to "read" the ticket, and returns it to the passenger. If the ticket is valid, a "Go" stencil indication above the gate on the right-hand wall is illuminated, and the power-assisted gate released.

If the ticket is not valid, it is returned to the passenger and the gate remains locked.

Ternary-coded ticket and electronic ticket-scanning machine in L.T.B. experimental installation

Railway Gazette **1964**

THE Forth Road Bridge, the greatest engineering achievement in Scotland this century and the fulfilment of a 40-year campaign for a road link between Fife and the Lothians across the Forth, was officially opened by Her Majesty the Queen yesterday. The event, in all its wonderful colour and splendour, the biggest royal occasion north of the Border for many years, was watched by tremendous crowds. A blanket of fog threatened to blot out the entire ceremony for the majority of the thousands who flocked to both ends of the bridge for the occasion, but it lifted partially in time to give the crowds a glimpse of a historic moment. A few words graciously spoken by Her Majesty, who was accompanied by His Royal Highness, the Duke of Edinburgh, followed by the deafening roar of a Royal Naval salute and this magnificent bridge, the entire project started in 1958 and costing in the region of £20 million, was officially open.

Several hours later, the first motorists turned another page of Scottish history by crossing the new bridge, paying the 2/6 toll as they did so.

For the whole of Scotland, and particularly Fife, this was indeed a memorable day and it was appropriate that such a magnificent achievement should be inaugurated by the Queen.

Dunfermline Press and West of Fife Advertiser **1965**

NOW WORKING AT FULL CAPACITY, the Coventry-Eagle factory at Grove Lane, Smethwick, Staffordshire will soon be replaced by a large new factory— the move will mean the start of a new chapter in the annals of the family concern.

Coventry-Eagle anniversary recalls a great past

The Coventry-Eagle Cycle and Motor Co. Ltd., is this month celebrating its 75th birthday, recalling what has happened since it was founded in 1890 and looking forward hopefully to the years ahead.

Motor Cycle and Cycle Trader **1965**

Damaging tactics

THE Concorde survives—at least so it seems as we go to press; and now it is the turn of the TSR.2 to be the subject of those go-stop tactics which, whatever the outcome, are so damaging to the British aircraft industry. Damaging, not only to morale, but in the uncertainty which is engendered in the minds of potential customers overseas.

Daedalus, writing in AeCAN for Nov. 5 last, suggested that the new Minister of Aviation would wish to review the importance to the country of the aircraft industry. News of the appointment of a committee came shortly after, but it was not to be expected that its task would be severely prejudiced before it had even sat. Perhaps this is overstating the case; perhaps the Government has no intention of deciding anything at this stage; perhaps they are only testing public opinion. We find it difficult to believe that such could be the case, but there are those who, searching for an explanation of the Government's handling of this situation, can find no other explanation.

We welcome the decision to continue with the Concorde because we are now convinced that a good economic case can be made for a supersonic transport to the current specification. But there are two misconceptions going the rounds which could be very damaging to the project. The first is that it costs less money, when developing a new aircraft, to go slowly or to ration the expenditure in any one year. All Research and Development projects carry a heavy burden of overheads. Many of these are fixed overheads that do not vary with the amount of progress being made.

Aeroplane **1965**

HOVERLLOYD INAUGURATES RAMSGATE—CALAIS ROUTE

THE world's first international hovercraft service was opened last week by Hoverlloyd SR.N6 equipment on the Ramsgate - Calais route.

The inaugural runs in poor weather — took 58 minutes for the outward crossing, and 53 minutes on the return journey.

Two SR.N6 craft are being used on the route: the Swift, christened in Ramsgate early last month, and the Sure named in Calais on March 30.

Hoverlloyd is to open its regular Ramsgate - Calais service on April 30.

There are to be ten round-trips a day from 07.30 hours to 19.00, and local 'round-the-bay' voyages during the middle of the day and late evening.

Journey time from Ramsgate to Calais will be between 40 and 55 minutes, depending on weather conditions.

The single cross - Channel fare has been established at 45s., while the pleasure trip rate is expected to be 12s. 6d.

Operations will be limited by poor weather conditions: anything more than a Force 5 wind or waves higher than five feet is expected to halt services.

The schedule is claimed to be a prelude to Hoverlloyd's plan to introduce SR.N4 craft, capable of carrying 250 passengers and 35 cars, on the route in 1968.

Travel Trade Gazette
1966

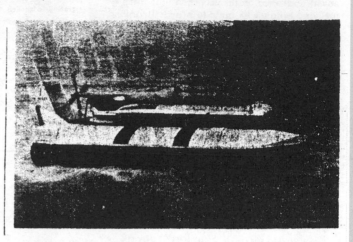

Flight 1966

Hawker Siddeley P.1127 (XS695)   One of the ex-tripartite squadron Kestrels appears in the static park, while the first P.1127 (RAF) development aircraft, which flew for the first time last week, was expected to take part in the flying shows later in the week. This BS Pegasus 5-powered aircraft, which followed the 90sec maiden flight in the hovering régime with a 42min conventional flight in the hands of Bill Bedford last Saturday, is the first of six which will all be flying early next year. At least the last two of these are expected to be completed to full production standard, with Pegasus 6 engines, and are likely to see squadron service.

The earlier static-display aircraft is shown with two underwing Matra Sneb rockets each able to accommodate 18 projectiles.

The name "Kestrel" is certainly being dropped by the manufacturer with regard to all future P.1127s and Hawker Siddeley is hoping that the RAF will choose a new name when production aircraft are delivered next year. "Kestrel" is thought to be too closely associated with the unarmed, very limited aircraft which equipped the tripartite squadron last year.

70 mph speed limit?

Fraser to make statement

By Gordon Jackson

A SHOCK decision to impose a 70 mph speed limit on all trunk roads throughout Britain including motorways is understood to have been reached by the Government.

This move will be accompanied by special fog limits to be imposed by local police chiefs on stretches of Britain's motorways whenever conditions get dangerous.

The Minister of Transport, Mr. Tom Fraser, was making a major statement to the Commons this afternoon about the Government's intentions.

These dramatic new measures are the result of grave concern within the Government over the alarming concertina pile-ups which have brought death and injury to the motorways during the past weeks.

Police forces with motorways running through their areas will get wide discretion to decide what speed limits should be clamped on as conditions become dangerous.

Special illuminated signs and other warning systems will be brought speedily into operation to warn motorists of the new restrictions.

The new proposals may be introduced experimentally at first to see how they work out during the winter.

The implications of the Government's decision on upper speed limits are far-reaching. It will mean that in future no one in Britain will be allowed to drive his car at more than 70 mph even if the conditions are ideal for high speed motoring. If the government's decision is made statutory it may seriously affect the high-powered car trade vital to Britain's exports and is bound to touch off a storm of protests.

But Mr. Fraser, after consultations with Britain's police chiefs, has decided that the time has come for drastic action. He will point out that the motorways were designed technically for speeds of 70 mph.

Reading Evening Post 1966

Hawker Siddeley P.1127, seen here with two Matra air-to-surface rocket pods

Bus driver's date with a ghost train

Every Saturday night a bus trundles a mile off its route to a railway station bus stop. But the driver knows, his passengers know, and the bus company knows there will be nobody waiting there. For the train the bus is scheduled to meet has not run for two and a half years.

It was 10 months ago—because of a rail closure—that British Railways asked the Wilts and Dorset Motor Services Limited to put on the service to Salisbury station every night except Sunday. But after a few passengerless Saturdays the company checked and found the train did not run on that day.

A spokesman for the company said last night: "Before we can take off a service a special order has to be made by the Ministry of Transport. This must follow an application by British Railways. We have written to the railways twice since we started the service but haven't heard from them yet." A spokesman for British Railways said: "There has not been a Saturday train at that time since September, 1964. The matter is being investigated."

Guardian 1967

One of the 24 30-ft. long A.E.C. Routemaster buses with Park Royal bodies turned out for London Transport

Transport World 1964

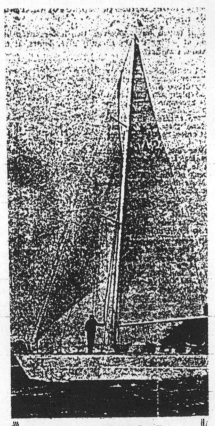

LONE VOYAGER LEAVES PORT

LAST glimpse of a lone figure as the 53ft. ketch Gipsy Moth IV. left Plymouth yesterday on the start of a 28,000 miles round-the-world voyage. At the helm, Devon-born yachtsman, 64 - years - old Francis Chichester, veteran of already three lone Atlantic crossings. He hopes to cover the distance within 200 days.

Plymouth Independent 1966

BRITAIN'S FIRST JET

On 15th May, 1941
just 25 years ago, this little aeroplane
opened the door to the future
for with its successful flight,
it proved the jet engine to be a practical power unit.
Twenty five years prior to this momentous flight,
frail wood, wire and fabric machines,
like the Bristol Boxkite, described on page 16 of this issue
were the wonders of the age—
such is the speed
of aeronautical development.
Who would hazard a guess at the likely shape
of the aeroplane
or its propulsion unit in 1991—
another 25 years on?

Meccano Magazine 1966

LAUNCH OF FIRST POLARIS SUBMARINE
BRITAIN'S NEW 'GRAND FLEET'

Navy News 1966

Queen Elizabeth the Queen Mother, at Barrow-in-Furness on September 15, launched Britain's first Polaris submarine, H.M.S. Resolution. Many of those attending saw for the first time the giant black cigar-shaped hull, twice the size of Dreadnought.

She is due to commission next autumn, and will be fully operational in the middle of 1968.

The Flag Officer Submarines, Rear-Admiral I. L. M. McGeoch, said that the Royal Navy's Polaris force of four submarines was the successor of the Grand Fleet of the First World War.

In the rapid state of evolution of the submarine, we were entering an era of underwater cruiser warfare.

The nuclear submarine, able to roam the seas and cover immense distances, could attack, shadow, or disappear at will. It could escort a convoy or act independently.

At a Press conference before the launch, Admiral McGeoch said: "Submarines like this are the ultimate guarantee against the destruction of Britain.

"They cannot be knocked out by sudden attack, so there is no need to get in the first blow. This means minimum risk of creating nuclear strife, and the maximum chance of preventing it."

Mr. J. P. W. Mallalieu, Minister of Defence for the Navy, said that whatever new types of surface ship emerged from studies on the future of the Service, it was already clear that the submarine fleet would form a most important part of the new Navy, representing the newest advances in so many fields of development, design, and naval capability

Drink-drive tests by the million

BY A STAFF REPORTER

The police are to be issued with a million breath analysis devices when new legislation affecting persons suspected of driving under the influence of alcohol comes into force in the autumn. The Road Safety Act received the Royal Assent on Wednesday. After the new legislation is introduced persons cannot be asked to give a blood or urine sample until they have undertaken the test.

The equipment is to be made by a west German firm, Drager, and distributed in this country by Draeger Normalair, of Blyth, Northumberland. The initial order is worth £200,000.

The Home Office said last night that if after breathing into the device – officially known as the Alcotest – a person is found to have an alcohol content exceeding 80 milligrams per 100 millilitre of blood, he can be taken to a police station for samples to be given.

Inside the Alcotest are yellow crystals which change colour when they come into contact with alcohol. No untrained officer will be allowed to use the device.

The Times 1967

Whitley Bay Guardian 1967

WHEN the Queen officially opened the Tyne Tunnel yesterday, she praised the skill of the men who built it.

From a dias near the entrance to the tunnel at Howdon, the Queen said. "It would be difficult to find a better reason for coming to Tyneside than for the opening of the new way of communication between the people who live on either bank of your great river and I am extremely glad to be here for such an excellent purpose.

"This new tunnel constructed on the most modern principles will certainly relieve the congestion of traffic in Newcastle and Gateshead.

"It will serve the communities and factories at both ends and by connecting the road systems of North-east Durham and South-east Northumberland, it will assist in the industrial development of this important area and will bring great benefit to the country as a whole.

Five Pass First Camden Motor Cycle Course

AT Camden's first Motor Cyclist and Scooterist Training Scheme course, instructors Bob Osborne and Jim Anker are seen demonstrating the technique of riding the ramp and negotiating obstacles, to trainee riders.

Camden and Holborn and Finsbury Guardian 1968

The Times 1967

BREATHALYSERS BY THE MILLION

By BASIL CARDEW

ONE MILLION breath-testing kits for the police are being ordered by the Government, it was announced yesterday as a new drunk-driving law took shape.

The kits, "blow-up," breathalysers for use on the roadside, are made in Germany.

They will be supplied through a firm at Blyth, Northumberland, said the Home Office. They will cost about 1s. apiece.

One hundred police forces will issue them to car and motor-cycle patrols when this aspect of the new Road Safety Act is brought into operation—probably in the autumn, said the Ministry of Transport.

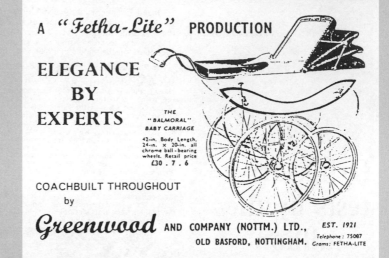

A new looking car for 15 bob

Or anything else, boats, doors, cases, you name it Stickers improve it. In five different colours, two black and whites, orange and pink, yellow and green, blue and green, in four different sizes. Send 15/- for a packet of nine to **INTERTRADE, 47 Fleet Street, London EC3**

Evening Standard 1968

AN Arizona group today claimed it had won the fight to buy London Bridge. The price was estimated unofficially as £1,000,000.

The group plans to re-build the 10,000-ton granite bridge as the centre of a vast international resort at the Lake Havasu City on the Colorado River.

A spokesman for the McCulloch Corporation at Lake Havasu City said a news conference had been called to announce the victory.

But the spokesman, Mr. Frederick Schumacher, a director of the corporation's Lake Havasu City Development, said: "If we don't win the bid, we'll just all have breakfast" at the conference.

North Sea gas is coming

"...the best bit of luck for 100 years!"

In 1969 a steam locomotive hauled the Golden Arrow for the last time. Here a locomotive of the Britannia class takes the Golden arrow through the London suburbs on its way to the coast.

South London Press 1967

LEWISHAM'S mayor, Councillor John Day, called to the scene by town hall officials from his Devonshire-hill home alerted Chief Welfare official Mr. Joseph Young and other council workers before leaving.

At the disaster he helped with removing the injured.

"It looked like a bomb had dropped," he told the *South London Press* yesterday.

"The carriages looked as if they had been smashed by a giant hand and the rails were like bent paper-clips.

"I helped a stretcher gang to carry the injured from the wreckage, down the embankment and into waiting ambulances.

"Despite all the moaning, sobbing and shouting of instructions, everything was performed well and there was no chaos."

As well as the police, ambulance men and local doctors, council welfare workers and Salvation Army officials helped with the dead and injured.

Yesterday the Mayor launched a disaster fund, the second resulting from a rail crash.

It is because of the pre-vious one, 10 years ago that the borough has £500 in hand to give immediate aid to victims of Sunday's disaster.

Councillor Day has his own views on why residents of Lewisham were so fast to act to help the survivors.

"We had a lot of practice during the war. We were on 'Bomb Alley' on the German path to Deptford and the docks," he said.

"Also we learned a great deal from the previous train disaster. There have also been some practice runs for welfare staff."

The mayor left the crash scene at 3 a.m. after making sure there were sufficient beds in the borough's old people's homes to sleep surviving passengers who could not go on to their destination.

Hand in hand with his wife Dorothy, Alec Rose stepped ashore at Southsea today to a deafening noise of boat sirens and bells and cheering of thousands.

His round the world solo voyage was over and waiting to greet him was the Lord Mayor of Portsmouth (Coun. F. A. J. Emery-Wallis).

As Alec stepped on to a raised platform to shake hands with the Mayor he was handed a telegram from the Queen and the Duke of Edinburgh which read: "Congratulations on your magnificent voyage. Welcome home.— Elizabeth and Philip."

Alec who had changed from his canvas sailing smock into a smart reefer jacket yachting cap and grey flannels was deeply moved by the fantastic clamour of welcome and by the turnout of craft which escorted him the last few miles home.

Portsmouth News 1968

Meet a star with a hobby
A CAT ON HORSEBACK

'I love my horse as much as I love you.

You may fade, my horse will always come through!'

These are the words of a pop-song that Cat Stevens hasn't written! The real hit was about his dog, but the sentiments apply just as well to a horse.

Cat is a great horse-lover and is completely at home in the saddle. 'A horse can sense immediately what sort of rider you are,' he says, 'and which of you is going to be the boss.' And to prove it, one light tap with his heels was enough to send his horse galloping smoothly away across the common. Mine stood stubbornly still, oblivious to all entreaty, and defiantly cropped the grass.

Cat started riding when he was about twelve. He had no burning ambition to be a cowboy, he just liked horses. However his first ride is implanted very firmly on his memory. 'It sounds really corny, but I was so sore I couldn't sit down, literally.'

While he was at school he started to learn the proper way to ride. 'In Rotten Row, it was, with all the gear!' He enjoyed the lessons, with the smartly cut riding jacket, the highly polished boots, and the admiring audience—until one day he fell off before crowds of tourists! 'Catastrophic.

It wasn't until the first hit record came along that Cat took up riding again. He found he needed some relaxation, and 'to get away into a forest with just a horse for company' was the ideal solution. Now while he's touring the first thing he looks for in a new place is the stables, and he practically lives on horseback in every spare moment.

He's now looking for a horse of his own: 'A big white one, with spirit. Something to conquer. That could be the start of a beautiful friendship.' He's most particular about the colour—it must be white or 'grey' as the technical term is, as black horses and Cat for some reason have never got along!

Luckily though, he's never had any real trouble with horses. Accidents are rare, he says, 'because a horse will always consider his rider and try to save him if there's a tumble coming up.'

At the moment Cat is debating what sort of car to buy. 'Although I don't know . . . I rather fancy seeing my "grey" tied up to an Oxford Street parking meter.'　GAY SEARCH

Radio Times 1967

A completely new Jaguar structure with 2.8-litre and 4.2-litre 6-cylinder engines

Coming as the first really new Jaguar since the Mark 10 in 1961, the XJ6—initially available with 2.8-litre and 4.2-litre six-cylinder, twin o.h.c. engines, will later have a new range of engines available. Very high standards of steering and roadholding allied to even greater refinement. 240, 420G and E-Type models continue.

WITHOUT A DOUBT THE NEW Jaguar XJ6 model announced today is the most important new British car of 1968 and will be the centre of attraction at the Earls Court Show next month.

First completely new model since the Mark 10—the S type and 420 were developments of the Mk 2—it proves that Sir William Lyons has in no way lost his touch for line and form. The XJ6 perpetuates the Jaguar line and at the same time contrives to be thoroughly up to date. The new model will be offered in 2.8-litre standard form at the attractive price of £1,797, including purchase tax, with the more powerful and more luxuriously equipped automatic 4.2-litre priced at £2,398, all-in. In between these price extremes a 2.8-litre de luxe model is offered and there are options of overdrive and automatic transmission.

Autocar 1968

The lesson of ELDO

The likelihood that the European Launcher Development Organization will collapse, see ("What follows ELDO," p. 225) raises the whole question of the reasons for supporting research. Mr Wedgwood Benn has referred to "economic justifiability"; but this is far too vague an entity to enable anyone to use it as a basis for decisions. If it means that there must be an economic profit in view, important research will be stopped. If the term does not mean this, then it means nothing.

Quite certainly, however, the fact that a politician's mistakes have landed the country with proposals to build a useless weapon is not a reason for starting a scientific programme, and the ELDO decision itself was long overdue. A lot of money has been spent and there has been virtually nothing in return. We have perhaps learned something about the realities of international cooperation —ours was the only stage that worked—but this lesson could have been learned before £72 million had gone down the drain.

The principle of maintaining a European initiative in space technology, on the other hand, could well be acceptable. Communications satellites will be big business, and no doubt the Americans will be ready to put up enough to capture all the profitable business going. But American initiative may not cater properly for European needs. Social demands could justify uneconomic satellite channels, as they justify uneconomic telephone lines; furthermore, the Americans might find public pressures driving them to refuse satellite channels to countries which, for example, trade with Cuba.

There are thus two good reasons for Britain staying in space—the hope of profit and the need for independence. The fact that this country's three Aeriel satellites have been so widely admired, suggests that we could provide the driving force behind a well planned and effective European space programme.

New Scientist 1968

Challenge of the new post–by Stonehouse

POSTMASTER-GENERAL Mr John Stonehouse told GPO men yesterday to 'meet the challenge' of the new two-tier postal system.

He said in a message to all staff that they had been under attack because 'we have been brave enough to introduce a new and different system.

'Now the challenge is with us all. I ask you all to meet this challenge. Be proud of our fine postal service and speed the mails.'

Priority

The new service starts today. 'Already more than 18 fully paid letters out of 20 are delivered by the day after posting,' said Mr Stonehouse.

'Now with the fivepenny first-class service, we can aim to increase this to 19 out of 20.

'After priority has been given to the 5d. mail, all efforts must be given to maintaining the schedules for second - class letters.'

Daily Mail 1968

Homework on Henley for Mr Teasy Weasy

THE horse-owning hairdresser 'Teasy Weasy' Raymond had never been to that sporting event in the social calendar known as Henley Royal Regatta.

And he decided it was time he put in an appearance with his wife, Rosalie, yesterday. But not before he'd done his homework. He had a session with Walter Skelton, an old rowing man who stroked the 1947 boat which won the Wyfold Challenge Cup.

'I was given a good hour's lecturing on how to behave, and how to say things,' Raymond remarked with refreshing candour. 'For instance, I didn't know an oar was always described as a blade.'

Daily Mail 1969

AT Earl's Court this year, combined stands 98 and 99 give **Ford** of Dagenham the biggest single display of the whole Motor Show. No less than twelve saloon models from the Company's comprehensive range are being exhibited.

On stand 84, Carbodies Ltd. is displaying the Consul, Zephyr and Zodiac convertibles, while the estate car versions can be seen on the E. D. Abbott Ltd. stand, number 83.

Although unchanged for the Show, every Ford model continues to offer a host of quality features at outstandingly competitive prices.

On the Ford stand can be seen: (1) Britain's best-selling car; (2) Britain's lowest-priced family saloon; (3) Britain's lowest-priced four-door car; (4) Britain's lowest-priced, full-sized six seater; (5) Britain's lowest-priced 6-cylinder car; (6) The world's lowest-priced saloon available with disc brakes.

Ford claim that value like this is made possible by their unique facilities for manufacture from the raw material stage to the finished product in the most advanced **motor** factories in Europe.

Woman's Home Journal 1968

EITHER/OR

THE last two years have shown that the introduction of automatic transmission on the Mini-Minor has been an unqualified success—proving equally suitable for the beginner driver unused to the problem of managing a clutch pedal, and the more experienced motorist appreciative of an opportunity to ease the strain of continual concentration.

The versatility of the system used on the Mini is its greatest attraction. The controls, as far as driving is concerned, consist only of an accelerator and a brake pedal—the " over-riding lever " providing a choice of automatic or manual driving, or a combination of both.

There is no clutch. With the lever in D—drive—the transmission becomes completely automatic. This makes for restful and relaxed driving—especially in town—as the system provides that the right gear is always in use for the prevailing road conditions.

The lever can also be used to give complete choice and control over whichever of the four gears is used and with manual control in operation the gears are changed manually as in a normal car—except that with the Mini system there is no clutch pedal.

When the automatic is in use a " kick-down " on the accelerator, or a quick flick of the lever—manual control—is the only effort needed to give exactly the right gear at the right time. Always an agile and sprightly little car, the automatic transmission has undoubtedly enhanced the Mini-Minor's qualities, bringing a new era of enjoyment to motoring. And because the automatic produces appreciably less power than the highly tuned Mini-Cooper versions, considerably less strain is imposed on the engine. As a result, the reliability of the automatic model's engine can be taken for granted. Brakes give a hundred per cent. efficiency and are capable of maintaining their efficiency for long periods of hard usage.

With a turning circle of just over thirty feet and only 2-3 turns of the steering wheel required to change from lock to lock, the car can be driven and parked with the greatest of ease.

Performance is not *quite* so good, and fuel consumption is slightly higher for the automatic than the manually-operated gearbox version, but these differences become unimportant when compared with the overall fascination and usefulness of the automatic model.

The bodywork retains all the good features of the original '59 Mini. It has the roomy pockets in both doors and the rear quarters, as well as a capacious shelf surrounding the instruments. A new feature is the provision of a special adjuster which allows tall drivers to set the front seat to give a more comfortable position. The hydrolastic suspension gives a pitch-free ride and, for a small car, comfortable transportation is provided for the three passengers.

With a maximum speed of over 70 mph, a fuel consumption of approximately 35 mpg, and the countless benefits of the excellent automatic transmission, this Mini-Minor must be the complete answer to many motorists' needs—especially women whose everyday driving is usually so demanding. Price approx. £630, including Purchase Tax, the Mini-Minor Automatic has proved itself to be a good buy indeed.

£25m government plan for the 70's

THE first stage of a £25m major development in Britain's air traffic control system will be introduced during 1971. Code-named Mediator, its object will be to provide greatly improved facilities for the safe flow of aircraft over the United Kingdom.

Roy Mason, President of the Board of Trade, announced this during a visit to the College of Air Traffic Control and Air Traffic Control Evaluation Unit at Bournemouth Airport, where the first training course for Mediator is being held this week.

Over the next 18 weeks, 500 experienced air traffic controllers will attend intensive one-week courses at Bournemouth. They will be instructed in the new skills necessary for operating the improved system.

Mediator will eventually replace the present wholly manual system of air traffic control. It will automate the supply, storing and display of flight information by the use of computers and will become a fully integrated operation.

In a later stage Mediator will be able to advise which aircraft are on collision paths and to offer solutions to prevent them.

Mason said that Britain's skies were becoming increasingly crowded each year and the country was holding its place as the "Clapham Junction of the air". In addition to scheduled and charter services, Britain had to cater for air taxi operations, and private and business flying. Last year over 1¼ million civil movements were totted up.

This, said Mason, was the background against which recent reports of air misses had to be weighed. He paid tribute to London controllers who handled 2,000 movements in one day last year, an all-time high and to Manchester (Preston) controllers who handled 13,000 movements in one month over one point. Lichfield. He also praised Prestwick Oceanic Control Centre, which handled 500 Atlantic flights on peak days last year, and West Drayton (Middlesex) controllers who handle all incoming and outgoing aircraft over south-east England, which totalled a record 70,000 movements last August.

The Mediator complex will be situated at West Drayton, but there will be a sub-centre at Manchester, and major developments in Scotland at Prestwick.

Freight News Weekly 1970

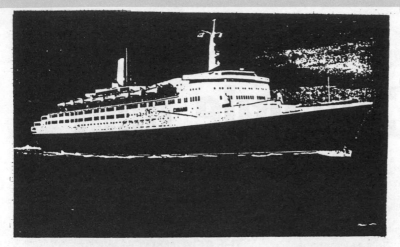

"Queen Elizabeth 2" enters service

65 863 gross ton, 28½ knot Cunard liner of 111 000 shp—the world's highest-powered merchant ship.

PRINCIPAL CHARACTERISTICS OF "QUEEN ELIZABETH 2"	
Gross register	65 863 tons
Overall length	963 ft
Breadth	105 ft
Draught, maximum	32 ft 6 in
Height (keel to funnel base)	134 ft 6 in
Height of funnel structure	69 ft 6 in
Height (keel to masthead)	203 ft 9½ in
Service speed	28½ knots
Shaft horsepower	110 000
Propellers	2, six-bladed
Main boilers	3
Steam pressure	850 lb/in²
Steam temperature	950° F
Evaporators, sea water to fresh water	1 200 tons daily
Drive on-drive off facilities	80 cars
Number of decks	13
Air-conditioning	full
Passengers	2 025
Crew	906
Theatre seats	531
Deck space	6 000 yd²
Swimming pools	2 outdoor, 2 indoor
Restaurant Capacities	
The Columbia	500
The Grill Room	100
The Britannia	815
Lifts	22
Keel laid	4 July, 1965
Launched by HM The Queen	20 September, 196

QUEEN ELIZABETH 2, which leaves Southampton tomorrow on her maiden voyage to New York, is the world's most expensive and most magnificent passenger ship. From an accommodation viewpoint she is the finest of Cunard's many fine liners, and her sophisticated machinery installation, computers, and satellite navigation system make her a world leader in technological achievement.

Sailing time tomorrow will be the great moment Cunard men have been anticipating during the long and anxious weeks of waiting when QE2 was laid up alongside Southampton's Ocean Terminal for turbine repairs and the completion of fitting-out work in cabins and public rooms.

Shipping World 1969

The Spectator 1968

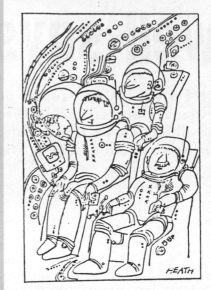

'It really is a great sight! From up here I can see the Grand Canyon, the Great Wall of China, student demonstrations . . .'

When to watch

ITV: Until 10 a.m.—Pictures of Moon walk. 10 a.m.-4 p.m.—Latest news, studio report and live TV from the Moon. After 4 p.m.—Moon headlines, different times in different areas. 5.50 p.m.—Latest reports, summaries, live pictures of blast-off back to Apollo. 10 p.m.—Extended News.

BBC 1: Until 10.30 a.m.—Pictures from Moon. 1-1.30 p.m.—Astronauts prepare to leave. 1.45-1.53—News. 4.20-4.40—Waiting for blast-off. 5.50-6—News. 6.20-7.5—Blast-off due. 8-8.50—*Panorama* on Moon landing. 8.50-9.10—News. 10.25-11—24 *Hours* as modules re-join. 11.10-11.17—News.

Daily Mail 1969

MAN ON THE MOON

Daily Mail 1969

From ANGUS MACPHERSON, Houston, Sunday

THEY'RE on the Moon! While the world held its breath Neil Armstrong and Edwin Aldrin touched down today dead on time in their landing craft Eagle and began preparing for man's first fantastic steps on another planet.

The big bird flies pretty well says Concorde pilot

Daily Sketch 1969

SHE'S off ! The Concorde giant, painted red, white and blue, leaves the ground for the first time—a year and three days late.

The maiden flight was first fixed for March 1968. Even today's take-off had been put off since Friday because of the weather.

But the £700 million Concorde made a triumphant debut with a 200 m.p.h., 26-minute "flip" from Blagnac Airport here.

And, back on the ground, test pilot Andre Turcat announced:

"The big bird flies — and I can say now that it flies pretty well."

The only snags reported by Frenchman Turcat were "minor malfunctions" in some instruments.

THE WAY WE LIVE
THE COLUMN YOU WRITE

❝ I'm always talking to strangers ❞
by Mrs. Dorothy Hammant

How many people do you talk to in a day? Ten, 20 perhaps? Then I wonder how you'd like my job—for I estimate that for every hour I work I speak to at least 100 people!

Mind you, I never see them, for they're just voices on the other end of the telephone. I'm the girl on the switchboard, or, to give me my full title, a GPO telephone operator, working at the busy exchange in Worcester, just six miles from my home in Broadwas-on-Teme.

I've been a telephone operator since 1960. Although I had several weeks' training beforehand, I'll always remember my first day at work. I was so scared that I didn't dare connect more than one call at a time, in case I connected up the wrong people or lost one of the calls! Today, although I have spells of manning the ordinary switchboard, I mainly work on Directory Enquiries, which means that when a caller dials 192 I'm there to trace that elusive telephone number for him. Believe me, that can be pretty tricky on some occasions.

It took me quite a few weeks to get to know which town was in which county—not surprising, considering that we deal with requests for phone numbers all over the British Isles. And, of course, when a caller rattles off the name of a town it's not always easy to catch the name straight away. Some callers get very impatient if I ask them to repeat the name; they seem to expect me to know the exact location and spelling of even the tiniest village! In fact, it's incredible how many people think I'm a veritable mine of information. I've had callers asking me things like what films are on at the local cinema, and whether the little grocery shop on the corner of such-and-such a street is open on Saturdays! We get children who like playing games and ringing us up, and I have to force myself to be firm to get them off the line.

Yet I love the work and I've made many good friends here on the exchange. The ages of my colleagues range from 15 to 50, and we enjoy swopping stories of our families in our coffee break. But, despite what some subscribers think, our working hours are very busy, and we certainly don't have time to knit or drink tea at the switchboard.

I get a lot of satisfaction, too, from quickly connecting people who are worried or impatient, in soothing an irate business man or reassuring a nervous, elderly person who may be unaccustomed to the telephone. With old people and foreigners you need a great deal of patience. You also need to be able to keep your temper —people manage to be a little ruder when they're not face to face with you! But subscribers are usually very pleasant, and sometimes I wish I had time to chat with them.

My family life is geared round my hours of duty : one week may see me starting my day on the switchboard at 8 am; another week I may work from 10 am to 6 pm. Luckily, my husband, Eric, and my two daughters, Karen, 16, and Joan, 11, are quite used to my dashing off to work on Christmas Day or on Bank holidays—because, like hospitals, a telephone exchange never closes. And despite STD there are still a tremendous number of people who need my help.

Woman's Own 1969

APOLLO 11

Space capsule

Marzine has gone to the moon. Travel sickness hasn't. Marzine was selected for the American space programme. *Recommended retail price 3/-.*

QUEEN ELIZABETH II

Q4 became *Queen Elizabeth II* when Her Majesty launched the new 58,000-ton Cunarder at John Brown's yard on September 20. It was a faultless launch, receiving widest possible publicity from the Press and BBC. The event itself has already passed into the history of British shipping and shipbuilding, and completion work now continues apace at the builder's fitting-out berth. The ensuing pages offer a detailed record not only of the building, but of much of the work to be done before *Queen Elizabeth II* takes a proud place next year among the world's passenger liners.

Motor Ship
1969

SOME of the current doubts regarding the economic future for the vessel, but none of the pessimism, were reflected in the Queen's speech which followed the launch. Every great enterprise had an element of risk and uncertainty about it, said Her Majesty, and no one could predict the future career of the *Queen Elizabeth II*. However, she was certain that in the experienced and capable hands of the Cunard company the ship would stand the very best chance of a happy and profitable lifetime.

"I particularly welcome the opportunity you have given me to launch this splendid successor to those two famous Cunarders *Queen Mary* and *Queen Elizabeth*," she continued. "I suppose these two ships were better known and loved, both in peace and in war by all of us living in these Islands, than any other merchantmen in our history. I have always had a very special affection for them because they were named after my grandmother and my mother, and it does not seem so very long ago that I was present with my sister when my mother launched the *Queen Elizabeth* in 1938.

***Southern Evening Echo* 1969**

MOTORWOMAN

EDITED BY JEAN BARRATT

WINTER DRIVING

If you look out of the window and see falling snow, no one can blame you if you decide to go by bus. But, except in extreme conditions, there isn't any need if you're competent and careful, your car's in good condition and the road is passable.

The big thing is not to be scared. Alert, yes—and very much aware of the extra hazards—but a bad case of nerves can make you act abruptly when the main aim is to do everything very smoothly and gently.

How can you not be scared?—by experience of bad weather driving, by having instruction and practice on a skid pan and by knowing how to handle the car to avoid trouble.

Suppose you're caught in a bad snowstorm. This is nasty because it makes the road slippery and it's difficult to see. The flakes may be driven against the windscreen so thick and fast the wipers can't cope properly and, in fact, bad snow can reduce visibility as much as fog.

So the same principles apply as for driving in fog. Keep windscreen wipers going and windscreen heated; use dipped headlights even in daylight and keep your speed down. Remember—you must be able to stop within the distance you can see to be clear and *the surface is slippery*.

If the snow has settled, it doesn't always pay to follow in the tracks of other vehicles as the ruts can get very slippery. Unless the snow is too deep, it's often better to keep the nearside wheels near the kerb where the tyres can get some adhesion in the virgin snow and the gravel thrown off the centre of the road.

If you have to stop and park, the car won't be able to move off again if the tyres can't get a good grip. If one driven wheel is in deep snow, all the drive may go to this wheel as you rev; it will just spin uselessly and you'll stay where you are. The answer is to make a good surface for both driven wheels by clearing away the snow or putting sacking or matting in front of them.

NEXT WEEK: Ice and snow

Woman
1970